Stan DeFreitas'
Complete Guide to
FLORIDA GARDENING

Complete Guide to

FLORIDA

Stan DeFreitas'

GARDENING

Taylor Publishing Company
DALLAS, TEXAS

**Library of Congress Cataloging in
Publication Data**

DeFreitas, Stan.
    Stan DeFreitas' Complete guide to
    Florida gardening.

    Includes index.
    1. Gardening — Florida. I. Title.
    II. Title: Complete guide to Florida
    gardening.
SB453.2.F6D43   1984   635'.09759   83-18132
ISBN 0-87833-341-X

Printed in the United States of America

In memory of my father and
mother, Frank DeFreitas and Edith
Lillian Miller, and with special
affection for my family, Peggi,
Marie and James.

Acknowledgements

The author wishes to thank his wife, Peggi, who lovingly, diligently organized and typed the material for this book, and Colleen Tracy for her original work in houseplants.

Special thanks also go to those horticulture professionals whose guidance, knowledge, inspiration and reviews made the book possible — Dr. Charles Peacock, Ph.D. turf specialist, University of Florida, County Extension Service; Dr. Gary Simone, Ph.D. pathologist, University of Florida, Extension Service; Jim Stevens, vegetable specialist, University of Florida; Lee Schmoll, landscape architect, landscape design instructor, Pinellas Vocational-Technical Institute; Ray Smith, landscape designer, owner-operator of Smith's Nursery and Garden Supply Center; Jerry O'Rourke, landscape designer, Smith's Nursery; Dave Smith, owner-operator of Smith's Nursery and Garden Supply Center; Mike Karr, annual specialist; Jack Sweet, 31 years experience in raising and growing orchids and National Certified Judge for the American Orchid Society; Jim Nau, Ball Seed Co.; Opal Schallmo, urban-horticulturist, Pinellas County Extension Service; Mitchell and Michelle Crose; Pursley Turf and Garden Centers, and Mildred (president of Suncoast Botanical gardens) and Ken Palmer, owners-operators of G.K. Palmer Nursery, specializing in flowering and fruit trees.

Many of the photographs in this book were taken by the author. Others came from Jim Nau, Ball Seed Co.; the Florida Citrus Commission; James Bennett, John and Bonita Lucas, Steve Carlisle and Polly Jones, and the author deeply appreciates their time and skill.

CONTENTS

CHAPTER 12: FLORIDA LAWNS

CHAPTER 13: HOUSEPLANTS

FOREWORD

Seems as if I've loved plants forever — I started growing them at the age of 6. In my early years I worked with neighbors, helping them care for their plants. In high school, I worked for a local nursery, which sparked an even greater interest in horticulture. After attending junior college, I completed a two-year horticultural program, during which time I was also a landscape foreman.

Much of my experience and knowledge came as an urban horticulturist for the Pinellas County Extension Service. In seven years there, I attended numerous short courses, meetings and seminars and was exposed to plant problems by thousands of local residents and nursery people.

Radio played a further role in reaching people throughout the state. Primarily for easy identification with my listening audience, I adopted the name "Mr. Green Thumb," and the label stuck.

Local newspapers have also given me a vehicle to touch Florida gardeners. I have taken a greater interest in educating horticulturists, and as a teacher I feel I have learned even more about this profession. Hopefully this has also been rewarding to others who share the same interests. Now television has become an important part of these education and communications activities. Through the media, I have been able to encourage the sort of enthusiasm for nature which gets everyone involved in keeping Florida green.

— Stan DeFreitas
Mr. Green Thumb
Clearwater, FL, 1984

INTRODUCTION

When most people think of Florida, they think of orange trees, bright sandy beaches and tropical foliage — correct perceptions, every one. But Florida also offers outstanding growing seasons, a semitropical season from May through September and a temperate season from October through April.

Florida is blessed with a marvelous climate that enables us to spend as much time outside our homes as inside. With our climate, we can design and build walls of thick foliage for beauty and privacy, lay a grassy carpet for relaxation and furnish our outdoor living area with flowers for an ever-changing environment that is both aesthetic and satisfying.

You don't have to be wealthy to have a great landscape in Florida. A small amount of money yields beautiful returns. Whether you are building a new home or improving an old one, your imagination can lead to an attractive living atmosphere around your house. Depending on your preferences, needs and lifestyle you can create a home landscape that will give years of pleasure. Like compound interest on an investment, your property value will increase, and literally before your eyes.

If you recently moved to Florida, you will find that different types of flowers, vegetables, fruits, and lawns grow here. The difference in growing seasons can be months apart. The soil is certainly different than in most other areas of the country. My radio listeners mention that, back home, they would pull out St. Augustine grass, calling it crabgrass or another weed. But I tell them, "When in Florida do as the Floridians do." St. Augustine is an excellent lawn grass when watered and fertilized properly. This book is designed to help you learn the differences so you can grow plants successfully in Florida.

The chapters of this book are organized to give you a basic approach to the care and feeding of Florida's most popular plants plus some general discussion of their use in the landscape. From the section on planning the landscape in Chapter 1, through trees, shrubs, flowers, vegetables, lawns, insect and disease control, to the discussion of houseplants in Chapter 13, my approach has been to review basic requirements for planting and care and then to cover briefly the specific requirements and growing conditions for the plants you are most likely to select for your landscape.

The charts, maps and photos used throughout the text not only help clarify certain parts of the discussion but offer additional tips for successful gardening. The color photos, in particular, should help you judge the look and the appeal of these various kinds of plants. Color clues are very important in selecting the right varieties for your garden. I hope they will help you make faster and more satisfying landscape decisions.

There are other important matters in the text which probably merit repeating here. The importance of following label directions with chemicals and other materials cannot be over-emphasized. No amount of fun in the garden is worth risking the safety of you, your family or your pets. To keep things safe and enjoyable, follow the rules. Secondly, your nurseryman should be your partner in making the perfect choice of plant materials, fertilizers and other products for the lawn and garden. I hope this book will give you plenty of information for making appropriate choices, but the nurseryman can help you in making final selections and in judging the value of certain materials for your specific growing conditions.

If you are in North Florida, you will need to plan for cooler winters and later spring planting; in South Florida and the Keys you will be dealing with tropical conditions and near year-round growing. In Central Florida, of course, the climate is temperate but has elements of both extremes, both heat and cold. These matters will invariably affect plant selection and watering practices.

All in all, gardening is one of the most enjoyable things you can do. It's healthy, productive, satisfying, and gives you an intimate relationship with your natural environment. Here's hoping all your gardening experiences are happy ones.

Stan DeFreitas'
Complete Guide to
FLORIDA GARDENING

CHAPTER ONE

Planning Your Garden

Never planned a garden before? Does the prospect of having to landscape your yard bring on an anxiety attack? Don't be disturbed. It's much easier than you imagine. Still, if the idea terrifies you into immobility, you may need help from a professional landscape company. Depending on the amount of work to be done, the cost can vary from very reasonable to a major expense.

Professional landscape companies will guarantee their work. Any weak or dying plants will be replaced, provided you have given them the required amount of care and feeding. You might even want to weigh the comparative cost of doing all the work yourself, and possibly having to replace some plants later, against the initial cost of turning the job over to a landscaper.

You could let a professional design your garden or landscaping and advise you on trees, shrubs and plants. Then you could proceed on your own from that point. Again, this will depend on your own capabilities and desires, as well as the amount you plan to spend. A good, reputable landscape company certainly can help those who feel creatively inadequate in planning the layout of a garden.

For the ambitious do-it-yourself gardener or landscaper, however, this book can help you get the results you want.

Your first concern should be your family's outdoor needs. How do you plan to use your garden? The front of most homes usually is the public area, to be designed merely as a setting for the house and to enhance its appearance from the street. The back yard and sides of the property usually are the living and entertaining areas, play areas or service areas, and functional areas for storage or a vegetable garden. To decide which areas to use and how much space you have to fill, you should draw a scale outline of your property. School graph paper is ideal. Scale your drawing down to one-fourth-inch to every foot, making the overall outline from fence-line to fence-line. Fill in all driveways and walkways, as well as the outline of the house itself. Any existing trees that you wish to retain should be marked, together with "hot spots" where shade is needed. You may want to check your deed map to determine the exact dimensions of your 1

2 property. The architect's drawing of your home also is useful to show the placement of doors, windows and the direction of the house on your lot. You may also have to check a contour map to discover any rises or hills in your yard. Some properties will drop a foot or two over the length of the yard, a factor that will affect your landscaping plan.

Once your scale drawing is complete, you can make decisions on where to put flower beds, trees, shrubs, rock gardens, etc. If you intend eventually to put in a pool, choose a large, open area away from any existing trees.

Landscape planning begins from the time you move into your new home, assessing the nature of your living environment and your gardening plans.

Common Florida soil tends to be sandy and poor in nutrients. Even muck-type soil needs major improvement.

Remember that digging a swimming pool requires working space for men and equipment. Be sure to leave at least twenty feet along the back fence to allow the pool construction crew room to get in and out of your yard. Once the pool is installed, you then can determine the placement of shrubs or trees along the fence.

While everyone envisions a landscaped yard or garden in its final form, remember that it often takes several years for such dreams to take real shape. Not only the expense but the growing time needed for plants

To begin landscaping remove all unwanted materials and prepare the soil. Healthy native trees should be left and developed into the landscape plan.

Flower beds around the home, pool or recreation areas should be established with enriched soil and with defined borders.

A touch of green can make your home both inviting and enjoyable for your family and friends. The plants you select should reflect your preferences but should be adaptable to native soil and climate conditions.

Especially in new homes, don't be surprised to find rubble and debris left behind by builders. All debris should be removed before beginning your planting routine.

makes many homeowners approach landscaping as a "five-year plan." This is especially true if a pool is in those plans. Whether you are able to begin everything you want to do right away or have to spread your budget over a period of time, you should stick to your original plan for landscaping. In this way, no matter how long it is before completion, you wind up with a garden or yard that is aesthetically appealing and creatively satisfying.

In Florida, patio landscaping serves as an extension of the living room. Patio landscaping makes small houses seem larger and provides a smooth transition from indoor to outdoor living and recreation areas. Similarly, the placement of trees, shrubs and flower beds in front should serve to lead visitors to the front door of the house.

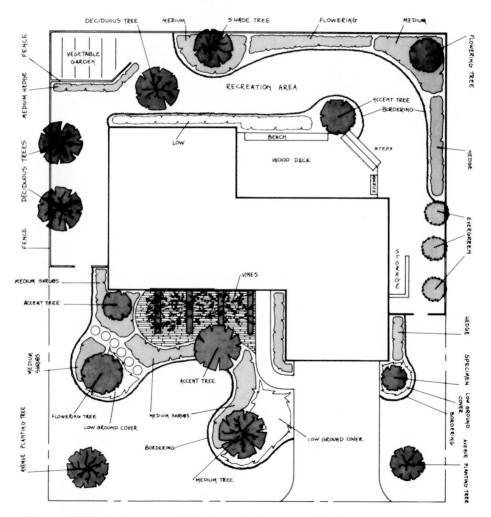

It is a good idea to draw up a sketch of your landscape and plan in advance how trees, shrubs, flowers and vines can be planted.

6 GUIDING GUESTS TO THE FRONT DOOR

Landscape architects plan their plantings at the front of a home to frame the house in the most appealing manner, and, at the same time, point the way to the front door. If your front yard is a jungle of foliage, visitors can wind up at the side or back door by mistake. A well-designed front landscape should have a welcoming appearance, a natural flow that guides people to your front door.

AVOID THE NOAH'S ARK EFFECT

For the front of your property, try for visual balance, not symmetry. Noah's Ark had two of everything, but this is not advisable for landscaping. Avoid having two of the same type of plant on opposite sides of a walkway. Vary your plant selection and give a balanced, but not identical, appearance to arrangements. If you have, for example, a large oak tree on one side of the property, you may balance it with two or three smaller trees on the other side. Always choose plants that will grow in proportion to your house. An 80-foot eucalyptus tree will look out of place next to a typical one-story Florida home. Check the ultimate height of any tree before deciding on it. Many people buy a small Norfolk Island pine or an Italian cypress and plant these close to the house, unaware that they inevitably will grow into the overhang of the roof.

By checking the full-grown size of a tree or shrub, you can avoid planting anything that will become a problem in a few years. The secret lies in maintaining visual balance — creating a pleasing flow of lines and patterns across the landscape and maintaining the right look to your property without any awkward visual distractions. The size and ultimate shape of shrubs and trees is very important, and something you should check out at a nursery before you make a purchase.

ADDING TO YOUR LANDSCAPE

Many of us do not know what specific types of plants to buy. Here again, your nurseryman can advise you, not just on size, but on overall appearance and texture. Take a walk through your nursery and examine the various plants and shrubs. Feel the leaves. Determine whether a shiny plant (such as *Philodendron*) would be right, or perhaps something light and feathery, such as a fern. Will the plant fit into your plans? Does the plant spread, or does it grow round-headed and upright? Should the plant be placed in a corner for best effect, or could it be a specimen by itself, surrounded by lawn? Try to visualize the plant in the location you have in mind before buying anything that might not enhance your overall landscaping ideas.

WALKWAYS AND PATIOS

One of the greatest joys is to be able to walk comfortably through a yard or garden without tripping over protruding branches or uneven ground. Patios and walkways not only add beauty, but also ease access to your yard and garden. Concrete often is used for this purpose. It is easily available and very frequently favored by Florida contractors. Gravel and wood chips also can be used for a decorative walkway or patio and formed into any desired shape by using strips of wood along the outer edges. Gravel can be pressed into wet concrete to form a more interesting surface. Bricks, too, are popular and can be laid into many interesting patterns, such as the basket weave (two bricks one way, two bricks at right angles to the first two). These various types of walkways can give you attractive and practical paths through your greenery, enabling you to enjoy it to the fullest. If you are laying a pathway yourself rather than hiring a contractor, be sure to place four inches of sand on the ground first. This provides a solid base, especially for bricks, and prevents shifting and buckling.

FENCES

Fences are essential for privacy and containment of pets, but they need not be unattractive. A variety of fencing materials can blend with the image you wish to create in your landscaping.

Chain-link fence is one of the most popular, though it does little for privacy or cutting down on outside noises. However, chain-link fence is ideal as a solid support for vines. A fast-growing vine of your choice soon will provide an attractive and impenetrable barrier against neighbors.

Wrought-iron fences lend a touch of elegance to any garden, but again afford little privacy. Still, a wrought-iron fence surrounding the patio area inside your property line can give a picturesque touch to your overall landscaping, sectioning off an outside area for dining or relaxing.

The most practical fences, however, are made of wood. The old-fashioned picket fence adds a traditional rustic touch and can be utilized as a solid support for climbing roses. Solid wooden fences can be installed in several different ways and — whether left natural or painted — they blend with any garden. For durability use pressure-treated posts, which are well worth the extra cost. For a Western touch to your Florida home, a split-rail fence is unusual and very attractive.

The longest-lasting and most secure fence is one of masonry or brick. These fences are common in Florida landscapes. A fence company can advise you on installation as well as show you a variety of styles from which to choose. Comparative costs between different types of fencing should be considered. A fence is a major expense and is not an item you should replace frequently.

COLOR IN THE LANDSCAPE

Your own taste and sense of color should determine the color coordination of your landscaping. Many perennial shrubs, such as azaleas, not only provide different shades of green in the foliage, but burst forth with eye-catching blossoms in the spring. Certain plants such as crotons and copper plants can be used in the central and southern parts of Florida to add year-round color with their variegated leaves.

For a changing palette of color in a garden, however, the annuals are your best bet, not only for variety of hues, but also for interesting flower

8   forms. Petunias, marigolds, zinnias, asters, nasturtiums and calendulas all do well in Florida. The perennials also contribute their share of color, including Gerbera or Gazzina daisies, carnations and everybody's favorite: roses. Annuals require more care, as do roses, but the rewards are well worth the effort. A detailed list of suitable annuals and perennials will be found in a later chapter.

Mixing flowers of various colors in the same bed can be exciting, but you should be careful that the final result is tastefully appealing and not

With a little imagination any Florida home can be developed into a tropical paradise.

Flowers in the land-scape are one of the nicest decorations for your home.

flashy or gaudy. Some gardeners like mixing various flowers in the same bed. This creates an interesting display, but it is a matter of individual taste. You may want to keep roses separate from the rest of the garden, but the addition of climbers and tree roses can add a nice touch of color to the landscape. I generally feel that a ratio of 40% tropical plants, such as hibiscus, copper plants and bird of paradise, should be mixed with 60% evergreens, such as podocarpus, ligustrums and viburnum. This should give you a good hedge against the severe cold we occasionally experience (remember the 1983 freeze), as well as a nice mixture of colors.

PLACEMENT OF TREES, SHRUBS AND FLOWER BEDS

After you have determined the overall layout of your greenery, the first step will be the proper placement of trees, shrubs and plants.

Trees should be planted first. They provide the landmarks on your property and create the general character of the landscaping. In selecting your trees, ask yourself why you want them. To add privacy? To provide shade? To balance the overall look of your property? Trees are the largest living things in the yard; they also are going to be your largest investment. In some areas, you may have to check with City Hall for a permit to remove any existing trees that you may not want included in your new landscaping. Bear in mind, too, that trees are the slowest growing of any plant. You may wish to spend a little more and buy a more mature tree rather than get a smaller one that will take years to give you the look you want.

Shrubs are the second item you should plant. Again, most shrubs are slow growing and may take several years to achieve the size and height needed to complete the impresssion you wish them to create.

Planter boxes add a certain appeal and are a convenient and easily-cared-for addition to the landscape.

10   The third step will be marking out and preparing your flower beds. If you plan these as raised beds, wooden or masonry edging will have to be installed. Whether you do this work yourself or have a contractor build them for you, room will be needed for equipment and workmen.

The last step is to install your lawn, which fills in all the space between flower beds, trees and shrubs and the edges of your property. Putting in the turf last ensures that it will not be destroyed by workmen or equipment needed for building walkways, the swimming pool, the edging to flower beds or any other major items.

These three steps are your major plantings, after which the main layout of your landscaping will be complete. All that is left will be vines, ornamental shrubs and annuals or perennials in the flower beds.

Vines should be placed so that they help screen heat and excessive light from the windows. Planted along a chain-link fence, they ultimately provide privacy as well as block any unsightly views beyond your property line. Along with vines, you can plant ground cover to conceal problem turf areas, such as beneath shade trees.

Try to avoid the "tunnel effect", which can obscure your house and make it less inviting.

The "Noah's Ark Effect", two of everything, can also make the landscape stale and boring.

With a little planning, trees and shrubs can be used as energy saving features of the home.

Ornamental shrubs, either in the ground or in decorative tubs, can be placed as accents wherever you feel they are needed. A row of various-sized clay pots with small ornamental shrubs can enhance a patio or walkway.

Finally, you can fill the flower beds with the annuals and perennials of your choice.

An extra incentive for planning your landscaping is the potential energy savings of judiciously planted trees, shrubs and vines. A large oak tree can reduce the temperature inside your home from ten to twenty degrees. It has been estimated that a large growing tree can equal ten-room air conditioners in cooling efficiency. Similarly, vines growing against sunny walls cut direct heat as well as indirect, reflective heat. A lawn also provides cooling, because it is always transpiring water. Concrete, on the other hand, retains and radiates heat.

Well-planned landscaping can benefit your home in winter as well as summer. Deciduous trees, such as the Golden Raintree, produce shade during the hot months and let sunlight and warmth through in the winter. Large evergreens planted on the north side can stop some of the north winds from cooling your home.

IMPROVING THE SOIL

The most important element in your garden is the soil . . . the good earth. Without it there would be no life in any form. Nothing is more important to the continued success of your garden than good soil. As in most other states, the soils of Florida vary from north to south. Northern Florida soils are mostly clay. The central soils consist mostly of sand. And

12 in the south, the soil is muck-type. All these soils need attention to transform them into the most suitable consistency and composition for maximum growth of plants.

Sandy soil provides good drainage but does not hold nutrients or water. Most Florida soils are low in nitrogen, phosphorous, potassium, iron, zinc, manganese and magnesium. On the other hand, there are plenty of nematodes, bacteria, fungi and weed seeds. As every gardener will discover, it takes more than merely turning over the dirt and planting seeds to achieve a truly rewarding display of flowers. Any undesirable elements in the soil have to be removed, and any shortages of essential minerals must be supplemented, much as we take vitamins to provide our bodies with the building blocks to replace tissues and keep us healthy.

For this reason, once you have completed your landscaping or gardening plan, you must give attention to your soil. A good, balanced soil mixture is essential for growth and good blooms, as well as for resistance to disease. To determine the quality of your soil, you first must learn its pH balance, which refers to the acidity (sourness) or alkalinity (sweetness). A measurement of 0.0 on the pH scale indicates the highest acidity, while 14.0 is the most alkaline. The halfway mark, 7.0, is neutral.

Soil pH is important because it influences several soil factors that affect plant growth, such as (1) soil bacteria, (2) nutrient leaching, (3) toxic elements, (4) nutrient availability and (5) soil structure. Bacteria that change and release nitrogen from organic matter, as well as the action of certain fertilizer materials, are particularly affected by the pH level of the soil.

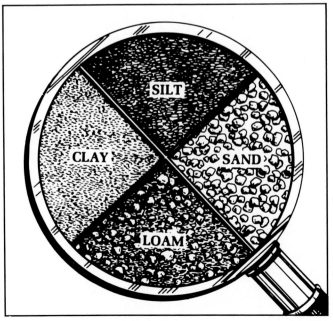

SOIL TYPES

Sand: This is the coarsest soil, well aerated, but drains rapidly.

Loam: Contains equal amounts of clay, silt and sand, plus some organic material. Ideal for garden soil.

Silt: Important in loam soil for texture and nutrients, but not adequate as garden material by itself. Needs enrichment.

Clay: The smallest particles of all soils; has high nutrient and water retention and helps bond sandy soil.

MR. GREEN THUMB RULE

Many gardeners tend to overlook the importance of knowing the pH of their soil. But most of the soil in Florida is poor and needs some enrichment. You must check the pH level in your garden and take whatever steps are necessary to adjust it.

The pH level in your garden soil must be tested chemically. You can do this yourself with an inexpensive kit obtainable from a garden shop or feed store.

With a small trowel or soil auger, dig a core sample from two to six inches. These are the main depths where plants feed from their root systems. Use this plug of soil to test for pH. Alternatively, you can send your soil sample to the University of Florida for analysis. For a small fee, you receive not only the pH factor, but a listing of all minerals and other elements in the soil. From this you can judge what remedial action needs to be taken. Bear in mind that most soil in Florida consists of silicon sand, which is devoid of nutrients. Pure sand has less than 1% organic matter, compared with the ideal soil composition of 25% organic matter, 25% air, 25% water and 25% minerals.

After you have learned the pH of your soil, you either will have to increase or decrease the pH to achieve the proper or neutral balance that is most desirable for optimum plant growth. To increase the pH, or "sweeten" the soil, use ground limestone or dolomite. Do not use hydrated lime, which will "burn" the plant roots. The greater the amount of organic matter or clay in the soil, the more lime or dolomite will be required to change the pH. To raise the pH one unit, add 4½ ounces of lime or dolomite per 10 square feet, 3 pounds per 100 square feet or 30 pounds per 1,000 square feet.

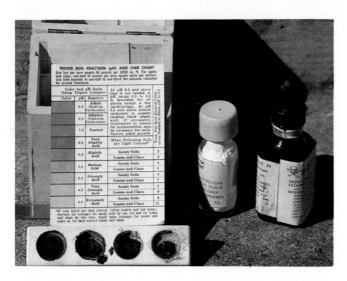

Soil analysis kits are available at many lawn and garden centers and can help you determine how to enrich your soil.

14   If a high pH reading is created by applying too much lime or dolomite, you can restore an acceptable balance by adding sulfur, ammonium sulphate or similar acid-forming chemicals that enrich the soil. However, it is difficult to bring about an appreciable change in the pH of naturally alkaline soils with only chemical additives.

To decrease the pH, use superfine dusting or wettable sulfur in the following amounts: not more than 1½ ounces of sulfur per 10 square feet, 1 pound for 100 square feet or 10 pounds per 1,000 square feet. Note that it takes one-third of the amount of superfine or wettable sulfur to decrease pH one unit as it does ground limestone or dolomite to raise soil pH by one unit. Applications of sulfur should not be made more than every eight weeks. In the ground, sulfur oxidizes, mixes with water and forms a dilute sulphuric acid, which can burn the roots of plants. Be careful. Too little sulfur is better than too much.

SOIL FERTILITY

The results you achieve with your plants are directly related to the degree of fertility in the soil, which is influenced by the amount of nutrients available. For instance, approximately one-seventh of protein is nitrogen, which is the element most used by all plants. Important for both the growth and greening of plants, nitrogen is an essential ingredient in most fertilizers. But since it dissolves very easily in water, nitrogen is leached out of the soil more easily than other elements. Nitrogen exists in the protoplasm and chlorophyll of all plants. It is an integral element essential for life and growth. Too much nitrogen applied during fertilization, however, can cause overly fast growth, as well as excessive growth. This will make plants more susceptible to disease and insects and less capable of withstanding strong winds, extremes of temperature and physical injury.

Other elements necessary to maintain a balanced rate of growth are potassium, phosphorous and iron. Potassium, or potash, strengthens plants, stems, leaves and the holding quality of flowers. Potassium is the main element that helps plants survive a long period of drought. Phosphorous helps in germination and development of seeds, provides rapid development of roots and is necessary for good flower color. Iron, meanwhile, is vital to the growth and life metabolism of plants. Iron deficiency in the soil will cause new growth to lack the green of a healthy plant. Iron-poor plants often will exhibit green veins in the leaves, while the remainder of the leaf turns yellow, a condition that can be remedied by spraying with chelated iron. Most good fertilizers contain some iron in the formula.

Several minor elements play important roles in plant metabolism. Calcium helps strengthen cell walls and assists in root hair development. Root hairs are essential to plant growth because most nutrients are absorbed into the plant through them. Magnesium is used in the cells of chlorophyll (green coloring) that assist in photosynthesis, the food production and respiration process of plants. Magnesium also aids in the distribution of phosphate within plants.

Manganese is essential in carrying iron throughout a plant, as well as helping the roots assimilate fertilizer, water, air and gases. Boron helps prevent the breakdown of structural tissues in the leaves and stems. Small quantities of copper and zinc also are needed by plants to strengthen the growth of young seedlings and ensure proper growth in mature plants. And sulfur is used in the formation of protein and aromatic oils in leaves and stems.

Since it is difficult to counterbalance excessive acidity with chemical additives (such as sulfur) only, compost and other organic soil-builders should be added for structural enrichment of Florida soil. For improving the fertility, chemicals certainly should be used, but generous amounts of organic matter also should be worked into the soil with a tiller, or by hand with a shovel.

Add 25 pounds of peat moss and 25 pounds of cow manure for every 100 square feet of growing area. Organic matter and fertilizers will enrich your soil and provide your plants with the greatest possible nourishment.

CHANGING THE GRADE

Many people spend thousands of dollars extra for a piece of property because of the trees. Then they change the grade, or the level of the soil, and proceed to kill their extra investment. Many people do not realize that it does the average tree less harm to remove soil than to increase the soil greatly around the roots. Before changing the level of the soil, try to select the trees that can be saved and the trees that may need to be replaced. Not only is increasing the level of the soil more than a few inches detrimental to the tree, but heavy equipment, such as bulldozers and dump trucks, can damage trees and plants. You may find that by building a barricade around the base of the trees you can protect them from damage and more easily control weed growth.

It is also helpful to install a drainage tile system. This is done with 4-inch agricultural clay tile or 4-inch perforated PVC or plastic pipe. Normally six to ten tiles or pipes should be placed to radiate away from the trunk of the tree. Vertical pipes rising to the new grade should be installed to ensure aeration of the old roots.

Lowering the grade is easier. You most likely will need to remove some of the larger, surface roots. Remember to trim some of the top back to compensate for the loss of feeder roots. This is similar to transplanting a tree (as covered in Chapter 3).

ORGANIC MATTER AND FERTILIZERS

All organic matter is derived from living material and contains the most essential building block of life: carbon. So a compost pile is a must in every garden. Not only does a compost pile provide you with a disposal site for grass clippings, leaves and small twigs, but in time it becomes a never-ending source of the best possible soil conditioner for your garden. Certainly, chemical fertilizers are needed, but these constitute a fast pick-me-up for plants, just as we get a daily boost from coffee, which contains caffeine, a strong stimulant. Caffeine, however, does nothing for our growth, while fertilizers do possess positive food value for plants

16 RAISING THE GRADE

Raising the grade is difficult and potentially dangerous to trees if some precautions are not taken. To ensure that roots receive adequate drainage, it is best to install a drain system, as shown, with four-inch agricultural clay tile or perforated plastic pipe, sloping away from the base of the tree to a storm sewer or drainage ditch.

Vertical pipes should be placed to the height you expect to raise the grade, then construct a retaining wall around the trunk, from three to six feet from the tree. These steps help ensure proper aeration and give the trunk natural exposure.

When filling the grade with new soil, cover pipe openings to keep soil out; then begin filling with coarse gravel, then medium, then fine gravel, then top off with sandy loam.

Once the grade has been raised to the height of the vertical pipes, re-move the coverings and fill with coarse gravel. Then cover the pipe openings with wire mesh to keep critters out. The new grade can give an attractive and functional design to your lawn or garden, but never fill to the base of the tree. Trees need to rest at natural root level. Tiles help to drain off excess water and keep roots from drowning.

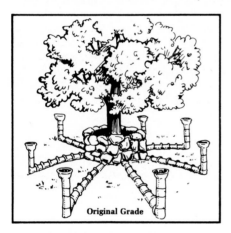

Original Grade

New Grade

through the process of photosynthesis. That word derives from the ancient Greek: "photo" meaning light and "synthesis" meaning putting together. This natural function within the body chemistry of a plant enables it to absorb and utilize chemical fertilizers, much as the human metabolism relies on minerals and vitamins for much of its function.

If you do not have a compost pile, you can start one right away. Any yard refuse may be used, such as grass clippings, leaves and small twigs, as well as any food scraps from the kitchen, including coffee grounds and tea leaves. Start with a six-inch layer on the ground, followed with a layer of chemical fertilizer or dehydrated cow manure; add another layer of organic refuse, continuing until you build a large pile. Make a small hollow at the top of the pile to catch and hold moisture, which aids in the breakdown of

FERTILIZER:

VITAMINS FOR PLANTS AND SOILS

Since Florida's soils are generally poor and deficient in texture and nutrients, you should be familiar with the properties of the common fertilizers available for enriching Florida soil. Whether you choose granular fertilizers, liquids, organic or inorganic materials, the basic properties are very much the same and those properties are spelled out on the product labels.

By law, all product labels must provide information by which you can judge the value of the material to be applied as well as standards of safe-handling.

WHAT'S ON THE LABEL?

Brand: Name of manufacturer, and standard product use.

Analysis: Gives the chemical analysis of the product in percentages. In the illustration below, 12 indicates 12% nitrogen (N), or high nitrogen for leaf and stem growth; 4% phosphorus (P) aids the plant in the growth of flowers, fruit and roots; and 8% potassium (K) affects the hardiness of the plant — its ability to resist extremes of heat and cold.

Contents: In addition to the basic elements, some products will contain other ingredients such as the trace elements, iron (Fe9, sulphur (S), or zinc (Zn), which affect coloration, tissue development and immunity to disease, etc. If present, they must be spelled out on the label. Some products, especially lawn fertilizers, may also contain insecticides or herbicides to help control, respectively, insects or weeds.

Inert Ingredients: The label will also tell what materials are included as carriers or fillers to facilitate absorption of nutrients by plants and soil but which are inert or inactive by themselves.

Precaution: Hazards, risks and chemical dangers must also be spelled out and suggestions for avoiding personal injury or damage to other plants and materials.

Weight: The label gives the weight of the product being sold.

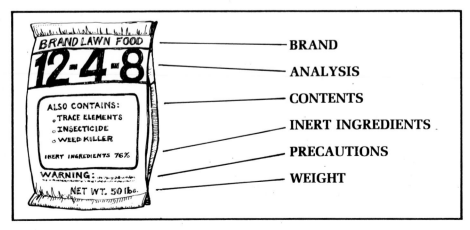

Peat moss is an excellent soil builder for flowers, lawns and vegetable gardens.

Commercial grade manure is also available as a soil-builder but apply according to direction.

the organic materials. Once a month, you should turn the pile over with a shovel. This keeps it well aerated, and it eventually will break down into a humus consistency.

To keep your compost pile from spreading, stake a fine wire mesh around it in a circle. This will allow oxygen and carbon dioxide to enter the compost pile and aid in the breakdown. During the process, heat and gas are generated, both of which affect the deterioration of the organic matter, turning it into the soft, crumbly humus that is the finest additive you can find for mixing with your soil.

MR. GREEN THUMB RULE

Working organic matter into the soil before planting is the best basis for good, healthy growth. But you still must apply fertilizer. Continued, strong growth will not result from only one application. Small amounts applied more often are advised, just as humans thrive better on three small meals a day rather than on just one large meal. Be sure to read label instructions on all fertilizers and consult your nurseryman for a steady nutritional program for your plants.

Fertilizer labels should give the following information:

1. Florida's registration code.
2. The brand name used by the manufacturer to identify the product.
3. The net weight, which tells the exact weight of the material in the bag.

4. The manufacturer's name.
5. The analysis, which lists the percentages of nitrogen, phosphorous and potash. This also should include secondary elements, if present, and the percentage of chlorine, which potentially can be toxic to plants when present in high concentrations.
6. Also important is the term "derived from," which gives the actual source of the ingredients.
7. A listing of inert ingredients, which are the fillers and carriers, or the inactive part of the fertilizer.
8. Details of any pesticide, contained on a yellow label with lettering in contrasting colors.

Florida laws concerning fertilizers have undergone many changes since they were first enacted in 1889. There is no magic combination of numbers to denote the best fertilizer. 6-6-6 often has been used. It is the lowest possible analysis that still can be termed a fertilizer under Florida law. By using more concentrated products, however, you will have fewer salt burn problems. You will save energy, time and effort in applying fertilizer, and, in general, you will get more for your dollar.

Fertilizers are sold in several forms: liquid, granular, pellets, capsules and spikes. Each has its own special value and particular application. Label directions will help you determine which will be most successful with your plants. Plants can only use fertilizer in liquid form, however. Even granular products must be dissolved in water before the tiny root hairs can absorb the needed nutrients for growth. Many people become confused over the relative merits of organic versus inorganic aids for plants. Organic aids are longer-lasting, but elements such as cow manure are more valuable as soil builder than as true fertilizer. Chemicals may not last as long, but they are less expensive and have a higher concentration of absorbable nutrients. Plants can use both chemical and organic fertilizers. Both should be included in your planned "diet" for your plants, as well as the all-important organic soil builders.

WATERING YOUR GARDEN

Eighty to ninety per cent of any plant is water. Water is vital to every form of life on Earth. Outside plants too often are killed by under-watering, just as indoor plants die from drowning, or over-watering. If a plant starts to turn gray, this is a sign of root stress, a danger signal that water is needed. In some cases, the leaves will cup and curl. What is termed the "critical wilt point" means the plant has become dehydrated and will die. Many enthusiastic gardeners complete a landscaping project, water it well for two weeks, them calmly forget it. When plants start wilting and dying, the nurseryman often is blamed when, in reality, the guilty party is the homeowner. A garden or landscaping is like having a new addition to the family, requiring daily attention and feeding to flourish. For healthy growth, you must check the moisture level in your soil every week.

In many areas of Florida, especially the coastal regions, salt is a problem that must be faced. A well can be a good source of water for your yard, but it is important to check its salinity. As a general rule, over a

20   THE VALUE OF DEEP WATERING

Plants with deep roots are hardier and more resistant to heat, cold and drought than plants with weak, shallow roots. By watering deeply, you encourage plants to develop deep roots, growing downward in search of moist soil.

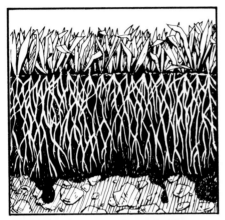

DO: Water deeply in order to develop deep, sturdy roots. Grass watered less often but more deeply will have greater durability to withstand extremes of cold and heat. The grass above ground is only part of the total plant. Without a deep root system, the grass above ground cannot have great durability.

DON'T: Watering lightly, even if it's more often, will not give the kind of saturation and penetration you want. Shallow roots promote weak growth above ground, and extreme temperatures and/or drought can dessimate your lawn. Don't let the healthy green color on top fool you; the plant's only as durable as the roots that support it.

thousand parts of salt per million parts of water will kill sensitive plants, such as azaleas; they may even succumb to as little as 700 parts per million. If you live in a beach community, you can reduce the effects of salt in your water and air by spraying plants regularly with fresh water and washing down any areas affected by flood or high-water conditions.

Many people become confused about watering their plants, shrubs and trees. "When?" and "How much?" are common questions, and there are no hard-and-fast rules. Plants use water at different rates according to the temperature, rate of growth and the season or time of year, as well as the type of soil.

For most plants, an inch of water a week will suffice, with two inches in the hot summer months. Florida usually gets 50-60 inches of rain each year, but this is not necessarily sufficient to keep the ground properly moist, day in and day out. You can test the soil by hand, pushing your fingers below the surface. If the soil is dry below two inches, you need to water. Remember that deep watering, especially for lawns, promotes a strong root system that spreads deep into the soil, enabling the plant to withstand heat and dry spells. Light watering tends to cause the root system to stay near the surface, where it is subject to damage during hot, dry days.

There are so many ways to water a garden, all effective, that it will be a matter of personal choice *how* you go about this necessary duty. Many Florida gardeners still use the old-fashioned watering can. It does the job as long as you have the time and energy. Its chief drawback is the inability to reach spots that may be too high or too densely surrounded by foliage. For convenient flower beds, however, the watering can is ideal, providing a gentle, effective rain that supplies the needed moisture without washing out the root system, especially around small plants.

A hose possibly is the most popular means of watering, both for efficiency and savings in time. Hoses come in several sizes, with the half-inch and ⅝-inch the ones most commonly used. Price ranges are determined by the quality of the hose. Very cheap plastic hoses may seem economical at first, but they tend to fold over and impede the water flow; also, their lifespan is limited. You should invest in a top-quality, rein- forced rubber hose which will not buckle. It will outlast any other type. The type of nozzle for your hose will depend on your personal preference. The adjustable type is the most popular. You can vary the flow of water from a wide spray down to a needle-sharp stream for reaching over shrubs and small trees. The higher-priced brass adjustable nozzle is best. With proper care, it should last a lifetime, while plastic nozzles will deteriorate and leak after a period of time. The breaker-bar type of nozzle also is recom- mended for watering flowers. It turns the flow into a wide, gentle spray that does not damage delicate plant foliage.

WATERING SYSTEMS

Some gardeners prefer automatic watering systems, and several are available. A water bubbler literally bubbles the water out gently like a spring. These also can be attached to wands for broader distribution. Soaker hoses are perforated, porous rubber or plastic hoses that distribute the water in thin, gentle streams. Mechanical sprinklers come in various types, from the stationary version that creates a large, circular spray to the oscillating sprinkler that can be adjusted to distribute a pattern, either square or rectangular. These are particularly useful in preventing water dropping onto undesired areas, such as pathways. For very large lawns or garden areas, the traveling sprinkler is recommended. These require laying out the hose in the desired configuration where you wish to water. The sprinkler creeps along the hose as it rotates and distributes the water.

For the ultimate in convenience, of course, there is the built-in sprink- ler system, which eliminates watering cans or hoses.

You can put in a sprinkler system yourself or have one installed. While it is best to have this done before planting your lawn, it can be done in existing gardens without major disruption of your landscaping. Check with a reputable company or discuss installation techniques with hard- ware stores that sell the pipe and sprinkler heads. Such a system can be operated manually or by an automatic timer. The automatic system en- sures that your garden and yard will be watered regularly, and one is advisable if you are away from home frequently for more than a few days at a time. Water is essential for the continued health and growth of your

Next to the soil itself, water is the most important factor in creating a healthy lawn and garden.

There are many sprinklers and spraying systems on the market. Select the best one for your own environment.

plants and lawn. If your soil dries out, you cannot expect your garden to flourish. Regular watering, either by hand or by a sprinkler system, is the most important element in gardening. Without water, your lawn, your trees and your flowers will die.

Another efficient system is drip irrigation, which refers to the slow application of water to soil through mechanical devices called emitters that are located along selected points from the main water supply. Most emitters are placed above ground, but some can be buried at shallow depths for protection. Drip irrigation introduces moisture to the soil through capillary action and is an excellent means of maintaining a proper moisture level. Because it uses less energy, drip irrigation requires less water and is considered 10 to 25 per cent more efficient than sprinkler systems. The savings in water alone makes this method very attractive.

Other advantages of drip irrigation:

1. Accelerated growth and increased yields.
2. Conservation of water while providing adequate moisture to root zones at all times.

3. Crops are not subjected to cycles of extreme soil moisture.
4. The area between rows remains dry, thereby reducing weed growth.
5. No runoff on hillsides or rolling ground.
6. Improved crop quality.
7. With water of poor quality, there is less damage to crops, because the water is applied only to the root area.

Despite its basic advantages, one problem in Florida affects drip irrigation systems. A sludge inhibits water flow under low pressure. Iron, sulfur and calcium in irrigation water can react with certain bacteria to produce an ochre sludge or slime that clogs the emitters. If you experience this problem, you should flush out your system occasionally with a solution containing chlorine bleach. While drip irrigation is very efficient for watering trees, shrubs, flower and vegetable gardens, tests have revealed that for watering lawns it is not as efficient as overhead sprinkler systems. Drip irrigation kits can be purchased at nursery or garden supply stores, where you also can get information on installation and maintenance.

Select the most efficient system for your particular needs, bearing in mind that water should be cherished and conserved. Using water efficiently will avoid wasting time and money. Water early morning for best results. Watering during the day is not harmful to plants, but it is less efficient due to evaporation in the hot sun. Watering at night, however, is not advised. It tends to promote fungus problems.

TEMPERATURES AND SEASONAL CHANGE

Florida is touted as the land of eternal sunshine, but we are subjected to low temperatures on occasion. Every ten to twelve years, we experience a freeze. Though Florida is largely a sub-tropical region, heat-loving plants that do well in the south end of the state are susceptible to injury in the colder areas inland and in the northern parts. Be warned, therefore, especially if you are a newcomer to Florida! Tropical plants can be placed outdoors from central Florida south. In St. Petersburg you will need to cover tropical plants during the cool season, while in Miami tropicals can flourish year-round with little or no protection. Before placing tropical plants outside, check the lowest temperature for your area. The color-coded map (page 24) also will help you be aware of the climate in your area.

As in most states, spring is a great season in Florida. Cool breezes mixed with warm, sunny days bring out the best in any garden. Azaleas burst forth with color in most areas, while in the northern and central areas, you will see occasional dogwoods in bloom.

Summer in Florida is warm to hot, with extremely high humidity. Day lilies appear, and the annuals such as zinnias and marigolds start giving the rich rewards of beauty that can be expected of them. But for all the blessings of spring and summer, fall is truly the most outstanding season in Florida, particularly favorable to petunias, both in the ground and in the popular hanging baskets which brighten patios. Fall is the time for planting cabbage, broccoli and cauliflower, all cool-season vegetables.

Winter demands that you take extra care of sensitive outdoor plants,

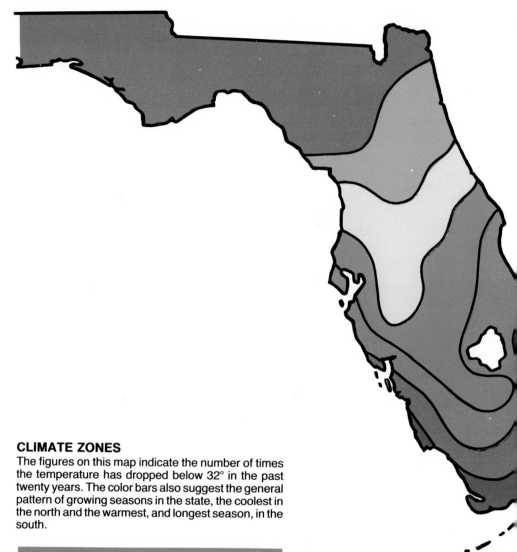

CLIMATE ZONES

The figures on this map indicate the number of times the temperature has dropped below 32° in the past twenty years. The color bars also suggest the general pattern of growing seasons in the state, the coolest in the north and the warmest, and longest season, in the south.

300	300
200	200
100	100
75	75
50	50
25	25
10	10

covering them with boxes to protect against cold nights. The only part of the state that does not drop to the 20s is the Keys; the rest of the state, especially areas around Tallahassee and Pensacola, can be cold enough to damage some of your plants. It is possible to hop into shorts and sun yourself on Christmas Day, but Florida in the winter can be chilly enough to inflict serious damage to some gardens.

PROTECTING PLANTS AGAINST HEAT AND COLD

The best insurance against possible plant loss in winter is to select the majority of your plants from cold-hardy species. But just as too much cold can permanently damage your garden, so can too much heat. Even hardy plants can suffer from prolonged exposure to the sun, especially if the temperatures are high, as they often are in Florida in summer. The wind and heat also can dry out foliage, as well as direct sunlight. No one has ever said that keeping a landscape or garden in top shape is easy. You must pay attention to every element that affects growth and appearance. Caring for your greenery, therefore, includes choosing the right annual for the right season as well as taking protective measures for perennials, shrubs and trees.

A vegetable garden, for instance, can last an extended season if leafy vegetables are planted in the shade, just as young azaleas are a natural for shady spots in the yard.

When a cold spell is anticipated, you must take steps to protect your plants. Burlap, a thermal sheet or a blanket are all good for protection against frost. You also can cover the ground itself to preserve the radiant heat stored in the soil. Large cardboard boxes are ideal for this purpose. Plastic (polyethylene film) also is excellent, but be warned: you cannot allow the plastic to touch the foliage, otherwise the plant will die. The plastic must be suspended over a framework of wood or wire. In this way, it creates a small greenhouse that holds in the heat and wards off the cold air.

For some special plants, you can use a low-wattage light bulb placed under a box or protective covering of plastic to raise the temperature a few degrees. Many beautiful theme parks in Florida use heaters on cold nights, but this system is too expensive and hazardous for the home gardener.

Water immersion is another way to save a garden from freezing. A third of an inch of water must be applied until the ground temperature rises above freezing. Again, you must be fully familiar with your watering system to employ this means. Also, there are hazards with water immersion: ice may form on branches or leaves and cause a plant to break. In reality, water immersion should be regarded as a desperate effort to save threatened plants during a freeze. It also increases the danger of rot and mold in the soil.

If you do suffer cold damage to your garden, do not trim off damaged branches until mid-April or May, when all danger of frost has passed. Some gardeners get out their pruning shears the day after a freeze, but trimming entices a plant to put forth new growth that may be killed by ensuing cold spells. Leave the dead leaves and branches alone. They provide some protection until the warm weather arrives. Once the plant

26

PREPARING YOUR PLANTS TO HANDLE TEMPERATURE EXTREMES

Whether you live in North, Central or South Florida, your plants will be exposed to temperature extremes at some point. The precautions illustrated on this page will help your plants develop hardiness to withstand the weather.

Apply fertilizers containing potassium (K), to protect against heat and cold damage.

Avoid reflected heat for sensitive plants.

Water during heat waves and before an expected hard freeze.

Mulch with compost, bark or leaves to hold moisture and protect against extreme temperatures.

Shelter cold-sensitive plants from winter winds.

begins to sprout, you can treat for cold damage. Starting at the end of a damaged branch, trim down until you come to fresh, healthy growth. Always paint the newly cut end of a branch with neutral copper and pruning paint to protect against infection and excessive sap drainage.

Remember the old adage: prevention is better than cure. It is far easier and cheaper to plan ahead than to try and save your plants once they are withered by winter chill, scorched by summer sunshine or infested with insects.

SELECTING YOUR PLANTS

While you may have many ideas of your own, it is advisable to check with a nursery about the type and size of plants to install in your yard or garden. When selecting plants at the nursery, pay special attention to the condition of the leaves. Make sure a leaf is healthy — rich, dark green rather than a yellowish-green (chlorotic) hue that denotes a deficiency or disease. Even plants with naturally variegated leaves should be firm, healthy looking and free of brown spots that could be fungus infection. Above all, a plant must be free of insects and any sign of insect damage.

Share your landscaping ideas with your nurseryman and ask about the ultimate size, height and width of any plants you consider purchasing. Check on any potential root problems, insect or fungus susceptibility. What are the nutritional requirements? Is the plant prone to nematode infection? Does it require a special pH? How much light and water will it need for optimum growth?

Take a pad and pencil with you to record the information you get from your nurseryman. Your notes will be helpful when you return home and begin putting in your plants. Above all, take heed of the advice you get from your nursery. Most of these stores have qualified personnel familiar with the stock and the growing requirements of each type of plant. They should be eager to help, because a satisfied customer is a repeat customer. Get to know your nurseryman, just as you get to know your doctor or dentist. He can be invaluable when it comes to resolving your particular gardening problems or selecting the right trees, shrubs and flowers for your yard.

CHAPTER TWO

Florida Trees and Palms

Florida is famous for many things, but most of all its abundance and variety of trees and palms. Our state truly is a growing paradise, with the widest range of palms, evergreens, deciduous and flowering trees to be found anywhere in the U.S. Trees may be the slowest-growing of all plants, but they are the most enduring, stately and impressive elements in any landscape. They are an artistic investment that pays off over the years not only in beauty but in increased value for your property.

SELECTING THE RIGHT TREE

Before purchasing any trees for your landscaping, check the existing trees to determine if you want to keep them or replace them with other species of a different size or shape and aesthetic appeal. Your plans may call for trees to balance out the overall look you desire on your property. Or you may decide on trees that not only provide foliage but also blossoms to add color in the spring, such as the exotic Royal Poinciana with its exquisite orange-red flowers or the Orchid Tree with its multi-colored blossoms that grow up to six inches across. Check with your nursery for recommendations. You may imagine a large tree standing in stately majesty in the middle of your front lawn. But a mature tree can cost ten times as much as a younger sapling that you can nurture and watch grow to its full size. Your decision, therefore, can be affected by the amount you wish to spend on a tree. Trees are the most expensive items in any landscaping, but they endure the longest and give the richest rewards in protection, beauty and improved value.

Some trees grow better than others in various parts of Florida. Knowing the high and low temperatures (micro-climate) of your location is helpful in making a decision about the type of trees to plant. And do not shop only for price; shop for quality. A cheap tree may save you a little now, but in time you may be dissatisfied and have to pay to have it removed. Trees are like everything else — you get what you pay for. Cheap trees seldom are a satisfying or good investment.

Years ago, most trees were field-grown, in the ground. Transplanting 29

30   resulted in shock, and often the transplanted tree did not survive. If you buy a field-grown tree, make sure it has a compact root system. Ask if the tree has been root-pruned to minimize transplant shock, then make sure the tree has been well watered, cultivated and fertilized.

These days, the majority of commercial nurseries grow trees in containers, which reduces transplant shock. A large metal or concrete ring surrounds the tree root system, holding the roots intact and allowing for expansion as the tree grows. Container-grown trees can vary from 10 to 25 feet in height. They can be transplanted without damage and will adapt to their new location at any time or season of the year.

Follow these guidelines before purchasing your trees:

1. Check your landscape plan. Make sure you have enough trees to complete the look you want.

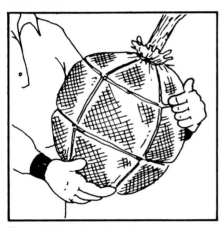

To avoid damaging the plant, always carry trees by the root ball, not the trunk.

To prevent damage in transit, secure the plant out of the wind as much as possible.

TRANSPORTING TREES FROM THE NURSERY

Selecting the right trees for your landscape is one of the most important decisions you will make. Once you have decided on the size and variety, you should also consider how to bring your trees home safely and without damage.

When carrying trees, hold them by the root ball, not by the trunk alone. If you use a truck or trailer, secure the plants and place them for the least wind abrasion. If you put them in the trunk of the car, place the root ball in first and secure the plant firmly. Tie the trunk lid down. In either case drive slowly and carefully. Wind will damage leaves.

If the tree is heavy, get help. Don't drag or pull the tree. Don't abrade the bark and don't crush the root ball.

Once you've selected the proper planting site where the tree will have a proper exposure and plenty of growing room, carry the tree by the root ball to the digging site.

Dig the hole twice as wide as the root ball. Place the plant straight upright in the center of the hole. Do not remove burlap material — the roots will grow through. Make sure the soil level does not come above the top of the ball or the top of the level of soil in the nursery container. Enrich with peat moss, refill soil, and water deeply immediately after planting.

2. Always deal with a reputable nursery that will guarantee its stock and replace any tree that does not survive.
3. Make sure the tree you select fits your height and width specifications in your landscape plan. Your nurseryman will be able to tell you the maximum height and width of any tree.
4. Always buy a tree that is vigorous and growing abundantly.
5. Check the leaves. They should be well formed and relatively free of insects or disease.
6. If the tree is dormant, scratch the bark to see if the cambium layer is green and moist. This is the green layer just beneath the outer bark. It is also called the growth layer. And examine the buds (tips of new growth). They should be ready to swell and starting to grow.

You may decide to have your nursery plant your trees, but if you prefer to do it yourself, here are some tips to help you guard against improper planting.

Many new trees must be staked for the first year to support them against wind and weather, especially trees that may be top-heavy with more foliage than the root system is able to support. Place three wooden stakes in a circle, three to five feet from the hole in which you place the tree. Attach guide wires to the stakes and, before wrapping these around the tree itself, thread a twelve-inch piece of old garden hose on the guide wires. Where the wire wraps around the tree trunk, slide the hose to this point so the wire does not cut into the bark. The hose protects the tree from injury. Do not nail pieces of wood to the tree to protect it from being cut by the guide wires. While this may be effective temporarily, the damage to the tree can lead to fungus and bore infections. The pieces of hose are far more efficient.

If the tree is small enough, you may drive one heavy wooden stake a few inches from the trunk and attach the tree to the stake to help support it. However, the three-stake method is the best way to ensure that your newly planted tree remains upright until the root system has taken hold, usually after the first year.

CARING FOR YOUR TREES

The root system is the key to a healthy tree. After properly planting and staking your tree, water and fertilize it regularly to help build a good root system. Deep watering promotes a strong root system that makes a tree more drought-resistant and better able to withstand Florida's torrential rains and thunderstorms. Trees should be fed at least three times a year. As a general rule, add fertilizer and soil builders in February/March, May/June and September/October. Your nursery can advise you on a good tree and shrub fertilizer for your area. There are several ways to apply this very necessary supplement: the punch-bar method, watering rods, spikes, liquid fertilizer or by applying fertilizer on the ground around a tree.

The *punch-bar* method uses a steel rod that is hammered into the ground to a depth of twelve inches. Make 12 to 24 holes beginning two feet from the trunk of the tree and continuing every two to three feet to the drip line (the overhang of the branches) and two feet *past* the drip line. If your

Florida Gardening

32

Hammer notched stakes into the ground on three sides of the tree.

STAKING NEW TREES

Newly transplanted trees will probably require staking against the strong Florida winds. Since new root growth is often tender and delicate, swaying can sever roots and, ultimately, kill young trees. Stakes may need to remain from one to two years, depending upon the strength, growth and vitality of the tree.

Your first concern is to give support without damaging the tree. The illustrations on this page will indicate how to brace your young trees by any of several practical methods.

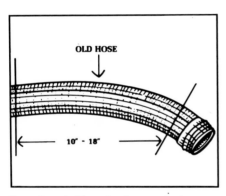

Cut strips of old garden hose or burlap to protect the tree.

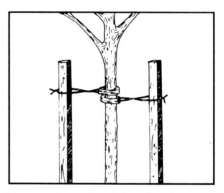

For some trees, two stakes placed as shown will give adequate support.

Run lengths of wire or twine through the hose and tie as shown.

Never nail into trees. This only encourages disease and insects. A single stake will help support larger trees.

rod encounters a root, move it over a few inches to avoid damage. When you have completed punching the holes, pour fertilizer into them and water thoroughly (about a half-inch of water).

The *watering-rod* method is the same principle as the punch bar, with the addition of water pressure. A watering rod is attached to the garden hose and inserted deep into the soil around the tree in the same manner described above. Some watering rods have an attachment for inserting a cartridge of fertilizer that dissolves in the water as it flows into the ground. This method can water and fertilize the tree at the same time.

Spikes are a relatively new product on the market and are most effective and easy to use. They are solid cores of fertilizer enclosed in a tube that is hammered into the ground. As the tree is watered, the moisture dissolves the fertilizer gradually, giving a long-term feeding to the root system.

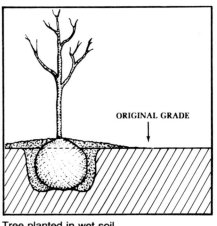

Tree planted in wet soil

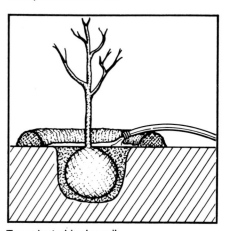

Tree planted in dry soil

TREE PLANTING IN WET OR DRY SOIL

Young trees need proper amounts of moisture to thrive and develop a strong root system. In dry soil, you may need to have a system for ensuring extra moisture. But in wet soils, especially in coastal regions, too much water can damage roots, encourage diseases, and insect problems. Here are a couple of ways for dealing with each.

In wet soil plant the tree so that the root ball stands a few inches above the grade level. Build up soil around the trunk. This should hold roots above the water table enough to allow proper growth and aeration of roots.

In dry soil, or in hot summer months, build a four-inch soil berm about fifteen inches from the base of the tree all around the trunk. The berm will hold extra water and help provide adequate moisture for young roots.

Liquid fertilizers are the easiest method of fertilization for everything in your yard or garden. They can be applied by watering can, siphoned into the hose or into the sprinkler system. They do not leach away any quicker than other methods of fertilization and are effective, economical and easy to apply.

Broadcasting granular fertilizer around a tree also is simple. Start about a foot away from the trunk and apply a few feet past the drip line. Normal watering will dissolve the fertilizer and carry it down to the root system.

TREE TRIMMING

Eventually, all trees must be trimmed, but this does not mean butchering a tree or topping it. It usually is best to hire a professional to handle any large trimming, not only to have it done properly, but to avoid the dangers of falling branches. For smaller branches, however, you should be able to do the job yourself, using a saw or a chainsaw.

Branches may grow over the house or into power lines. Or, you may suffer tree damage during the hurricane season. You may wish to eliminate heavy shade from part of your yard. Diseased limbs also should be removed. If you see mistletoe growing in the tree, you should remove this parasite, which usually requires cutting off a branch. When cutting, remove the small leafy growth first, then trim branches out in sections. Try to retain the aesthetic balance of the tree so that you do not wind up with a lopsided appearance. Try to retain the natural "look" of the tree: balanced on all sides under normal growing conditions.

If you have to remove a major branch, determine where you will make the cut, then undercut a "V" a few inches closer to the trunk. Next, proceed with your top cut. The weight of the branch will cause it to break evenly at the point of the undercut. Sometimes, you may need to attach a rope to the branch to hold it in place while cutting and to prevent it from falling into an undesired spot, such as a flower bed or other shrubs. The branch then can be lowered gently to the ground.

During the hurricane season, it is advisable to check trees for diseased areas that denote weakened limbs. These could fall during high winds and damage your property. Sawdust and blackened areas on the bark can indicate questionable parts that need attention. It is well worth a horticulturist's fee to have your trees examined periodically so you can maintain them in top condition.

TRANSPLANTING TREES

Good initial planning of landscaping will eliminate the need to transplant a tree, such as when you put a patio or pool in your yard. If at all possible, however, leave your trees where they are. Transplanting a large tree is equivalent to major surgery, and if improperly done, the patient may not recover. Call in a professional to move any large tree. Smaller ones you can move yourself, remembering the following guidelines:

1. Transplant only in the dormant season, December-January.

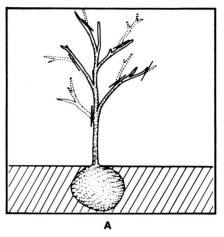

A

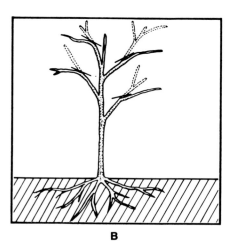

B

SHAPING AND PRUNING OF YOUNG SHADE TREES

Shaping and pruning will help give young trees their distinctive shape and encourage growth. Newly transplanted trees should be pruned back to compensate for roots lost in transplanting. About 25 percent of top growth should be trimmed back if the tree was balled-and-burlapped; about 40 percent should be trimmed if the tree was transplanted bare-rooted.

Trimming from the top, example B, will encourage lateral growth and outward spread, for best shade.

For vertical, upward growth, trim limbs and branches facing outward above buds, as in example C.

Growth at the base of the trunk encourages thicker trunk development, but this also creates a bushier, shrub-like appearance. For shade trees with a tall, erect trunk, trim lower growth as shown in example D once the tree has become established.

Normally pruning paint is not required for stripling trees, but limbs of an inch or more in diameter on larger trees should be painted to prevent loss of sap and possible insect or disease damage.

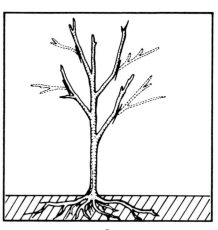

C

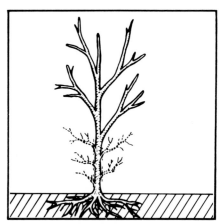

D

2. Be sure you move the tree to a location large enough for the tree's ultimate height and width.
3. Dig the hole at the new location twice as wide and twice as deep as the root ball of the tree you are transplanting.
4. When digging the hole, save the top soil and mix it with an equal amount of peat moss before filling it back around the roots of the transplanted tree. To get the hair roots off to a good start, hose the mixture of peat moss and topsoil around the root ball and force it into the space between the roots. Make sure there are no air pockets beneath the root ball. After filling the hole, make a ring around the base of the tree with the soil that is left over. This forms a basin to catch water and allows it to drain down around the roots.
5. To minimize transplant shock, apply a root stimulator-type fertilizer, one high in phosphorous (the middle number on the bag). Place this along with the peat-moss mixture around the root ball. A good liquid plant food also may be used, but avoid high-nitrogen lawn fertilizers. These can burn the roots.
6. Prune the tree, both in height and width, unless you are transplanting a container-grown tree. These rarely need pruning after being moved. Bare-rooted trees should be pruned 30 to 50 percent. Balled and burlap trees should be pruned 25 to 30 percent.
7. If the transplanted tree is taller than five or six feet, you should stake it for the first year until the roots grow out and are able to support it.
8. To prevent sun scald on certain trees, wrap the trunk with tree-wrap, obtainable at your nursery. Ask which trees need this added protection after transplanting.
9. Water is the most vital factor to a newly transplanted tree. Be sure to water every day for the first two weeks, dropping to once every two days for the following two weeks.

The following is a list of suggested trees from which you can make your selection:

Cercis canadensis — Red Bud — Height: 20-30 ft.

Native to Florida, the red bud is fairly cold-hardy and grows mostly in the northern and central parts of the state. A deciduous tree in winter, the red bud bursts into an umbrella of rose-pink flowers in spring, followed by the leaves that replace the blossoms and remain until they fall at the end of the year. Also available with white flowers.

Cornus florida — Dogwood — Height: 20-30 ft.

The flowering dogwood is a traditional spring delight for nature lovers, with silvery-white bracts its main attraction more than the actual flowers, which are relatively inconspicuous. The dogwood enjoys being shaded by other trees and protected from excessive heat, and grows well in enriched soil. An azalea-gardenia fertilizer is recommended for improved growth and appearance. The dogwood retains its attractive appearance even in the deciduous stage in winter.

Dogwood Tree   Dogwood blossoms

Koelreuteria formosana — Golden Raintree — Height: 20-30 ft.

An exceptionally beautiful specimen for landscaping, the Golden Raintree is one of Florida's most popular trees. It is best adapted to north and central areas of the state. It sometimes grows in a graceful, irregular pattern, with brilliant yellow panicles on the tips of the branches in October, followed by attractive pink seed pods almost two inches across. A deciduous tree, the Golden Raintree can be planted on the east and west sides of the house, providing leafy shade in summer and allowing sunshine through in the winter after the leaves have fallen.

Jacaranda acutifolia — Jacaranda — Height: 50 ft.

Growing in central and south Florida, the jacaranda is a beautifully balanced tree, often as tall as it is wide. Its pale-blue, trumpet-shaped flowers appear in May and June, making it one of the most appealing trees for landscaping. However, because of its size, it may not be suitable for smaller gardens. A deciduous tree, it sheds its graceful, feathery leaves in winter. It enjoys full sun and will tolerate sandy soils but is not salt-tolerant.

Golden Raintree   Jacaranda

Peltophorum

Green Ash Tree

Peltophorum inerme — Peltophorum — Height: 40-50 ft.

Sometimes called the yellow poinciana or the yellow jacaranda because of similar foliage, this evergreen tree bears spikes of golden yellow flowers that bloom in early July.

Fraxinus pennsylvanica — Green Ash — Height: 40 ft.

Growing in north and central Florida, the green ash is a tall, upright tree with beautiful, dark-green leaves during the warm months. But it loses its foliage for longer periods than most deciduous trees.

Acer rubrum — Red Maple — Height: 75 ft.

For wet areas, the Florida swamp red maple is ideal. It looks a lot like the northern maples, with three-lobed leaves that turn red in November and drop. Growing in full sun to partial shade, the red maple flowers from December through January. However, it is not salt-tolerant and is prone to tree bores.

Magnolia grandiflora — Magnolia — Height: 40-75 ft.

This Florida-native tree is a large, stately evergreen with big, white, fragrant blossoms in late spring. Like most flowering trees, the magnolia does best in full sun. Large amounts of peat moss and cow manure are recommended for maximum growth.

Pinus elliotti — Slash pine — Height: 40-60 ft.

Like the sand pine (clausa) and the long-leafed pine (palustris), the

Slash Pines

Carrotwood Trees

slash pine is native to Florida. If you have some of these trees on your property, leave them where they are. The slash pine does not tolerate grade change. This tree also does not flourish with heavy equipment close to the root system, which is why barricades often are built around them to protect them from builders.

Cupania anacardioidres — Carrotwood — Height: 30-40 ft.

A native of Australia, the carrotwood has excellent salt tolerance but may be injured by freezing temperatures. An evergreen, this tree is best adapted to central and south Florida. It grows into a round, spreading shape that is most graceful.

Salix babylonica — Weeping Willow — Height: 25-40 ft.

Wet areas, ditch banks and ponds are natural settings for this tree. Its graceful branches droop to the ground. Be sure to plant a weeping willow in moist soil areas. These trees are ravenous water consumers. Their roots have been known to spread immense distances in search of moisture. Never plant a weeping willow close to a house or sewer pipes. The hair roots will wind up clogging the sewer line.

Melia azedarach — China Berry — Height: 40 ft.

Like the weeping willow, this tree is prone to spread its roots into sewer lines, so be careful where you plant. An excellent shade tree with dense foliage, the china berry has blue blossoms in summer but drops both its berries and leaves in winter. Many people regard the china berry as a "messy" tree. It is salt-tolerant and grows in every part of Florida.

Liquidambar styraciflua — Sweetgum — Height: 50-70 ft.

Where an upright, tall tree is desired, the sweetgum is an excellent choice. It spreads its foliage 30-40 feet across and is colorful. Its leaves turn

Sweetgum Tree

Sweetgum Foliage

red, orange and yellow in the fall before they drop in the winter. Be warned, however. The sweetgum produces a spiny fruit that is most uncomfortable to walk on barefoot! A well-drained spot is best for the sweetgum.

Taxodium distichum — Bald cypress — Height: 75-100 ft.

Some of Florida's famous gardens, such as Cypress Gardens, owe their unique beauty to this impressive tree that grows throughout the state, in water as well as on dry land. Young trees are pyramidal in shape, shooting up and out into a "flat top" that can reach over 100 feet. This widely acclaimed tree is prized for its useful, long-lasting lumber and for its "knees," which enable it to grow up above water level in swampy terrain. A very hardy tree, the bald cypress has few problems with insects or diseases.

Bald Cypress

Bald Cypress knees in water

Ulmus parvifolia — Chinese Elm — Height: 20-35 ft.

Semi-evergreen and semi-deciduous, the Chinese elm has small, fine-textured leaves. It will grow in most soils in Florida but has only a fair salt tolerance. It is an excellent choice where a small, fast-growing tree is needed.

Ilex opaca — American Holly — Height: 30-50 ft.

There are several varieties of this plant: the East Palatka, which has large, beautiful berries; the Howard, Taber #4, Savannah, Fort McCoy, Croonenberg and the Dupre. Used for centuries for bordering avenues, American holly grows well in north and central Florida.

Ilex cassine — Dahoon — Height: 30-40 ft.

Native to swamps, including the Biscayne Bay area, the dahoon has more salt tolerance than most hollies and displays the traditional red berries during the Christmas season. Ideal as a small tree, it grows well in moist soil.

Ilex cornuta — Chinese Holly — Height: 20 ft.

Although it usually grows to tree size, the Chinese holly often is used as a shrub. Not very salt-tolerant, it grows well in full sun and will tolerate partial shade. The dark, shiny leaves are edged with sharp spines. One popular and very common variety is *Burford*.

Juniperus silicicola — Southern Red Cedar — Height: 25-40 ft.

Cone-shaped when young, the red cedar gains a flat top at maturity, grows throughout Florida and is quite salt-tolerant. It can be grown as a landscape specimen or used as a hedge. As with other junipers, mites can become a problem for the red cedar.

Sapium sebiferum — Chinese Tallow — Height: 30 ft.

Attaining a width of 30-35 feet, this fast-growing tree has orange, red, yellow and wine-colored leaves before it drops them during the winter. It prefers slightly acid soil.

American Holly

Deodar Cedar   Camphor Trees

Cedrus deodara — Deodar Cedar — Height: 40-50 ft.

Resembling the northern spruce and hemlock, the deodar cedar grows moderately into a blue-green pyramid of foliage. It can be planted anywhere in Florida.

Cinnamomum camphora — Camphor Tree — Height: 40-50 ft.

The camphor tree does best in north and central Florida, although it can be grown throughout the state. This magnificient tree grows to mammoth size.

Delonix regia — Royal Poinciana — Height: 30-40 ft.

Best adapted to lower protected areas in central and south Florida, the deciduous royal poinciana is covered in exquisite orange-red blossoms in May and June. It is one of the most beautiful trees to use as a backdrop for your landscaped garden and grows as tall as it does wide.

A well-established Camphor Tree

Bottle Brush   Indian Rosewood

Callistemon rigidus — Bottle Brush — Height: 15-20 ft.

This tree has super spikes of red flowers in spring that resemble the old-fashioned bottle brushes. It makes an outstanding, small specimen. In a corner planting or as an accent plant, it is an excellent accent in the landscape. The bottle brush has only fair salt tolerance but grows throughout the state.

Dalbergia sissoo — Indian Rosewood — Height: 40-45 ft.

This tree is considered semi-evergreen, or semi-deciduous. It has an upright, rounded head and can be used for avenue planting or as a specimen tree in the landscape. In northern Florida, it is sometimes totally bared of its foliage in a hard frost.

Bauhinia spp. — Orchid Tree — Height: 25 ft.

This deciduous tree is grown in central and south Florida. It is admired for its orchid-like flowers, which can grow up to 3-4 inches across and come in a number of different colors such as white, red, purple and pink. Some varieties have flowers as large as six inches across. As a specimen or a small framing tree, the orchid tree is superb.

EVER-POPULAR OAKS

Quercus virginiana — Live Oak — Height: 40-50 ft.

A moderate grower, the live oak is considered the best tree for Florida, encountering few problems with disease or insects and having a lengthy life span. It is salt-tolerant and, being evergreen, it maintains its leaves year 'round. However, the live oak does spread as much as 50 feet, so allow plenty of room for it in your landscaping plans.

Quercus nigra — Water Oak — Height: 40-60 ft.

Unlike the live oak, the water oak grows upright rather than spread-

Live Oak

Laurel Oak

ing, sometimes to heights of over 100 feet. A moderate-to-fast grower, it takes alkaline soils well, though it may show some iron deficiency. In fall, some leaves do drop, but the tree is never devoid totally of foliage.

Quercus laurifolia — Laurel Oak — Height: 50-60 ft.

Like the water oak, the laurel can grow in excess of 100 feet tall and also is partially deciduous. Its life span is at least 80 years, making it a permanent fixture in most locations. Its long, slender leaves (2-3 inches) create thick, robust foliage. Often used along public streets and avenues as well as in private homes, the laurel oak has only fair salt tolerance.

Grevillea robusta — Silk Oak — Height: 50-60 ft.

Despite its name, this is not a true oak tree but belongs to the Proteaceae family that originated in Australia. A rapid grower, it flourishes in central and south Florida with an attractive display of golden flowers. Because it drops a lot of leaves and small twigs, the silk oak is considered a "messy" tree. Allow plenty of room for its maximum growth.

FLORIDA PALMS

Florida is famous for many things, including its incredible variety and size of palm trees. Every visitor remarks on the majestic Washingtonian palms that line our boulevards, the beautiful, curved elegance of the coconut palm, the stately royal palms standing like living concrete poles, crowned with green, glossy foliage. Easier to grow than trees or shrubs, palms can be a picturesque addition to any yard, with a size and shape to satisfy your landscape requirements.

There are many palm varieties. Some are very tropical, others are moderate and a few are cold-hardy, able to withstand near-freezing temperatures and survive in the coldest parts of Florida. For a lush, tropical look to your property or garden, you cannot choose any plant more suitable than a palm tree.

Study your available space and your proposed landscape plan before you choose your palms. Whatever size you select, the palms should remain in scale with your landscape and not upset the intended artistic balance. In some areas, a tall, slender palm will enhance the overall look you want. In other spots, you may need a palm with a short, fat trunk. Always remember the light requirements of the species you choose, as well as its cold-hardiness.

Most palms are tolerant of Florida's sandy soil. But you can improve the growth and appearance of your palms by adding peat moss, cow manure, chicken manure or wood chips to the soil. In addition to a good palm food or general fertilizer, you should apply manganese and magnesium at the rate of one pound per inch of trunk diameter, up to five pounds. One pound of palm food or general fertilizer should be applied for every inch of trunk diameter, as well. These applications should be done three times a year, in February, June and October. Palm trees are like every other living thing: they need feeding. Palms need high levels of both manganese and magnesium. They also need watering on a regular basis. Although mature palms are among the most drought-resistant plants, it is advisable to water them once a week. Newly planted palms, like trees, need more frequent watering until they become established: daily for two weeks after planting, then once a week thereafter.

As a palm tree grows, it sheds its fronds at the bottom of the trunk. When you observe fronds turning yellow, then brown, it is advisable to trim them off, using a palm saw. This tool has a large curved blade on a long extension pole. Never try to trim the center of a palm. This is the bud from which new fronds emerge. Trimming the bud will kill a palm tree. Trimming should be done when the fronds turn yellow and are still tender. Once they turn brown, they become hard and are difficult to cut.

Adonidia merrillii — Manila Palm — Height: 20-25 ft.

This salt-tolerant, small palm has a green crown shaft and is sometimes called the baby royal palm. The foliage is elegant with bright-red clusters of fruit.

Roystonea spp. — Royal Palm — Height: 100 ft.

This stately palm requires a great deal of moisture to look its best. Its

Royal Palm

erect, white, cement-like trunk is topped with a three-foot green shaft from which feathery fronds grow, often as long as ten feet. It is the most widely grown palm from Sarasota to Miami. A native variety grows in the everglades.

Cocos nucifera — Coconut Palm — Height: 80-100 ft.

Best known for its fruit, the coconut palm has feathery fronds from ten to fifteen feet long, and the coconuts have a rough, fibrous husk. To avoid lethal yellowing (described in a later chapter on diseases), you should plant the dwarf Malayan variety, which is immune to this disease.

Chrysalidocarpus lutescens — Areca Palm or Cane Palm — Height: 20 ft.

Very salt-tolerant, this palm can be used in south Florida as a landscape specimen. In north and central parts of the state, it is best used as a potted specimen for patios and indoor plantings. With its long, arching, feathery fronds, the areca is a very attractive and versatile palm for landscaping.

Caryota spp. — Fish-tail Palm — Height: 40 ft.

A clump-type growing palm, the fish-tail grows in lower and central parts of Florida, preferably in protected areas. An impressive landscape addition, this palm gets its name from the shape of the fronds.

Chamaedorea elegans/Neanthe bella — Household Palm — Height: 8-10 ft.

Here is one of the few palms that produces a variety of mature leaves after germinating from seed. Placed near a bright window, it will grow and flower indoors, and has both male and female plants.

Areca Palm

Palms in a tropical setting

Chinese Fan Palm

Livistona chinesis — **Chinese Fan Palm** — **Height: 20-30 ft.**

Sometimes called the Chinese fountain palm, this one is only moderately salt-tolerant and should be grown in full sun to partial shade. A moderate-sized palm, the Chinese fan creates a nice effect with the ends of the palmate curling slightly on the edges. There are downward-pointing spines along the petiole, making this palm easy to identify.

Arecastrum komanzoffianum — **Queen Palm** — **Height: 40 ft.**

A straight-trunk palm requiring full sun for best growth, the queen palm is not very salt-tolerant. Once called the *Cocos plumosa*, it is the most popular palm in central Florida.

Queen Palm

Queen Palm with frizzle top

Phoenix roebelenii — Pygmy Date Palm — Height: 8-12 ft.

Frequently grown in central and south Florida, this is a graceful, well-shaped dwarf palm with large, three-inch thorns at the base of each leaf petiole. An excellent choice for a planter or entry, this small palm must be protected from hard freezes.

Paurotis wrightii — Paurotis Palm — Height: 30-40 ft.

A native of the Florida everglades, the paurotis palm loves wet areas but also will grow on higher, dry ground. It has good salt tolerance and grows well in full sun to partial shade.

Acrocomia spp. — Gru Gru Palm — Height: 40-50 ft.

The large thorns on the leaf stalks and trunk of this palm give it a menacing appearance that causes a lot of comment, especially from tourists. It thrives in sandy soil and full sun. Look for it at nurseries specializing in unusual palms.

COLD-HARDY PALMS

Butia captita — Pindo Palm — Height: 15-20 ft.

Once called *Cocus australis*, the pindo palm is one of the most cold-hardy palms in Florida, as well as being very salt-tolerant. It is a slow-growing, very attractive specimen palm with beautiful, blue-green pinnate and gracefully curved fronds.

Paurotis Palm (Saw Cabbage)

Pindo Palm

Cabbage Palmetto

Sabal palmetto — Cabbage Palmetto — Height: 60-80 ft.

The state tree of Florida, the cabbage palmetto is our most cold-hardy native palm. It grows in any part of the state and in any type of soil. It is so salt-tolerant that it will grow right down into salt water. From the southern Keys to Tallahassee, this palm can be seen growing wild.

Phoenix canariensis — Canary Island Date Palm — Height: 50-60 ft.

This is one of our most beautiful specimen palms, often used to border avenues. In landscaping, it needs plenty of room because of its large size. With its straight, thick, bulging trunk and the diamond pattern formed where the fronds grow, it is sometimes called the pineapple palm.

Chamaerops humilis — European Fan Palm — Height: 15 ft.

A native of southern Europe, this palm grows in north, central and southern Florida. It is tolerant of many different soils and grows best in partial shade to full sun. A slow grower, the fan palm is considered a dwarf variety. It has fan-shaped fronds and often puts out several trunks at the same time.

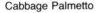

Canary Island Date Palm

Washington Palm

Washington Palm

Rhapis Excelsa — Lady Palm — Height: 8-10 ft.

Used as foundation plant or grown in containers for patios and decks, this is another clump-growing palm with an abundance of fan leaves extending from the base. The lady palm prefers shade to partial shade, and is not salt-tolerant. But it can be planted on the side of a house that is protected from salt spray.

Washingtonia robusta — Washington Palm — Height: 60 ft.

For avenue planting, this palm is unequalled. It is too large for small properties, and its height makes it difficult to trim. It does best in full sun, has good salt tolerance and can be grown throughout Florida. When the old fronds begin to droop, they hang down like a petticoat around the trunk.

Lady Palm grown as a decorative hedge   *RHAPIS   LADY PALM*

Florida's Finest Trees

Common Name	Scientific Name	Growth Rate	Shape	Color	Season	Salt Tolerance	Height	N, C, S
Banana-Leaf Acacia	Acacia auriculaeformis	Fast	Upright	Yellow	Summer, Fall	Good	20'-30'	C,S
Woman's Tongue	Albizzia lebbek	Fast	Spreading	White, Green	Summer, Fall	Good	30'-35'	N,C,S
Mimosa	Albizzia julibrissin	Fast	Spreading	Pink	Summer, Fall	Good	25'-35'	C,N,S
Araucaris Norfolk Monkey Puzzel	Araucaria spp. Excelsa Bidwilli	Moderate Moderate	Upright Upright			Very good Very good	75'-100' 60'-80'	C,S C,S
Orchid Tree	Bauhinia — spp.	Fast	Upright to Spreading	White, Pink, Red, Purple	Spring	Good	20'-30'	C,S
Lipstick Tree	Bixa orellana	Fast	Round Headed	Pinkish Red	Fall	Good	20'-30'	C,S
Toog	Bischofia jauanica	Fast	Round Headed			Fair	30'-45'	C,S
Shaving-Brush Tree	Bombax spp.	Fast	Spreading	Red	Winter	Fair	30'	S
Flame Tree	Brachychiton acerifolium	Fast	Upright	Red	Fall, Winter	Fair	25'-30'	S
Black Olive	Bucida buceras	Moderate	Spreading			Poor	25'-30'	S
Golden Shower	Cassia-alata	Moderate	Spreading	Yellow Gold	Summer	Good	20'-35'	C,S
Australian Pine	Casuarina equisetifolia	Fast	Upright			Excellent	60'-80'	C,S
Camphor	Cinnamomum camphora	Moderate	Upright to Spreading	Yellow	Spring	Fair	50'-60'	N,C,S

Common Name	Scientific Name	Growth Rate	Shape	Color	Season	Salt Tolerance	Height	N, C, S
Sea Grape	Coccolobis uvifera	Moderate	Upright to Spreading			Excellent	20'-25'	C,S
Redbud	Cercis canadensis	Moderate	Spreading	Dark Pink	Spring	Fair	25'-30'	N,C
Fringe-Tree	Chionanthus virginica	Slow	Upright	Greenish White	Spring	Fair	20'-30'	N,C
Geiger Tree	Cordia sebestena	Moderate	Round-up	Orange-Red	Spring, Summer	Excellent	20'-25'	S
Flowering Dogwood	Cornus Florida	Moderate	Upright	White	Spring	Poor	18'-30'	N,C
Carrotwood	Cupania anacardioides	Fast	Upright			Excellent	30'-40'	C,S
Indian Rosewood	Dalbergia sissoo	Moderate	Upright			Fair	35'-45'	C,S
Royal Poinciana	Delonix regia	Fast	Spreading	Red-Orange	Summer	Good	30'-40'	C,S
Pink Ball	Dombeya-wallichii	Fast	Upright	Pink	Summer	Poor	15'-30'	C,S
Ear Tree	Enterolobium cyclolarpum	Fast	Spreading	Greenish White	Spring	Good	60'-75'	C,S
Loquat	Eriobotrya japonica	Fast	Upright	Fragrant not Showy	Fall	Good	15'-25'	N,C,S
Coral Tree	Erythrina cristagallii	Slow	Upright to Spreading	Red	Summer	Fair	20'-30'	C,S
Australian Bush Cherry	Eugenia paniculata	Moderate	Upright	White	Summer	Poor	20'-25'	C,S
Cuban Laurel	Ficus nitida	Fast	Spreading			Excellent	60'-80'	C,S

N — North Florida   C — Central Florida   S — South Florida

CHAPTER THREE

Landscape Shrubs

There are more evergreen and flowering shrubs in Florida than in any other state. While trees are important to your landscape plan, they take years to achieve their full height, width and beauty. Shrubs, on the other hand, develop quickly and give almost immediate results in completing the picture you are trying to create in your garden. Similarly, lawns do not sprout into their ultimate rich carpet of green overnight. Shrubs can serve to screen the lawn area while it is growing, and they can shade your home and add overall beauty and charm to your yard or garden.

Shrubs are a versatile decorating item in completing your dream landscape. They soften the lines of a wide area, creating a natural balance between flower beds, lawn expanse and trees. A tall shrub fills in a corner very well — the corners created by a fence as well as the corners of your home. Shrubs also constitute a break between separate areas, becoming a "transition plant" from lawn to walkways or between lawn and ground cover, allowing the eye to flow smoothly from one area to the next. Shrubs also can be planted as specimens by themselves in order to break up large areas of lawn. Ligustrum and Viburnum are good for this purpose, grown as standard shrubs or trimmed as trees. Whether you use a shrub as a shrub or as a small tree is up to your imagination and wishes for your landscape design.

The same principle applies to vines, such as Bougainvillea and Allamanda. These can be left as vining plants or trimmed into shrubs. The ultimate use of shrubs in your garden depends on their placement and the way you care for them.

Shrubs are sold in containers or balled and burlapped. There is no transplant shock with container-grown plants. You merely slide them out of the plastic containers and lower them gently into the ground. Balled and burlapped plants, on the other hand, should be put into the ground as soon as possible to minimize deterioration from exposure. Occasionally, roses, crape myrtle and some other plants are sold bare-rooted, but this is not a common practice in Florida.

When planting your shrubs, pay attention to the spacing between the holes you dig. A minimum of two feet apart is recommended for small 55

Container grown shrubs offer the best transplant potential.

BUYING SHRUBS

Nurseries will sell most shrubs in any of three forms: container grown, balled-and-burlapped, or bare root. Whether you want a young shrub or a full-grown variety, container grown plants generally offer the best root protection and the best transplant success, since they remain in their natural soil. Balled-and-burlapped are also popular, but will suffer some root damage and will need to be trimmed back about 25%. Bare root shrubs will lose most feeder roots and should be trimmed back from 40 to 50 percent.

Balled-and-burlapped shrubs will need some pruning after planting.

Bare-root shrubs require major pruning after planting.

shrubs, three to five feet apart for larger shrubs. Check with your nursery and learn the ultimate size of the shrub you purchase. Then allow sufficient space for the plants to spread naturally without becoming crowded.

PREPARING THE SOIL

Not only is spacing important, but also soil. It is often wise to dig your hole somewhat larger than needed, and after lowering the shrub into the ground, fill up the space with good planting soil, plus peat moss, cow manure and compost to ensure a nutritious base in which your plant can thrive. This is especially important near the foundation of your home, where there is always an accumulation of lime from the bricks and mortar, as well as from the concrete slab.

ESTABLISHING SHRUB BEDS

Shrubs look best and are easier to care for when planted in beds. Although you may have a special planting for some shrubs, plan your shrub beds well before planting and prepare the soil according to your plan and expected use. Consider the following pointers:

1. Measure and stake the area for your shrub beds.

2. Spray the staked area with a short-lived weed killer to get rid of established weeds. Wait two weeks for the herbicide to work completely.

3. Rototill the soil in the staked area to a depth of 8 to 12 inches. Remove any roots, rocks or other debris.

4. Add organic material, compost, peat moss or shredded bark and till again. If you need to fumigate the soil, use a product such as *Vapam,* following label directions carefully, then wait four weeks before planting.

5. Dig holes in the soil to the depth of the root ball or container and wide enough to accommodate the roots. If root ball is too wet or too dry, it may come apart. Make sure it is just moist.

6. Place plants in the soil so that the top of the root ball is level with the grade. Cover the roots with soil and water immediately. Apply root stimulator for one to two months before beginning a fertilizer program.

7. Place bricks or other edging material to separate lawn areas from shrub beds. Although lawn grass may creep into this material, it will provide a border for edging.

8. A bark mulch or other mulch will aid in water retention and temperature protection. Also remember to prune back approximately 25 percent of top growth from balled-and-burlapped material and about 40 percent of top growth from bare-root plants. When using weed killers to control weeds under shrubs, follow label directions carefully to ensure the chemical does not damage the shrubs themselves.

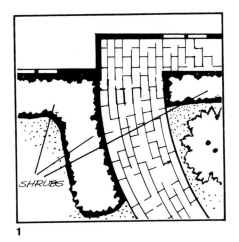

1

2

3

4

5

6

7

8

WATERING YOUR SHRUBS

Shrubs are often watered at the same time you water the lawn; however, lawn sprinklers may not always reach bedded shrubs adequately, so you may need a system to ensure shrubs get deep watering to the roots and not on the leaves, which can encourage disease or damage blossoms.

Drip irrigation allows a slow stream of water to trickle to the shrub's root system. The method is slow and reliable and provides uniform moisture for the soil.

Soaker hoses come in many types. Some are capped on one end with perforations around the entire hose, others are perforated on one side only, sprinkling directly into the soil. Both types are excellent for shrub beds.

If you select watering rods which penetrate directly to the roots, insert the instrument to a depth of six to eight inches. Try not to damage roots or to pass the critical root area by going too deep.

Some automatic sprinkler systems come with special adapters for shrubs, sending a fine spray to the soil and lower greenery. These are generally effective and less time consuming for the gardener.

60

Specific application fertilizers for shrubs and flowering plants are available with chemical concentrations suited to specific types of plants. Explore the possibilities and consult your nurseryman before selecting one of these.

TYPES OF FERTILIZERS

There are many brands of fertilizer on the market, many with special concentrations of elements for specific types of growth. In determining which may be the best for your needs, it will be helpful to remember the value of the three major chemical ingredients.

The standard combination is nitrogen, phosphorus, potassium: N-P-K. Nitrogen encourages leaf and stem growth, especially important for trees and shrubs which develop dense foliage. Phosphorus encourages growth of flowers, fruit and roots. Potassium helps plants develop sturdy tissue and temperature hardiness.

For specific plants and specific soil conditions, fertilizers with added iron, sulphur and zinc, and other trace elements, are available.

Some root-watering systems allow you to insert fertilizer cartridges which add nutrients directly into the root system. If you use one of these, be sure to keep the watering element, the spike, at root level, or about six to eight inches deep.

Plant food spikes, available at most garden centers, allow nutrients to dissolve into the soil slowly and naturally over a period of time. These can be very beneficial for bedded shrubs.

Newly planted shrubs need plenty of water every day for the first two weeks, after which twice a week is adequate. With established shrubs, it is better to deep-water twice a week than to merely sprinkle them daily. Daily watering can promote fungus growth on the leaves. Soaker hoses or drip irrigation are especially recommended for shrubs. If you have a sprinkler system, make sure your shrubs are included in the spray pattern.

Fertilizing also is very important because there is little natural fertility in Florida soils. Make sure you apply the right combination of elements. Nitrogen promotes leaf growth, but too much will cause stress and possible damage. Phosphorous aids root growth and flowering. Potassium helps in the overall strength of the plant.

Some gardeners prefer an evenly balanced formula such as 6-6-6 or 10-10-10. For best results in Florida, use a 12-10-20, which offers a healthy and natural balance of needed nutrients. With some evergreens, especially if you desire heavy growth and dense foliage, use a tree and shrub fertilizer with a high nitrogen content. Fertilizing should be done immediately after planting and thereafter three times a year in spring, summer and fall.

Certain varieties of shrubs work better as hedges than others do. Most hedge material will remain full from top to bottom. By tapering the top slightly, you allow more sun to enter. This gives thicker growth below. Tapering the top is recommended with newly planted shrubs, but once a hedge has matured, you can leave it to grow and form a living wall around your yard or patio.

Of course, all hedges should be trimmed occasionally to prevent them from becoming untidy. Power trimmers are useful for this purpose, making the job easier. But be warned: one can get carried away with power tools. You must be cautious when dealing with live material such as a hedge. Sometimes, without realizing it, you can remove large chunks that leave unsightly scars and damage the plant. Hand trimming is far better for shaping a hedge and helps you avoid stubs and notches that can mar the beauty of the hedge.

SELECTING SHRUBS

Choosing your shrubs demands that you pay attention to the climate in your particular area. Crotons may be inappropriate for Tallahassee, but in central Florida, they can give an added burst of color in your landscaping. Location of cold-sensitive plants also is important. Some shrubs can be protected from the cold by positioning them close to water, such as a pond or a lake, where the ground is warmer. During a cold spell, you should protect your shrubs by covering them with sheets, burlap or plastic. However, remember to build a frame for a plastic covering to hold the polyethylene away from the plant. If not, the cold will pass through the plastic to any leaves it is touching and burn them. You also should cover the ground around the shrub in order to hold heat in the ground.

Mulching can help prevent rapid changes in soil temperatures. Mulch can be raked away from the plant base during the day to allow the sun's warmth to penetrate, then raked back at night to hold in the heat. A plant can withstand extreme cold if the soil is moist. A well watered and fertilized plant can withstand extremes of heat and cold far better than one which has been neglected. Even in periods of drought, well watered plants can survive freezing temperatures if they have been watered adequately. While good soil and fertilizer contribute to the health and growth of a plant, it is water that is essential above all else, particularly in those areas of Florida where the temperature drops drastically in the winter.

RAINTREE

Copper Plant, used as
shrubs and specimens

LANDSCAPE SHRUBS FOR FLORIDA

Acalypha wilkesiana — Copper Leaf Acalypha
Height: 15 ft.
Spread: 5 ft.

Often used as a background plant in landscaping, the acalypha grows best in full sun. This shrub spreads rapidly and needs trimming to keep it from getting out of hand. It is used mostly in protected areas in lower central and south Florida. Reconsider this shrub before buying. Its bright color may be too glaring for your particular landscape needs. Mealy bugs and aphids occasionally are a problem, and this shrub does suffer injury when the temperature drops to freezing. But it normally will grow back.

Abelia sp. — Abelia
Height: 10 ft.
Spread: 4 ft.

Useful as a border, hedge or screen plant, the abelia is a hardy evergreen seen mostly in the Gainesville area and the northern parts of Florida. During summer, this shrub is covered with white, tubular, bell-shaped flowers. The abelia can be propagated both by seeds and cuttings and has a good salt tolerance.

Variegated Century Plant

Century Plant

Agave americana — Century Plant
Height: 8 ft.
Spread: 7 ft.

This shrub grows only in sandy soil and does best in full sun, but *do not* plant a century plant in areas where children play. Its large thorns can be quite dangerous. They are stiff, sword-shaped leaves with needle-like points at the end. Every six to 12 years, the century plant grows a large stem 15 to 25 feet in height with flowers on top.

Illicium anisatum — Anise Tree
Height: 15-20 ft.
Spread: 5-8 ft.

Grown in central and north Florida, this hardy evergreen is an ideal accent or enclosure plant for full sun or partial shade. It grows best in improved, organic soil, so mulching is a definite asset for this plant. It needs trimming once a year.

Azalea Bloom

Azalea Bloom

Rhododendron — Azalea
Height: Dwarf variety: 2 ft.
Others: 10-15 ft.
Spread: 1-3 ft.

Azaleas are the "Queen of the Garden" from January through April. They come in a wide range of sizes and color variations: white, red, pink, purple, orange and all shades between. Flowers can be single or double and often vary in the way they open. Azaleas are not salt-tolerant and must have an acid soil. A 50/50 mixture of peat moss and existing soil is helpful in promoting good growth and a healthy plant. Shallow rooted, azaleas need frequent watering — at least every two days. They are used for masses of color, as an informal hedge, or as bedding and background

Azaleas grown as a hedge make an attractive addition to the landscape.

plantings. Pruning the shrubs after they flower promotes the formation of more flower buds and prevents the branches from growing out of control and giving a straggly look to the plants.

Caution: Do not trim after July 1. This is when azaleas set buds for the next season's flowers. Mulching is of utmost importance in growing good-looking azaleas.

INDIAN AZALEAS:

These plants produce an abundant display of color in late winter and early spring:

Duc de rohan — An early, compact, spreading azalea that is semi-hardy and grows about two feet high.

Elegans — An abundant flowering shrub that reaches ten feet in height, is quite hardy and produces blossoms that are single, medium size and pink in color.

Formosa — A vigorous, long-lived, hardy azalea with large, singular, lavender blossoms. Grows from 10 to 15 feet in height and blooms early to mid-season.

KURUME HYBRIDS:

Kurumes are a Japanese species of azalea, with leaves and flowers smaller than those of the Indian variety. For best blooms, the kurumes need cooler weather. They do best in rich, acid, organic soil in partial shade, and are prone to petal blight.

66   *Coral Bells* — A hardy bloomer during mid-season, this hybrid grows
to four feet in height and produces small, shell-pink flowers.

Hexe — This hardy hybrid grows to two feet in height with an abundant display of violet-red flowers.

Snow — As its name implies, this hybrid produces small, white flowers in mid-season. A dense grower, the plant matures to two feet in height.

Buxus sp. — Boxwood

Height: 6 ft.
Spread: 3 ft.

Flourishing from St. Petersburg to northern Florida, this evergreen shrub is extremely cold-hardy and will grow in full sun and partial shade. A versatile shrub for landscaping, it can be trimmed into virtually any desired shape. The sister variety (English boxwood, *buxus sempervirens*) is not well adapted to Florida's alkaline soils and heat. This plant thrives best in rich, acid, organic soil. Disease problems include root rot and leaf spot.

Camellia japonica — Camellia

Height: 5-15 ft.
Spread: 5-10 ft.

The camellia's shiny, dark-green, toothed leaves are almost four inches long and create an interesting contrast to the brown twigs from which they sprout. During winter and early spring, camellia bushes make beautiful framing or accent plants. They grow best in north and central Florida. Like azaleas, these plants thrive in an acid soil and prefer partial shade during part of the day. They need to be sprayed regularly to prevent

Camellia Blossom

Camellia Blossom

Crape Myrtle

accumulation of tea scale insects on the foliage and thrips and botrytis disease in the flowers. Mulching is especially important for your camellia plants. Florida's winters pose a special problem for camellia plants. The cool periods alternating with short heat waves produce a condition called "bull nosing" or "bud blast." When this occurs, flowers start to open and then simply fall off the branches.

Lagerstroemia indica — Crape Myrtle
Height: 20-25 ft.
Spread: 6-8 ft.

One of the few beautiful deciduous shrubs, crape myrtle is appealing in appearance even without leaves because of its smooth, light-brown bark. A fast grower, it does best in full sun, is hardy and flourishes in all parts of Florida. With attractive flowers (pink, red and white varieties), it can be grown as a free-standing specimen or used to highlight other evergreen plantings. Locating the crape myrtle where the morning sun can dry its leaves will lessen any potential powdery mildew problems. Pruning branches after flowering will help increase the following year's yield of blossoms. Mushroom root rot is a potential problem when planting the crape myrtle in poorly drained soil.

Prunus caroliniana — Cherry Laurel
Height: 40 ft.
Spread: 15 ft.

Clipped or unclipped, the cherry laurel can be used as a hedge or as a large shrub where a screening plant is desired. Like the boxwood, it can be cut into almost any shape. A member of the true cherry tree family, it grows best in a slightly acid soil. Do not allow water to settle around this plant. It does not thrive in very wet soil. *Caution:* The cherry laurel foliage is poisonous.

Gardenia in bloom

Gardenia jasminoides — Gardenia

Height: 8 ft.
Spread: 5-6 ft.

Like azaleas and camellias, these evergreen shrubs grow best in acid soil. They prefer filtered shade and cannot withstand temperatures below 20 degrees. Their exquisite white, double, waxy, fragrant flowers appear from April through early June, making an impressive show, especially against an all-green background in the garden. Particularly susceptible to nematodes, gardenias should be grafted on the Thunbergia root stock to minimize this threat. Other disease problems include leaf spot, algal leaf spot and mushroom root rot.

Hibiscus rosa-sinensis — Hibiscus

Height: 10-15 ft.
Spread: 5 ft.

One of central and south Florida's most popular plants is the hibiscus, a pleasant addition as an informal hedge or screen, foundation plant or background for other garden plants. Varieties often are selected on the basis of plant growth, habit and size, the form and color of the flowers and adaptability to specific environments. Six basic colors exist — red, orange, yellow, white, lavender and brown — but many variations show up between varieties. Some of the newer varieties grow well only as grafted plants and are not widely available.

Given proper fertilization, hibiscus will grow fine in most of our sandy soils. A well-draining soil with a pH of 5.5 to 6.5 is preferred. Nutrient deficiencies may occur in alkaline soils.

Hibiscus should be planted at the same depth as they were in the container. Staking may be necessary on the tree types. Most hibiscus should be spaced at a minimum of 4-5 feet apart. The planting hole should be at least 6 inches deeper and 6 inches wider than the root ball. Add

Yellow Hibiscus

Hibiscus Blossom

Red Hibiscus

Hibiscus Blossom

organic matter such as peat moss, dehydrated cow manure or compost to the planting hole. This normally should be mixed one-third by volume with the existing soil. Plants should be watered throroughly after planting. A mulch will conserve water, reduce weed problems and give some control of nematodes. Mulches include cypress, oak leaves, pine bark and pine needles.

MR. GREEN THUMB RULE
Keep the mulch a couple of inches away from the hibiscus trunk. Mulching too close to the trunk increases the chances of root rot.

70   Hibiscus should be watered heavily once a week during dry periods. A regular fertilization is essential. These plants do their best blooming when fertilized lightly and often, three to four applications per year, as a rule, in March-May-June-November.

Hibiscus should be pruned to maintain a desired size and shape without disrupting their blooming or appearance by cutting only the longest third of the branches at one time.

Some hibiscus plants grow upright like a tree or bushy like a shrub. They can be used in many ways: as an enclosing plant; as a background; a screening plant; an informal hedge or formal hedge; even as a specimen. They grow best in full sun but can withstand partial shade. In either location, the soil should be well drained. There are many different varieties, enabling you to have a hibiscus in bloom almost year 'round. During cold snaps, protection is advisable. Freezing temperatures can injure these plants.

HOLLIES

Holly *(Ilex sp.)* usually is considered part of a northern landscape, but while it is not tropical, holly grows well in most parts of Florida. All types of holly prefer slightly acid soil and are moderate in their growth pattern. The varieties that bear the traditional red berries will produce their Christmas color only during winter. There are many hybrid varieties, with new ones being developed each year. Holly makes an ideal hedge, on the outer perimeter of a garden as well as along pathways and to separate areas within a yard.

Ilex cornuta — Chinese Holly
Height: 10-15 ft.
Spread: 5-8 ft.

This is a large, compact shrub with glossy, dark-green leaves that have one sharp-pointed spine at the top of each leaf. Bright-red berries appear in late fall and winter. The Burford is a sport, or bud, variation of

Chinese Holly

Chinese Holly, Container grown

East Palatka Holly

Yaupon Holly

the Ilex cornuta. The dwarf Chinese holly *(Ilex cornuta rotunda)* has similar leaves but grows only to 24-36 inches at maturity and has a rounded shape.

Ilex cassine — Dahoon
Height: 30-40 ft.
Spread: 6-10 ft.

Often considered a small tree, the Dahoon's leaves are three to four inches in length, shiny on top and velvety beneath. Originally from Florida's swamplands, the dahoon has red berries in the winter and sometimes yellow berries as well.

Ilex opaca — American Holly
Height: 40-50 ft.
Spread: 10 ft.

Normally grown as a tree because of its size, the American holly comes in many varieties, the most common being the East Palatka type, found throughout the state.

Ilex crenata — Japanese Holly
Height: 3-5 ft.
Spread: 3 ft.

Japanese holly is grown mostly in upper central and northern Florida. It has medium to dark-green foliage and compact, shrubby growth. It grows best in shady locations and should be protected from afternoon sun.

Ilex vomitoria — Yaupon Holly
Height: 20-25 ft.
Spread: 10 ft.

Dwarf yaupon holly has become the most popular in Florida. In regular or dwarf variety, this plant can be trimmed to any height and any shape, making it ideal for imaginative landscaping.

72 **Nellie R. Stevens Holly**

   Height: 15-20 ft.
   Spread: 5-8 ft.

One of the new hybrids, this variety of holly is a very attractive, vigorous-growing plant with dark-green leaves and a rounded growth pattern. Disease problems include dieback, various fungi, leaf spot and mushroom root rot.

HYDRANGEA

Hydrangea macrophylla — Hydrangea

   Height: 4-5 ft.
   Spread: 2-3 ft.

Hydrangea has long been admired for its enormous clusters of flowers that resemble pom-pom. The hydrangea is a natural pH indicator, giving blue petals in acid soil, pink in alkaline soil and off-white in near-neutral soil. By changing the pH of your soil, you can change the color of a hydrangea. This deciduous shrub grows best in shade or filtered sun. Moderate moisture is preferred, with a fairly high level of fertility in the soil. Hydrangeas, with their medium to dark-green leaves and large clusters of flowers, make an outstanding shrub against a wall or a fence or in the protected entranceway to your front door.

SLOW

Hydrangea

Indian Hawthorne

Rhaphiolepis indica — Indian Hawthorne
Height: 5 ft.
Spread: 4-5 ft.

Ranging in size from dwarf to standard, the Indian hawthorne is a popular landscape shrub with a good salt tolerance. The foliage is similar to that of the pittosporum, with small, rose-like flowers a half-inch across in pink, white and rose. The blossoms are fragrant, and the fruit is drupe-like in shape, with a purplish-black color. This plant can suffer from fireblight.

Plumbago Capensis — Leadwort Plumbago
Height: 4-5 ft.
Spread: 6-8 ft.

The plumbago is a shrub that tends to be sprawling. It looks like it wants to vine but doesn't vine much. It has very attractive, tubular, baby blue flowers that are 1 inch across and flower throughout the warm season. The plumbago grows mostly in central and south Florida because it tends to be killed back to the ground by temperatures below 28 degrees and can grow back quickly. It is sometimes used as a color mass and as a transition plant or an informal flowering hedge. It flowers best in full sun and has fair salt tolerance. It should be planted in a nematode-free soil. There is also a white variety called alba.

Plumbago

Leadwort Plumbago bloom

Ixora

Ixora showing cold damage in
upper leaves

Euphorbia Pulcherrima — **Poinsettia**

Height: 10 ft.
Spread: 8 ft.

The poinsettia is a tender shrub that is killed back at 32 degrees. It will grow back and can be protected so it is seen growing in north, central and south Florida. It is loved in the Christmas season for its bright red floral leaves called bracts. It grows well in full sun, though it should be protected from night lights. This plant will grow in any improved, well-draining soil. Normally trim back about one-third after flowering. Do not trim later than September 1, as this may interfere with the timing of the Christmas blooms. Scab is an occasional problem and can be treated by trimming out the infected area and spraying wth a good general fungicide. The poinsettia has poor salt tolerance.

Ixora coccinea — **Ixora (Flame of the Woods)**

Height: 6 ft.
Spread: 4 ft.

Grown mostly in central and south Florida, this shrub has glossy green foliage with 2½-inch leaves and masses of brilliant red, orange and yellow flowers from May through July. The ixora requires full sun for best flowering and will freeze at 30 degrees, but normally grows back. It can be used as a hedge. Set plants about 24 inches apart. Disease problems include leaf spot, stem gall and mushroom root rot.

JUNIPERS *(Juniperus sp.)*

This useful and dependable evergreen grows best in full sun. Junipers are ideal for Florida. They can withstand the heat, the dry spells and the lowest temperatures without damage. They do not like very wet soil and need to be fertilized every two months with a good liquid plant food, or every three months with a tree or shrub fertilizer. Junipers can be started from cuttings in the summer. For excellent ground cover, try the blue rug or blue carpet species, as well as the shore juniper *(Juniperus conferta)*, which grows to two feet, and the Torulosa juniper.

Juniperus chinesensis 'pfitzeriana' — Pfitzer Juniper
Height: 5 ft.
Spread: 8-10 ft.

This juniper is a horizontal-spreading plant with branch tips pointing outward.

Torulosa Juniper

Juniper (Italian Cypress)

Spreading Junipers with Ilex plants

Pfitzer Juniper

76 *Juniperus chinesensis columnaris* — Japanese Juniper
Height: 20-30 ft.
Spread: 6-10 ft.

With a staight trunk and a column-type growth, this juniper has both a scale-form and needle-form growth on every branch. This shrub is one of the best tall evergreens with dark green foliage. Disease problems include twig blight, rust and leaf spot.

Elaeagnus pungens — Elaeagnus (Silver Thorn)
Height: 12-15 ft.
Spread: 15 ft.

As a hedge or screening plant, this juniper has a sprawling growth pattern, is quite tolerant of salt and will grow in light shade to full sun. The leaves are dark green with a silver dot pattern underneath. Elaeagnus produces brown, drupe-like fruit from which jams and jellies can be made.

JASMINE *(Jasminium sp.)*

Many species of jasmines flower and grow well in Florida, in full sun as well as partial shade. Jasmines can be trimmed as standard shrubs or grown as vines. Their height will vary depending on how they are used. Jasmine can suffer from algal leaf spot, anthracnose and mushroom root rot.

Jasminium multiflorus — Downy Jasmine — Height: 20 ft.

This variety has dark-green, hairy stems and leaves. Downy jasmine will freeze at 26 to 28 degrees but grows back fast. Like other jasmines, it can be started by misting soft wood cuttings in the summer.

Jasminium nitidum — Shiny Jasmine — Height: 4-6 ft.

Grown as a shrubbery border in central and south Florida, shiny jasmine can be trimmed as a shrub. But it is more often used as a vine because of its strong, twining, sprawling growth pattern. In fact, the branches have to be trimmed to keep them under control.

Jasminium gracillimum — Australian Jasmine — Height: 4-5 ft.

Often used as a background or enclosing plant, Australian jasmine is a slow-grower requiring full sun. It has glossy, dark-green leaves about two inches long and an inch wide, and freezes at 30 degrees.

GOLDEN DEWDROP

Duranta repens — Golden Dewdrop
Height: 18 ft.
Spread: 6 ft.

Golden Dewdrop sometimes is known as the pigeon berry. This ever-green shrub has beautiful, lilac-blue, half-inch flowers that hang from the branches like the Northern lilac. With its drooping habit, it can be used as

a background shrub or espaliered on a wooden framework against a wall. It
is susceptible to nematodes.

LIGUSTRUM

Ligustrum lucidum — Ligustrum (Glossy Privet)
Height: 40 ft.
Spread: 15-20 ft.

Grown throughout Florida, this very popular shrub is sometimes called the wax leaf ligustrum. The ligustrum grows very fast, especially when fed regularly, and can be used as a background plant, screening, hedge or enclosure. The leaves are pear-shaped, dark-green and glossy, reaching four inches in length. It produces cream-colored flowers in panicles during the spring. This evergreen shrub is very hardy and has become one of the most popular landscape items in the state. It will self-sow, and

Ligustrums are commonly sold in containers.

Ligustrums come in shrub and tree varieties.

78   the dozens of small seedlings can be transplanted easily, growing to four or five feet within two years with very little care. With regular fertilizing, growth and foliage improves rapidly. The ligustrum is one of the easiest shrubs to grow and one of the most rewarding. Disease problems include anthracnose and leaf spot.

Ligustrum japonicum — Japanese Privet

Height: 15 ft.
Spread: 5 ft.

The Japanese privet can be grown in full sun and partial shade and often needs heavy pruning to keep it from growing too large. It can be used as an enclosure plant or a sheared hedge. It is a very versatile plant for any landscape.

NANDINA

Nandina domestica — Nandina

Height: 8 ft.
Spread: 4 ft.

Used from Orlando in central Florida to Pensacola in the north, nandina grows in an upright, compact shape. This deciduous shrub has small, white terminal flowers that give way to strikingly bright red berries in the fall and winter. It can be used as a background shrub against a fence, or to break up green borders and provide color in the winter. *Caution:* A rather slow grower.

PITTOSPORUM

Pittosporum tobira — Pittosporum

Height: 15 ft.
Spread: 10 ft.

This hardy evergreen is very popular, with glossy, oval, leathery leaves that are dark green. A variegated variety offers white, marbled, cream-colored leaves. Pittosporum grows well in full sun, though the

Pittosporum

Pittosporum in full sun

variegated variety has a better mixture of coloring when grown in partial shade. The plant has a thick, compact growth habit and does well near salt water. As a hedge plant or for an informal shrubbery area, the pittosporum is an excellent choice. Disease problems include angular leaf spot, crown gall and dieback.

PODOCARPUS *(Podocarpus sp.)*

For a sheared hedge, podocarpus is one of the best choices. This very hardy shrub can be used anywhere in the state.

Podocarpus macrophylla — Yew Podocarpus
Height: 25 ft.
Spread: 10 ft.

One of the best for hedge plantings, the yew podocarpus has dense foliage from the ground up, with long, flat, linear leaves up to three inches in length. It grows well in full sun to partial shade and is salt-tolerant. It should be planted in well-drained soil; it does not thrive in wet soil. Yew podocarpus has a purple, edible aril attached to a green drupe and can be started from soft wood cuttings in summer. Suffers from angular leaf spot, crown gall and dieback.

Podocarpus nagi — Nagi
Height: 25 ft.
Spread: 10-15 ft.

A strong accent plant, this podocarpus has large, green leaves three inches long and almost an inch wide, with parallel veination. Nagi can be grown in full sun or in shade and has good salt tolerance. It has a strong central growing habit and does well as a large hedge. It can be propagated from seed or from cuttings in the summer.

Podocarpus needs well-drained soil and full to partial sun.

Podocarpus gracilior — Fern Podocarpus
Height: 30 ft.
Spread: 15 ft.

Fern podocarpus is more cold-sensitive than similar plants and should be planted in protected areas in central or south Florida. It makes an excellent corner plant or an outstanding accent plant. It also is used as a screening plant or espaliered on a frame against a wall or fence. It can be air-layered or started from cuttings.

PYRACANTHA

Pyracantha coccinea — Firethorn
Height: 20 ft.
Spread: 15-20 ft.

A large, spreading shrub, this hardy evergreen usually is espaliered, making a very attractive display against a wall with its small, white, fragrant flowers followed in the fall and winter by bright, orange-red berries. Firethorn flowers best in full sun but has some problems with fire blight, especially when over-fertilized. A low-spreading variety called "low dense" grows only six feet in height. Firethorn has good salt tolerance and always attracts birds, which enjoy the berries. These actually are pome-like fruit. It suffers from mushroom root rot.

PHOTINIA

Photinia glabra — Red-Leaf Photinia
Height: 10 ft.
Spread: 8 ft.

Found mostly in north and central Florida, the photinia grows best in full sun and should be used inland because of its moderate salt tolerance. It needs organic-enriched soil upon planting. This shrub is greatly admired for its leaves, which are three inches long and about three-quarters of an inch wide. They change from bright red to green as they mature. The cooler winters in northern Florida tend to bring out better color in this plant.

LANTANA

Lantana camara — Lantana
Height: 10 ft.
Spread: 3 ft.

This is a versatile shrub that can go wild if not kept under control. In fact, in California it is regarded as a weed. Nevertheless, the lantana can be a colorful addition to any landscape, flowering ten months out of the year with small blossoms colored red, lavender, orange, yellow, pink or white. Lantana can be used in hanging baskets or as ground cover, or allowed to grow into a dense, rather prickly bush. It will freeze at 28 degrees but will grow back. Has few disease problems.

Sweet Viburnum *ODAR*   Sandankwa Viburnum *SUSP.*

VIBURNUM *(Viburnum sp.)*

This popular shrub has a number of varieties that do well in Florida. The following are two of the most popular:

Viburnum Odoratissimum — Sweet Viburnum

Height: 40 ft.
Spread: 30 ft.

Often used as a hedge, a screening plant or an enclosing plant, this shrub has white, fragrant flowers in the spring. It can be grown in full sun or partial shade, with medium-to-bright-green oval leaves four to six inches long. It has fair salt tolerance and is considered a fast grower that makes a nice, thick privacy hedge.

Viburnum suspensum — Sandankwa Viburnum

Height: 8-12 ft.
Spread: 4-8 ft.

A moderate grower, this shrub has dark-green leaves four inches long and small white and pink flowers from late winter through early spring. It grows well in full sun as shade and is often used in shady areas around a house. Sandankwa viburnum also makes an excellent hedge plant and can be used as a foundation plant. It has good salt tolerance and tolerates very wet soil.

Oleander

OLEANDER

Nerium Oleander — Oleander

Height: 20-30 ft.
Spread: 10-15 ft.

The Oleander has pink, white or red flowers on long, straight stems with stiff, green leaves eight inches long. It has been a very popular shrub for centuries. It can be grown as a specimen or as an informal hedge. Left alone, it grows into a tree and needs pruning to keep under control. Oleander has excellent salt tolerance but needs spraying with Diazinon to control caterpillars. A dwarf variety grows from three to five feet.

Caution: All parts of the oleander are toxic — branches, foliage and sap. Do not burn any part of this shrub because the smoke also is toxic. Disease problems may include bacterial gall and leaf spot.

CROTON

Codiaeum variegatum — Croton

Height: 10 ft.
Spread: 6 ft.

A tender, colorful shrub, the croton does well in south Florida and in a few protected areas in central parts of the state. There are numerous combinations of leaf color, shape and size. For best leaf color, crotons

Crotons grow rich and full in Florida sun.

Note the multi-colored leaves of the Croton.

should be given full sun. Because they will freeze at 32 degrees, it is best to plant them against the house or fence for protection. Crotons have eye-catching colors and should be used sparingly in your landscape. Can suffer from anthracnose and root rot.

NATAL PLUM

Carissa grandiflora — Natal Plum
Height: 15 ft.
Spread: 10 ft.

Natal plum is ideal for growing in central and south Florida. This plant has single, white flowers over an inch across in spring, summer and fall. The flowers are followed by dark red, elliptical berries that not only are decorative but edible and can be used in making jellies. Natal plum has excellent salt tolerance. It will freeze at 28 degrees but grow back. It has two sharp-pointed thorns on each branch, with opposite, dark green leaves and a milky sap. Natal plum is best used as a background plant. A dwarf variety *(Boxwood Beauty)* can be used as a hedge. Natal plum does best in full sun. Disease problems include leaf spot, dieback, root rot and sphaeropsis.

Flowering Shrubs

Type of Shrub	Height	Flower Color	Zone	Blooming Season
Abelia	3'-8"	White	N	Spring, Summer, Early Fall
Allamanda	4'-10'	Yellow	C,S	Spring, Summer, Fall
Bottlebrush (Callistemon rigidus)	10'-20'	Red	N,C,S	Spring, Summer
Carissa grandiflora	8'-18'	White	C,S	Spring, Summer, Fall
Camellia	4'-15'	White, Pink, Red	N,C,S	Late Fall, Winter, Spring
Cassia palata	5'-10'	Golden Yellow	C,S	Summer, Fall
Cassia Bicapsularis	5'-10'	Golden Yellow	N,C,S	Summer Fall
Flowering Quince Chaenomeles	3'-6'	Red	N	Late Winter
Pampas grass (cortaderia)	5'-8'	White, sometimes Pink	N,C,S	Summer, Spring, Fall

N — North Florida
C — Central Florida
S — South Florida

Flowering Shrubs (Continued)

Type of Shrub	Height	Flower Color	Zone	Blooming Season
Clerodendrum speciosissimum	5'-10'	Red	C,S	Most of year
Gardenia	2'-8'	White	N,C,S	Spring
Calliandra haematocephala Powder Puff	5'-8'	Red	C,S	Spring, Summer, Fall
Hibiscus Rosa sinensis	2'-12'	Red, Pink, White, and many colors	N,C,S	Most of year
Hydrangea macrophylla	4'-10'	White, Blue, Pink	N,C,S	Spring, Summer
Crape Jasmine Eruatamia coronaria	5'-10'	White	C,S	Spring, Summer
Hamelia patens Scarlet Bush	3'-7'	Scarlet red	C,S	Most of year
Jasmine Primrose	4'-8'	Yellow	N,C,S	Spring, Summer

N — North Florida
C — Central Florida
S — South Florida

Flowering Shrubs (Continued)

Type of Shrub	Height	Flower Color	Zone	Blooming Season
Jasmine Multi Florum	4'-8'	White	N,C,S	Spring, Summer
Ixora Coccinea Ixora Flame of the Woods	3'-6'	Red, Orange Yellow	C,S	Late Spring, Summer, Fall
Lonicera Winter Honeysuckle	5'-8'	White, turn Yellow	N,C	Spring, Summer
Lantana camara	2'-5'	Lilac, Red, Yellow, Purple	C,S	Most of year
Oleander (Nerium)	5'-20'	White, Yellow Red, Pink	N,C,S	Most of year
Pomegranate	2'-12'	Cream, Orange, Red	N,C,S	Spring, Summer
Osmanthus gragrans Sweet Olive	5'-20'	White	N	Fall 'til Spring
Crepe Myrtle Lagerstroemia	3'-20'	White, Red, Pink, Purple	N,C,S	Summer to early fall
Plumbago (capensis)	2'-5'	Blue	C,S	Most of year

N — North Florida
C — Central Florida
S — South Florida

Flowering Shrubs (Continued)

Type of Shrub	Height	Flower Color	Zone	Blooming Season
Indian Hawthorn (Raphiolepis)	2'-8'	White, Pink	N,C,S	Spring
Spiraea Cantoniensis	2'-5'	White	N,C	Spring
Azalea	2'-8'	Pink, Red, White, Purple	N,C,S	Spring
Thryallis Glauca	2'-8'	Yellow	N,C,S	Most of year
Sweet Viburnum	5'-35'	White	N,C,S	Spring
Beloperone Guttata	2'-5'	White-yellow, Reddish	C,S	Most of year
Stenolobium Stans Yellow elder	3'-6'	Yellow	C,S	Fall, Winter
Tibouchina semidecandrea	3'-10'	Purple	C,S	Spring, Summer, Fall

N — North Florida
C — Central Florida
S — South Florida

CHAPTER FOUR

Fruits, Fruit Trees, Nuts

Thanks to the Florida Citrus Board, many people believe the only fruit that grows in Florida is the orange! Actually, our state has much more to boast about: avocadoes, mangoes and lychees grow better here than anywhere else, and several other fruits do very well, including apples and peaches. Although Florida is not a major nut-producing state, pecans and macadamias do well here. In actuality, Florida is a tropical-fruit paradise, and the secret to having a successful orchard is selecting the trees that do best in the state's climate. All fruit and nut trees have basic but vital growing requirements. Care should be taken in buying the best stock, planting the trees properly, then caring for them and feeding them so you will get a good harvest.

Always buy from a reputable Florida nursery and discuss your purchases with the nurseryman, making sure you get the right species for your area. Get advice on the best location and the proper care of the tree. Mail-order catalogues may have cheaper prices, but the results usually are not as good as buying from a local nursery.

Always buy fruit trees that are at least two to three years old. Not only will you get fruit quicker, but you eliminate going through the potential troubles that can afflict a tree in its early stages of growth. A tree two to three years old usually will be three to five feet tall. To achieve good pollination, you may need to plant more than one tree of the same variety. Your nurseryman can advise you on this matter. Normally, though, it is good to have several trees of the same species. One apple or peach tree can look rather lost on its own. But two or three can create a lush, full appearance that enhances the look of your garden. Plus, you get more fruit at harvest time!

Planting fruit and nut trees must be done carefully to ensure proper growth. If a tree has a two-foot ball, you should dig a three-foot-wide hole to allow proper positioning. Plant the tree only as deep as it is in its container or ball. Make sure the trunk points upright, and, if necessary, stake the tree for the first year. Before planting a nut tree, you should improve the soil two feet below the surface by adding compost and other organic material. This also is advisable with apple, peach and other fruit trees. The organic material raises the pH of the soil.

89

The glorious Florida sunshine is the key factor in promoting production of fruit and nuts. Your trees must be planted in a bright, sunny location, and a soil pH of 5.5-6.5 (slightly acid) is best.

BUDDING AND GRAFTING

The T-bud and the cleft graft are the non-professional's two easiest methods of budding and grafting. Budding is usually done during the spring — the most active growing period — or when the bark will slip. Grafting is done the early part of the growing season or during the dormant season.

INVERTED T-BUD

This common method is used on some ornamentals and citrus. Make a vertical slit in the bark of the stock or seedling plant about 1½ to 2 inches long. Make a horizontal slit in the form of an inverted T on the lower part of the vertical slit. The slit must be deep enough to peel back the bark to form flaps. Cut a bud from a twig of the plant to be propagated and slip this beneath the bark of the stock. Make sure that the cambium or inner bark of the stock and scion (bud) come together. Without this contact the graft will not take. Tie the bud in place with waxed cloth, rubber bands or other binding material. When the bud tissues have united with the stock (usually within 3-4 weeks), remove the bindings and prune the stem off above the bud. It's a good idea to bud more than you will need to allow for the buds that do not take.

CLEFT GRAFT

Here's the non-professional's favorite method. Cut off the root stock close to the ground, squarely. Trim the cut surface smooth, using a sharp knife, then make a cut across the diameter of the stock. Place the knife blade on the face of the cut stock and hit it sharply wth a wooden mallet. The knife is usually then removed and reversed to hold the cleft open.

Select a scion from the parent plant. This can be a tip cutting 1½ to 3 inches long, having several pairs of leaves, or a cutting from farther down the stem. Make two sloping cuts about three-quarters of an inch long from a bud. These cuts should make the outer side of the scion wider than the inner side. Insert the scion into the cleft and line up the cambium or inner bark. Remove the wedge and tie and wax the scions in place.

WRAPS FOR BOTH THE T-BUD AND THE CLEFT GRAFT

Cotton cloth strips from half an inch to 1 inch wide and soaked in grafting wax make excellent wraps. Similar strips of rubber or other binding material may be used. Apply the wax on top of the bindings. To make grafting wax, heat 4 pounds of resin, 1 pound of beeswax, 1 pint of raw linseed oil and 1 ounce of lampblack. Or forget all that and buy a mixture at your local nursery or garden supply.

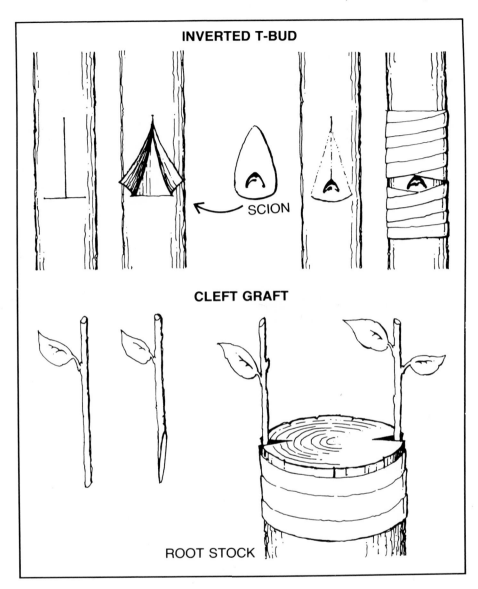

INVERTED T-BUD

SCION

CLEFT GRAFT

ROOT STOCK

PROTECTION OF THE GRAFTS

After the plants have been budded or grafted, keep them watered to prevent drying. Protect these plants, especially broadleaf evergreens, from the sun's direct rays. Cloth shade is ideal protection.

Commercial growers use cleft grafts, mound sand around the grafted area and then cover the plant with a wide-mouthed jar. Of course, this type of special treatment may not be possible with grafts on larger plants and trees. In these instances, use the proper wrapping and waxing to prevent the scion and the adjacent part of the stock from drying out.

92 PLANTING FRUIT TREES

Fruit and nut trees, like any other plant, should be planted in enriched soil. Tilling or digging-in organic materials, such as peat moss, compost, manure or straw, will help give your fruit trees a headstart. Also make sure the roots remain moist but not wet when planting, and follow these basic steps.

1. Dig the hole large enough to accommodate the entire root system, but keep the top of the root system just below ground level.
2. Prune off damaged and broken roots from bare root trees.
3. Plant the tree to the same depth as it was grown at the nursery, normally at the top of the root system or at a point on the trunk where you may detect soil marks or rings.
4. Fill the hole immediately after planting about half way with enriched soil made up of dirt from the hole mixed with organic material/compost. Water thoroughly.
5. When the water has drained off, fill the hole to ground level and pack soil lightly.
6. Since some roots will have been lost in transplanting, prune back from 25 to 40 percent of the upper growth. You may also begin to shape the tree at this point, as described on page 35, for either lateral or vertical growth.
7. If you wish to protect the young tree from sunscald or other injury, you may choose to wrap the trunk with a commercial tree wrap to a point just below the first bud union. While this is merely a precaution, it can be helpful for new trees, but should be removed from two to six months after planting.
8. During the growing season, it will help to apply a root stimulator about once a month. You should keep the tree well watered, and begin a regular fertilization program during the second year.

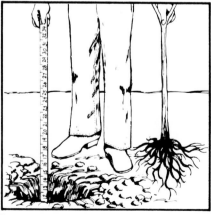

1

2

3

4

5

6   PRUNE
        HERE →

7

8   ROOT
        STIMULATOR

94 TREE WATERING

The most important element of all, however, is water. Proper watering ensures that you will get higher grades of fruit at harvest time and maintain the overall health of your trees. Lack of water will result in dry fruit. The Florida climate can change drastically, with heavy rains at times and long dry spells between.

When planting your trees, don't scrimp on the water. Although you may plant a tree in a dry hole and water later, it is a good idea to fill up the hole with water and sink the tree into it. This ensures plenty of water around the root system and gets rid of air pockets in the soil. A root stimulator or liquid fertilizer can be added to the water at planting. If you add peat and cow manure as well, there will be additional small amounts of fertilizer in this material.

After planting, your trees will need watering daily for the first two weeks. A half-inch at a time is recommended. After two weeks, check the soil moisture before watering. You should apply one to two inches at each application. For juicier fruit, water on a regular basis.

After a tree has three months of growth, a citrus special fertilizer can be applied. Use one pound the first year, increasing to one pound per foot of tree spread in spring, summer and fall. Do not use a high-nitrogen fertilizer for the fall feeding. This would produce a lot of new growth that could be injured by freezing temperatures in the winter.

Florida winters can be a problem for fruit trees. The frequent cold days often are followed by warm, tropical days with temperatures in the eighties. When this occurs in December, many plants and trees suffer unless they are protected from the cold.

COLD WEATHER PROTECTION

Follow weather reports closely. When a cold spell is predicted, take steps to guard your plants. Small trees can be covered with a sheet or blanket reaching all the way to the ground. Placing a small electric light bulb under the cover will help raise the temperature a few degrees and provides additional protection against damage.

As an emergency measure only, you can ice your trees with a continuous spray of water, maintaining the flow until the temperature rises above freezing again. As the ice forms and thaws, latent heat is given off. However, the weight of the ice can break delicate limbs. This method should be used only in extreme cases of bad weather when no other form of protection is possible.

Freezing temperatures damage all plants in varying degrees, but low temperatures also are a factor in promoting buds and blooms in the spring. Most deciduous fruit crops have a "biological clock-thermostat" that measures dormant season exposure to cold. Fruit growers call this clock the plant's "chilling requirement."

Specifically, the plant measures its exposure to cold below 45 degrees and above freezing. Each fruit variety has its own needs, a minimum number of hours' exposure to low temperatures that it must have before it

can bud and bloom in the spring. This is true especially of peaches, apples,   95
nectarines and certain other varieties.

CHILLING REQUIREMENTS

The following map indicates the chilling time needed for these trees. Locate your area on the map to determine its average winter exposure and plant only fruit varieties that coincide with that figure. This is essential to achieve best results. If you plant a tree with a much higher chilling requirement, it usually will fail to bud and bloom properly. It may not even leaf out and grow. Plant a variety with a much lower chilling requirement, and it will bloom too early almost every year and be frozen when cold weather hits again.

Chilling requirements of fruit crops vary, even within the same type of fruit. Peaches once needed as many as a thousand hours of chilling, but in the last few decades, varieties have been developed that need only 250 hours of chilling. Check with your nurseryman to find the varieties most suitable for your particular area of Florida.

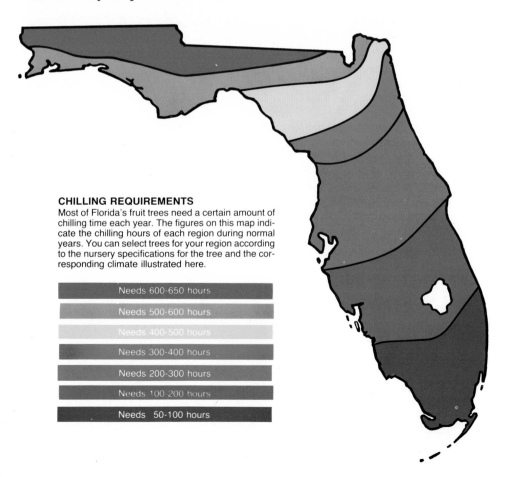

CHILLING REQUIREMENTS
Most of Florida's fruit trees need a certain amount of chilling time each year. The figures on this map indicate the chilling hours of each region during normal years. You can select trees for your region according to the nursery specifications for the tree and the corresponding climate illustrated here.

Needs 600-650 hours

Needs 500-600 hours

Needs 400-500 hours

Needs 300-400 hours

Needs 200-300 hours

Needs 100-200 hours

Needs 50-100 hours

The following fruit trees are recommended for planting in Florida:

Malpighia punicifolia — Barbados Cherry (Acerola)
Height: 10-12 ft.
Spread: 8-10 ft.

Thriving in partial shade or full sun, the Acerola cherry has one of the highest concentrations of Vitamin C known, making this delicious fruit a favorite with health-conscious dieters. The fruit grows one-inch across with a bright-red, thin skin and yellow flesh. The flowers are rose-colored and appear intermittently throughout the year, followed in 60-90 days by the fruit. The plant is thick-growing and spreads in all directions. It is grown mostly in southern Florida because it cannot stand temperatures below 32 degrees. Sterilizing the soil before planting is recommended because nematodes are a problem with the Acerola. Plenty of organic matter should be added to the soil before planting to ensure beautiful fruit and a large, healthy crop.

Malus domestica borkh — Anna Apple
Height: 15-20 ft.
Spread: 8-12 ft.

Many residents of Florida have tried and failed to grow apples, but three new varieties do very well: the Dorset Golden, the Ein Shemer and the Anna. The Anna grows to 2½ inches in diameter, with a shape similar to the Red Delicious. The flesh is firm, and the skin is about 40 percent reddish-blue color. This apple can be eaten fresh or frozen for later use. The trees last a minimum of fifteen to twenty years with good production. Flowering mid-February through mid-March, the Anna grows best in well-drained soil. But if the soil is sandy, you will have to water more frequently to retain sufficient moisture for growth and juicy apples. The Anna does best in full sun but tolerates partial shade. Spraying with Captan is recommended to control bitter rot.

Persea Americana — Avocado
Height: 30-60 ft.
Spread: 20-35 ft.

Introduced in 1833, the avocado is one of the oldest trees in Florida as well as one of the major tropical fruits in the state. Leaves are six to ten inches long and tough and leathery, making the tree a beautiful evergreen that graces any landscape. The pear-shaped fruit can weigh as much as two pounds. Blooming normally from January through April, the avocado has fair salt tolerance and grows best in full sun. Grafted trees are best for their true-to-type fruit, though they can be grown from seed. Many people start avocado seedlings indoors, supporting the seed with three toothpicks, the root end about half an inch below the surface of a glass of water. The stem grows up rather rapidly. Then the seedling can be transplanted to soil outdoors.

Young Avocado

Musa hybrid — Banana
Height: 15 ft.
Spread: 20 ft.

Several varieties of banana do well in Florida. The best is the Apple banana *(Manzana)*, which grows to a height of fifteen feet and has very flavorful fruit about four inches in length. Another good choice is the Cavendish, a dwarf type similar to the large bananas available in supermarkets. Large banana varieties do not grow well in Florida. The Cavendish grows from six to eight feet tall, with good quality, thin-skinned fruit. The leaves are fairly wind-resistant, and the plant is more cold hardy than others. The Ladyfinger offers thin-skinned fruit three to four inches long. The Red Jamaica banana has fruit four inches long and two inches wide, with an attractive pink skin. The Red Jamaica makes a striking plant in the garden but is quite sensitive to cold.

All bananas thrive in good, enriched moisture-retentive soil. They are heavy feeders and need light fertilizing once a month except in December and January. This herbaceous plant suffers damage below 32 degrees,

Banana Tree

with both leaves and stems showing injury below 26 degrees. Bananas require two years without frost to bear fruit that, once set, takes 90 days to ripen. After a stem has produced fruit, it should be trimmed back to the ground to allow suckers to emerge. Once bananas have appeared on a stalk, the bottom male bloom, called the "tail," can be cut off. While the fruit will ripen naturally on the plant itself, a stalk of green bananas may be cut off and hung upside down in a cool, dark place indoors to ripen.

Rubus hybrid — Blackberry
Height: 4-5 ft.
Spread: 4 ft.

Blackberries are loved for their large, succulent fruit. The best variety for Florida is the Brazos, developed at Texas A&M University. Very thorny, vigorous-growing plants, blackberries can be used as a privacy hedge that definitely will keep out intruders. The berries are very tasty when eaten fresh, but they also make excellent jellies and jams. Only semi-tropical, Brazos grows best in full sun and can suffer damage at 26 degrees. This is a semi-fertile plant, meaning that just one plant is needed to produce fruit.

Vaccinium myrtillus — **Blueberry**

Height: 3 ft.
Spread: 3 ft.

Two varieties — Sharpeblue and Floridablue — do best in our state and are grown from Gainesville, Ocala and Jacksonville to the south and central areas rather than in the northern parts of Florida. Blueberries grow poorly in alkaline soil, so add plenty of organic material and sulfur to the soil before planting. They thrive in acid soil with a pH of 4.2-5.2. To promote growth of strong, new wood, prune off the small, twiggy growth during the winter. Blueberries have no major pest problems, but be careful with watering. Too much water leads to root decay. The soil should be kept moist but not wet.

Averrhoa Carambola — **Carambola (Star Fruit)**

Height: 20-30 ft.
Spread: 15-25 ft.

Several varieties of the carambola — the Golden Star, Pei Sy Tao, Newcomb and Thayer — are all admired for their yellow, wax-like fruit. When cut across, the fruit resembles a star; hence the common name for the plant: star fruit. These trees of small to medium size have beautiful, alternate, compound leaves with larger leaflets at the end of each odd pinnate. Fruit is produced on the branches and the trunk of the tree.

Like most fruit trees, the carambola grows best in full sun but will thrive in partial shade. Older trees withstand temperatures as low as the mid-20s, though young trees are damaged in 32-degree weather.

Carambola (Star Fruit)

100 ### *Ficus carica* — Fig
Height: 10-12 ft.
Spread: 10 ft.

Growing in full sun very rapidly, the fig tree can be planted in all parts of Florida. Fruit is from one to three inches in length and yellow, green, brown or black in color, depending on the variety. The best two types are the Celeste and the Brown Turkey. Fig trees suffer from nematodes, which can be controlled by sterilizing the soil before planting. Vapam is very good for this purpose. Fig trees also should be mulched regularly with three to four inches of a quality mulch. This will conserve moisture and help keep down nematodes. Rust, a fungus, can be a problem. Spraying with Zineb or Dithane M-45 should give control.

Vitis rotundifolia — Muscadine Grape
Height: 8-10 ft.
Spread: 20-40 ft.

Bunch grapes such as the Blue Lake, Lake Emerald, Norris and Stover have been adapted to Florida, but the northern European bunch grapes suffer from Pierce's disease and usually die within a year or two. However, the Muscadine varieties such as Fry, Dixie, Cowart Welder and Southland all do well. Though they have thick skins and seeds, their flesh is sweet and juicy — great for eating as well as juices, jellies and wines.

Grapes must have an arbor, fence or trellis to grow along. They are vigorous growers and do best in full sun. They prefer a slightly acid soil with a pH from 6.0-6.5. Every winter the side shoots must be trimmed back, but there is no need to trim the main stem. Grapes suffer occasionally from fungus problems. Check in the chapter on insects and diseases for treatment directions.

Grapes can be grown along a fence line, and they also make a very appealing display when grown up a trellis at the side of a patio.

Psidium guajava — Guava
Height: 20-25 ft.
Spread: 15-20 ft.

The guava is a pear-shaped, sometimes round fruit from two to three inches across, with a waxy, smooth skin in various colors of pink, yellow and white. Guavas grow quickly and flourish in full sun, flowering in early summer to produce fruit throughout summer and fall. They suffer damage at 28 degrees but grow back again. Mulching is recommended for best growth.

Psidium cattleianum — Cattley Guava
Height: 15-20 ft.
Spread: 10-15 ft.

The Cattley guava has deep-green, glossy leaves only two to three inches long, compared with the five- to six-inch leaf on the Guajava guava tree. More of a bushy shrub with hard seeds, the Cattley has rounded fruit one to one-and-a-half inches across and purple-red in color. Mulching and a sunny location are recommended for good growth. The Cattley is more salt-tolerant than the common guava. Both the Guajava and the Cattley fruit can be eaten fresh or made into a delicious jelly.

Myrciaria cauliflora — Jaboticaba
Height: 10-15 ft.
Spread: 5-10 ft.

Growing well in full sun to partial shade, this small tree — a large bush, really — has round, tough-skinned fruit similar to the older Muscadine-variety grapes and with similar flavor. The fruit is dark purple and can be eaten fresh or made into jelly or wine, or frozen without losing much flavor. Jaboticaba grows in most protected areas of central Florida and in all southern parts of the state. It will take temperatures down to the low 20s. It often suffers from nutritional deficiency, needing application of Perk, Essential 6 or Minor-El.

Eriobotyra Japonica — Loquat (Japanese Plum)
Height: 20-30 ft.
Spread: 15-20 ft.

The loquat has large, leathery leaves ten to twelve inches long, with a fluffy white underside. The fruit is one to two inches in length, golden-yellow to orange in color and egg-shaped, with a distinctive taste. The loquat, found throughout Florida, is a moderate grower with excellent salt tolerance. Like most fruit trees, it must be watered during dry spells and responds well to regular fertilizing. Good varieties are the Fletcher, Oliver, Premier, Wolfe and Golden Nugget. It suffers from fire blight. Over-fertilization tends to increase bacterial disease. Trim out diseased wood and spray with Streptomycin.

Loquat (Japanese Plum)

Litchi Chinensis — Lychee
Height: 20-30 ft.
Spread: 20-30 ft.

A native of China, the lychee tree has a beautiful, rounded head with leathery leaves that are shiny and dark green. The fruit (called the lychee nut) has a hard, leathery skin that turns bright red when ripe, with white flesh that has an excellent flavor and can be eaten fresh or frozen. The tree flowers in January and produces fruit in June and July. Mulching is recommended, plus extra watering when fruiting. Tender young trees suffer damage at 28 degrees and must be protected in central and south Florida. Older trees survive down to 20 degrees. The most popular variety is the Brewster. Susceptible to spider mites.

Mangifera indica — Mango
Height: 40-50 ft.
Spread: 30-40 ft.

Called "the apple of the tropics," the mango has trees of many different sizes and fruit colors ranging from green to red, orange, purple and yellow. Its delicious flesh is yellow to golden orange around a large seed about three inches long. Tender young trees will freeze at 28-30 degrees. The fruit ripens normally from July through late September. As this tree is a moderate grower, very sensitive to temperatures when young, grafted trees are recommended and well worth the additional cost. A good citrus fertilizer will improve growth and hardiness. The original variety, the Haden, is good, but the improved varieties are excellent for Florida, including the Edward, Kent, Tommy Atkins and Parvin. Diseases include anthracnose and scale mites.

The Mango is a perennial favorite, but is relatively cold sensitive.

Papaya Tree

Pruning a young Peach Tree.

Carica papaya — Papaya
Height: 15-20 ft.
Spread: 5-10 ft.

The papaya's herbaceous trunk grows straight up, and the fruit emerges from a cluster of leaves on the top. The fruit varies from three-quarters of a pound to as much as twenty pounds. It looks like a melon, with firm, orange flesh that is delicious. The papaya does best in improved, organically enriched soil. Young plants are killed at 32 degrees, and the tree will die if the roots sit in water for too long. Sterilize the soil with Vapam before planting because the papaya has severe problems with nematodes. Another potential hazard is the papaya fruit fly, which can be held off by bagging the fruit after it emerges. A dwarf variety, the Hawaiian Solo, also can be grown in Florida.

Prunus persica — Peach
Height: 20 ft.
Spread: 15 ft.

This deciduous tree grows small and open. Its long, slender, light-green leaves have fine, serrated edges. The fruit is rounded, with a small peak at one end and fuzzy skin. The flesh is yellowish-orange, with a large seed. Peach trees did not always do well in Florida. The Jewel and Red Ceylon varieties were the only ones that thrived. Today, trees are grafted onto the Okinawa or Nemaguard root stocks, which are resistant to nematode damage, one of the major problems with peach trees. Peach trees also suffer from San Jose scale. Peach trees should be thinned each year. Thinning allows more light to reach the center of the foliage and produce more vigorous growth. For peaches and nectarines, chilling time is very important. Plant only those varieties which match the chilling time for your area of Florida. The map on page 95 indicates the chilling hours throughout the state, the varieties of peach trees recommended and their respective chilling hours.

104 *Pyrus lecontei* — Pear

Height: 15-20 ft.
Spread: 20-25 ft.

Pear trees grow best in northern and central Florida. This upright, deciduous tree is self-fruitful. It flowers in late winter with white, showy clusters of blossoms, with fruiting in early fall. Pears are vigorous growers for the first ten years and have a very poor salt tolerance. Mulching is beneficial, and judicious fertilizing with low nitrogen and high potash is recommended. Excessive fertilizing with high nitrogen can cause fire blight, a bacterial disease. The Baldwin and Orient varieties are best. They have a crisp, white flesh. The Pineapple or Sand pear is used more for cooking. Diseases include anthracnose and fire blight.

Ananas Comosus — Pineapple

Height: 3-4 ft.
Spread: 4-6 ft.

The pineapple has herbaceous leaves that resemble a long, narrow saw with little spines along the edges. The fruit grows out of the center of the plant on a long stem. The plant is damaged at 32 degrees and will be killed at 28 degrees, so protection is needed during cold spells. Sterilizing the soil with Vapam is recommended before planting because of nematode problems. Pineapples do well in full sun and can tolerate partial shade. This delicious fruit can be grown by planting the leaves and top one-inch of a store-bought pineapple in a good potting soil. New plants also can be grown from ground suckers and suckers on the stem. Mulching and weed killers are recommended as the spiny leaves make weeding difficult. Plants should be placed eighteen inches apart. As soon as they become established, place some organic material, such as well-rotted compost, in the buds to keep out sand and fertilizer, which will kill the plants. To force bloom, drop ten to twelve grains of calcium carbide into the bud in July, but only after plants are at least eighteen months old. This method, known

The Pineapple is a marvelous picnic and party fruit.

The Pineapple develops large spiny leaves and thrives in full sun.

as "gassing," will speed up fruit production from five to seven months. Spraying with Malathion will control mealybugs, which are the worst insect pest for pineapples. Red spiders also are a problem, controllable with a miticide. When planted in March, pineapples take 17 months for suckers, 26 months for slips and 29 months for crowns.

Rubus albescens — Raspberry
Height: 4-6 ft.
Spread: 4 ft.

Very similar to the blackberry, the raspberry has thorny canes, a bramble vining habit and reddish-purple fruit that can be eaten fresh or made into delicious jams, jellies and juice. Fresh raspberries do not last long after picking, which is why they are not sold in stores. The Mysore variety is the only common raspberry available in Florida. It grows best in full sun and is killed at 28 degrees. Diseases and insect problems include anthracnose and stink bugs.

Fragaria sp. — Strawberry
Height: 8-10 inches
Spread: 12-15 inches

Set out in October, strawberries will fruit in December, January and February. It is advisable to purchase new runners each year from your nurseryman, who can advise you on the best variety for your area, such as the Florida 90, Tioga or the Sequoia. These will bloom not only in winter but also in early spring. In northern parts of the state, strawberries have to be covered with newspapers or straw to protect them from freezing. Diseases include anthracnose and leaf spots.

NUTS

Macadamia integrifolia — Macadamia (Queensland Nut)
Height: 25 ft.
Spread: 15-20 ft.

A semi-tropical fruit tree, the macadamia has dark-green, waxy leaves eight inches long and two inches wide, with small spines along the edges. The nuts are three-quarters of an inch in diameter, have very hard shells and can be eaten fresh or roasted. The plants can be started by air-layering or from seed. They do best in full sun and are moderate growers.

Carya Illinoensis — Pecan
Height: 40-50 ft.
Spread: 30-40 ft.

A large-growing, upright tree, the pecan flourishes in well-drained soil, is totally cold-hardy and can be grown in northern and central Florida. It is a slow grower and has poor salt tolerance. Nuts are produced on the tip growth and appear between October and November. Spraying with a nutritional fertilizer containing zinc will eliminate zinc deficiency, a

The Pecan is one of Florida's favorite nut crops and produces an abundant harvest.

problem with pecan trees. Good varieties for Florida are the Moneymaker, Desirable and Curtis, all of which thrive best in full sun. A mature pecan tree needs thirty to fifty pounds of 8-8-8 fertilizer each year to maintain good growth and a fruitful harvest.

The following plants are recommended by the Florida Audubon Society as being attractive to Florida birds:

TREES:

Blackhaw *(Viburnum Ovovatum)*
Black Cherry *(Prumus Serotina)*
Cabbage Palmetto *(Sabal Palmetto)*
Camphor *(Cinnamonum Camphora)*
Cherry Laurel *(Prunus Caroliniana)*
Chinaberry *(Melia Azedarach)*
Citrus Sp.
Date Palm *(Phoenix Canariensis)*
Flowering Dogwood *(Cornus Florida)*
Hackberry *(Celtis Lavigata)*
Holly *(Ilex Opaca, Ilex Cassine)*
Loquat *(Eriobotrya Japonica)*
Magnolia *(Magnolia Grandiflora)*
Oaks *(Quercus Sp.)*
Red Cedar *(Juniperus Silicola)*
Red Mulberry *(Morus Rubra)*
Shining Sumac *(Rhus Copallina)*
Sparkleberry Tree *(Vaccinium Arboreum)*

SHRUBS AND VINES:

Amur Privet *(Ligustrum Amurense)*
Boxleaf Eugenia *(E. Myrtides)*
Beautyberry *(Callicarpa Americana)*
Brazilian Pepper *(Schinus Terebinthofolius)*
Downy Myrtle *(Rhodomyrtus Tomentosa)*
Elderberry *(Sambucus Simpsonii)*
Feijoa *(F. Sellowiana)*

Firethorn *(Pyracantha Coccinea)*
Grapes *(Vitis Sp.)*
Hawthorn *(Crataegus Floridana)*
Natal Plum *(Carissa Grandiflora)*
Pigeonberry *(Duranta Repens)*
Pokeweed *(Phytolacca Rigida)*
Seagrape *(Coccoloba Uvifera)*
Silverthorn *(Elaeagnus Pungens)*
Surinam Cherry *(Eugenia uniflora)*
Sweet Viburnum *(Viburnum Oratissimum)*
Wax Myrtle *(Myrica Cerifera)*
Wax Privet *(Ligustrum Japonicum)*
Yew Podocarpus *(P. Macrophylla)*

PLANTS THAT ATTRACT HUMMINGBIRDS AND BUTTERFLIES:

Butterfly Bush *(Buddleja Sp.)*
Cape Honeysuckle *(Tecomaria Capensis)*
Coral Honeysuckle *(Lonicera Sempervirens)*
Dwarf Poinciana *(P. Pulcherrima)*
Flame-of-the-Woods *(Ixora Coccinea)*
Glorybower *(Clerodendrum Speciossissimum)*
Hibiscus *(H. Rosa-Sinensis)*
Japanese Honeysuckle *(L. Japonica)*
Lantana *(L. Camara)*
Macaw Flower *(Daubentonia Punicea)*
Morning Glory *(Ipomoea Sp.)*
Pandorea *(Podranea Ricasoliana)*
Pentas *(P. Lanceolata)*
Plumbago *(P. Capensis)*
Shrimp Plant *(Beloperone Guttata)*
Red Cardinal *(Erythrina Arborea and E. Herbacea)*
Scarlet Bush *(Hamelia Patens)*
Scarlet Sage *(Salvia Coccinea)*
Slipper Plant *(Pedilanthus Sp.)*
Turk's Cap *(Malvaviscus Arboreus)*

When to Harvest

Variety	Season	Ripening Period
Apple	May-June	
Blackberry	May-June	
Blueberry	May-July	
Citrus	Early Oct.-Late July	
Figs	May-Oct.	
Grapes	May-June-July	
Pears	Sept.-Oct.	Will ripen off the tree in 5-7 days
Peaches	April-May-June	Will ripen off the tree in 5-7 days
Nectarine	April-May-June	Will ripen off the tree in 5-7 days
Strawberries	Feb.-March	Some will ripen off in a few days
Raspberry	March-April-May	
Avocado	Just about all year with different varieties	Will ripen off the tree in 4-7 days
Guava	June-July-Aug.-Sept.	
Mango	May-June-July-Aug.	Will ripen off the tree in 4-7 days
Papaya	Just about all year	Will ripen off the tree in 4-7 days
Banana	Summer-Fall	Will ripen off the tree in 4-7 days
Cattley Guava	June-July-Aug.	
Loquat	Jan.-Feb.-Mar.-April	
Oriental Persimmon	May-Oct.	
Carambola	Much of the year	
Pineapple	May-June-July-Aug.-Sept.	
Pecan	Oct.-Nov.	
Lychee	June-July	
Jaboticaba	Much of the year	

*Most fruits will taste better when they are ripened fully on the bush or tree. Fruits can normally be picked with a slight twisting pressure.

Spacing of Florida Fruit and Fruit Trees

Variety	Suggested Spacing
Apple	20'-30'
Blackberry	4'-8'
Blueberry	6'-10'
Citrus	20'-30'
Fig	15'-20'
Grapes	10'-15'
Pear	20'-30'
Peach	20'-30'
Nectarines	20'-30'
Pecan	35'-50'
Strawberries	3'-4'
Raspberry	4'-8'
Avocado	25'-45'
Guava	20'-30'
Mango	25'-45'
Papaya	5'-10'

CHAPTER FIVE

Citrus Trees

Citrus trees not only grow well in Florida, but they have helped the state establish itself as the nation's leading producer of orange juice. Florida growers also supply the country with grapefruit, lemons, tangerines, tangelos, kumquats and limes. Whether you live in the Panhandle of northwest Florida or as far south as the Keys, there is an adaptable citrus tree for your area that can be included in your landscaping plans.

Citrus trees are easy to grow and are evergreens with a lush look to their foliage. When covered with ripe fruit, they are one of the most rewarding sights for any gardener. The beauty they add to a landscape is supplemented by the joy of picking and eating your own fruit as the years go by.

Most citrus trees available in nurseries range from three to six feet in height, with a trunk diameter of one to two inches at the base. Select a tree with a good, straight trunk and healthy, dark-green leaves. The graft union should be smooth, clean and well-healed. Make sure there is no dead wood and that the union is sound. Be sure the roots are not protruding from the base of the container. Citrus trees tend to become root-bound, so before planting, pull the roots apart gently to allow them to continue growing out and down into the ground.

Stone fruit trees, such as peaches, are thinned out by a method called the modified leader system. But citrus trees require very little thinning to maintain continued good production of fruit. Compared with some fruit trees, citrus trees need very little care, though they do need spraying to control insect problems. Citrus trees are moderate in their water needs, but the soil should not be allowed to dry out. A moist, but not wet, soil is ideal. They need fertilizing with a "citrus special" — a formula higher in the minor elements. The analysis will be lower in nitrogen, such as 4-6-8, or with equal amounts of nitrogen and potassium, such as 6-4-6.

Citrus trees always should be planted in well-drained soil. If your garden does not have natural drainage, you should plant your citrus trees on a raised mound of soil six inches high and eight feet across, into which you have mixed peat and dehydrated cow manure.

Your selection of citrus trees will depend on the type of fruit you prefer and the area of the state in which you live.

112   **Kumquats:** Residents of the upper-north part of Florida may have to choose kumquat, the most cold-hardy citrus. The Nagami kumquat is very tart, about one inch long and oval shaped. It is used for making preserves and marmalade. The Meriva variety is rounded, sweet in flavor, and both the flesh and the skin can be eaten fresh.

Grapefruit: The Duncan is considered the best variety for Florida, with only one major drawback: it is seedy. It matures early, from October through January, and has the best flavor of all the grapefruits. For a seedless variety, the Marsh is recommended for superior quality. It matures from December through April. For lovers of pink grapefruit, try the Thompson, a bud sport of the White Marsh. As flavorful as the Duncan, the Thompson has a pink flesh that enhances its appeal.

Lemons: The largest lemon, often called the Florida pie lemon, is the Ponderosa, bearing from December through February and sometimes during the rest of the year as well. But the most common Florida lemon is the Meyer, maturing from December through April, and the one most often found in grocery stores. Lemons are not cold-hardy, though they are more tolerant of low temperatures than limes.

The ever-popular Grapefruit is a favorite for commercial and domestic growing.

Beautiful fruit salads like this begin with fruits from your own garden.

Oranges are not only one of Florida's most famous fruits, but one of the most attractive varieties of trees.

Oranges: This legendary Florida citrus has several varieties. The most widely grown is the Valencia, brimming with top-quality juice and usually the latest orange available because of its extended growing season. The Hamlin is an early-season orange, maturing from October through December, and is blessed with very few seeds. The Navel is a large, thick-skinned orange grown mainly to be eaten rather than juiced.

The Tangelo is a delicious hybrid of the Grapefruit and the Tangerine.

Tangerines: Large in size and spritely flavored, the Robinson tangerine is a hybrid of the Clementine tangerine and the Orlando tangelo. It produces fruit from September through October.

The Dancy tangerine bears from December through February, with easy-peeling skin typical of tangerines and flesh that easily separates into sections. The Lee tangerine produces from October through November and is another hybrid of the Clementine tangerine and the Orlando tangelo. For colder areas of the state, the Satsuma tangerine does well, though the fruit is smaller than average. The fruit appears from October through December.

Tangelos: The Orlando tangelo is a hybrid of the grapefruit and the tangerine. It is large and easy to peel and appears from November through January. The Minneola tangelo produces from January through March. It has a pear-shaped neck and reddish-orange flesh.

Limes: The Key lime is small and lemon-yellow in color and produces from October through December. The Tahiti, sometimes called the Persian lime, bears year 'round but has most of its fruit in early spring and fall. This is not a cold-hardy variety and must be grown in protected areas in lower-central and south Florida.

MR. GREEN THUMB RULE
Never mulch citrus trees. Mulching promotes root rot and other fungus-type diseases and encourages shallow root development.

Citrus trees are susceptible to a number of diseases and conditions
that can be controlled by regular spraying with Malathion, Diazinon or
Citrus Spray.

Black soot (a black, sooty mold) indicates an invasion of insects such as
white fly, aphids and scale. Spraying should be done immediately before
the problem gets out of hand and your citrus trees suffer damage.

The white fly is closely related to the scale insects. The adult stage,
which can be seen, is not harmful to citrus, but the transparent, silvery
larvae insert their stylet into the leaf and feed on the plant's sap, causing
damage. Any of the above-mentioned sprays will control this dangerous
pest.

Aphids are tiny, pear-shaped insects (often called plant lice) with very
small, soft bodies no more than a fifth of an inch in length. Aphids suck the
sap from new leaves and stems, producing a secretion called honeydew, on
which sooty mold will grow. These pests can be controlled by spraying with
the chemicals recommended.

Scale is found in several different types: the cottony cushion scale is in
reality an egg sack and looks like a cocoon about a half-inch long. The
actual scale is reddish-brown in color, about a quarter-of-an-inch long. The
hemispherical scale (sometimes called the round scale) is a twelfth-of-an-
inch high and dark brown in color.

All these pest problems can be controlled by regular spraying. Your
nursery can advise you on the best chemicals to use for each particular
problem on your citrus trees.

The following chart will specify treatment for your citrus trees:

Citrus Spray Schedule

When to Spray	Description	What to Use
March–April	(Before) Post bloom spray If scab or greasy spot has been a problem.	Neutral Copper Nutritional Spray Malathion Kelthane
May	Kelthane is for mites Pre-summer spray for white fly and aphids.	Malathion Kelthane
June–July	Summer spray Check temperature restrictions	Spray either Ethion and oil or oil emulsion
October–November	Fall spray	Malathion Kelthane
January	Dormant Spray If scab or greasy spot has been a problem.	Nutritional Spray Neutral Copper

*NOTE: Always cover upper and lower surfaces of all leaves and branches.

Citrus Varieties

Oranges	Seasons	Seedless or Seeds	Skin	Juice or Hand eaten fruit
Early Season				
Parson Brown	October-December	5-10	Rough	Good juice
Hamlin	October-December	1-5	Smooth	Good for juice
Middle Season				
Navel	Sept.-December	Seedless	Smooth	Hand eaten fruit
Queen	Dec.-March	8-12	Smooth	Juice & hand eaten
Pineapple	Dec.-March	7-10		Juice & hand eaten
Jafa	Dec.-March	2-6	Smooth	Juice
Temple	January-March	1-5	Smooth Reddish-orange	Hand eaten
Late Season				
Valencia	March-July	1-5	Smooth	Good for juice
Grapefruit				
Early Season				
Duncan	October-Jan.	10-20	Smooth	
Marsh Seedless	Dec.-April	1-5	Smooth	
Thompson Pink	Oct.-January	1-5	Smooth	

Citrus Varieties

Tangelo				
Minneola	Jan.-March	1-5	Smooth	Hand eaten
Orlando	Nov.-January	5-10	Smooth	Hand eaten
Tangerine				
Dancy	Dec.-February	5-10	Zipper skin	Hand eaten
Robinson	Sept.-October	5-10	Zipper skin	Hand eaten
Lee	October-Nov.	5-10	Zipper skin	Hand eaten
Osceola	November	5-10	Zipper skin	Hand eaten
Satsuma	October-Nov.	5-10	Zipper skin	Hand eaten
Limes				
Persian Tahiti	Spring — throughout the year	1-5	Dark green	Juice
Key Lime	All year	1-5	Yellow lemon	
Lemon				
Ponderosa	All year	2-8	Large size	Pie, lemon
Meyer	Dec.-April	5-10	Lemon yellow	Jiuce
Rough	All year	5-10	Large	Juice, pie
Calamondin	Oct.-Jan.	2-8	Round	Acid-marmalade, Juice
Meiwa Kumquat	Oct.-Jan.	1-5	Round	Sweet skin flesh can be eaten
Nagami Kumquat	Oct.-Jan.	1-5	Oval	Acid-marmalade

CHAPTER SIX

Annuals

When Juan Ponce de Leon discovered our part of the world in 1513, he named it *La Florida*, which is Spanish for "the flowered place." As gardeners have realized since, Florida's climate is ideal for growing many of the most beautiful varieties of flowers in North America. While temperatures in Florida may be more moderate than in many parts of the country, there can be extreme fluctuations during the cooler months, November through April. Whereas in May through October you may have all the heat problems of the tropics. Spider mites and other insects are a big problem during these times. Certain less hardy flowers and shrubs may have to be protected during Florida's infrequent cold spells, but in general, a garden of flowers can survive year 'round and provide color, beauty and satisfaction for the home owner, if he is aware of the changing seasons and plants accordingly.

Admittedly, a flower garden of annuals and perennials does demand more care and attention than evergreen shrubs. But considering the rewards, the time and effort spent is well worth it. Flowers are no more difficult to raise than vegetables. Both require some preparation of the soil, frequent watering, fertilizing and spraying for insects and various plant problems. Yet the baskets of cut flowers for the home and the canvas of color you create in your garden are more than sufficient compensation. Framing your home with an imaginatively landscaped flower garden not only will enhance the appearance but the value of your property. You also can realize a deep inner joy when you work with nature to produce a feast for the eyes and the soul.

If you feel some apprehension over starting a flower garden, start small, with perhaps one flower bed by the front door and some pots on the patio. Within a year, you likely will be eager to transform your entire property and enjoy the rewards inherent in painting your landscape with living color.

Just as you plan landscaping, you will have to plan flower beds. Four to six hours of good, direct sunlight are essential for most flowering annuals and perennials. Position your flower beds so that they are not shaded excessively by trees or buildings. Studying the requirements of 119

120 various flowers also can help you plan certain beds and areas and choose plants that tolerate the existing ratio of sun to shade.

Apartment dwellers with an itchy green thumb but no yard can compromise with planters and window boxes to fulfill their gardening desires. Flowering vines can be grown over balcony dividers or a trellis to add color to apartments and condominiums. Remember to let your imagination run wild when planning any gardening project, large or small. It is surprising what some people have achieved on large properties or on apartment porches and balconies.

SOIL ENRICHMENT

Whatever your situation, your initial concern must be for the soil in which you will be growing flowers. The ground in Florida is sorely lacking in nutrients and always must be enhanced with peat moss, manure and compost. About the only annual flower that grows well in poor soil is the nasturtium, which experienced gardeners humorously refer to as "a masochistic plant." The more it is neglected, the better it seems to thrive!

A good beginning is to take 25 pounds of cow manure, 23 pounds of peat, two to three pounds of a good, general fertilizer and one inch of colloidal phosphate and rotor-till this mixture into the soil to a depth of six inches. This should be sufficient for a flower bed approximately ten feet by twenty feet. After tilling, apply Vapam to kill nematodes, fungi, bacteria and weed seeds. Then rake the flower bed level and smooth, and let it sit for three weeks. This will allow the Vapam to dissipate, preventing injury to your flowers, and will let the new soil mixture settle down. Be aware that Vapam is a toxic material and should be used with care. If you decide not to sterilize, I recommend that you improve the soil, as described in Chapter I.

Next, check the pH of your soil. Most annuals grow best with a soil pH of 5.5 to 6.5. If your analysis shows less than 5.5 pH, add dolomite. If the reading is above 6.5, add sulphur until the desired pH of the soil is reached.

The next step is to decide on the flowers you will plant. If you opt for planting from seed, buy seeds from a reputable seed company or from your

SOIL PREPARATION
FOR FLOWERING PLANTS

Once you've selected a proper site for your flowering plants where sun and shade are most appropriate for the plants, you will need to prepare the soil carefully. To create a suitable bed for annuals, you should rototill the soil to a depth of eight to twelve inches, remove all roots, rocks or other debris, then add soil improvers such as peat moss, compost, or commercial quality manure.

You may also want to add sand to improve aeration and drainage. Rototill the mixture, then rake smooth prior to planting.

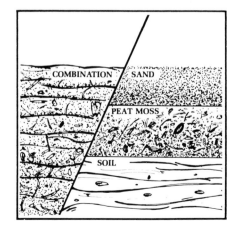

PLANT ACCORDING TO PLAN

Be sure to plan when each variety should be planted, fed and watered. Keep a record of fertilizer applications, and make sure each plant is properly spaced for future growth. A good plan is your best security for a beautiful flower garden.

Space plants according to their expected mature height and width.

nursery. It is not always advisable to buy seeds at a dime store or supermarket. These sometimes are old stock and poor quality. Follow directions on the package for planting, either in the ground or in jiffy pots (compressed peat pots that dissolve and improve the soil when sunk into the ground after the seeds have sprouted and grown a few inches). You also can plant seeds in six-pack plastic containers filled with potting soil or in large pots filled with prepared, sterilized soil.

PLANTING WITH SEEDLINGS

Seedlings may be purchased at a nursery, eliminating the waiting time encountered with seeds. Nurseries offer the newest and best varieties. Seedlings usually come in four- or six-packs. Be careful removing the young plants from their temporary home. An easy method is to slit the sides of the plastic containers with scissors, thereby releasing the soil so that it slips out easily. Prepare a hole in the ground slightly larger than the soil around the roots of the seedling. Gently lower the plant in and

WATERING FLOWERS

Flowering plants are delicate and should be watered either by ground-level drip irrigation, soaker hoses, or water breakers which spray a fine mist that will not damage the plants.

These plants will also require plenty of moisture; watch them carefully for signs of wilt. In well-drained soil, they need frequent deep watering.

A water breaker sprays a fine mist which helps protect delicate plants.

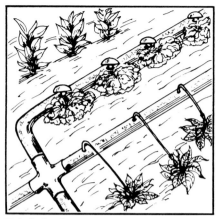

Drip Irrigation

Soaker Hose

press soil around it firmly to hold it upright. Space your plants apart as recommended for the particular variety. To minimize transplant shock, water each seedling immediately after planting with about a cupful of a fertilizer, such as Nutri-Sol, which helps the plant get off to a good start. The next day, you can begin a regular watering schedule.

A breaker-bar watering device minimizes possible damage to flowers and is used by many nurseries. A soaker hose or drip tubing is excellent and a very effective method of watering. Annuals should receive at least two inches of water per week. If you are unsure whether your soil needs watering, press your fingers into the ground around the flowers to test for moisture. Depending on the needs of the particular flower, you may need to water or allow the soil to remain moist, but not dry. Dried out soil can kill a flower quicker than an overnight freeze. Improper watering can be fatal to your flowers, or it can cut down the potential number of blooms on a plant. Check the requirements for your flowers, and water accordingly. Watch for any plants that may turn gray and withered-looking. This denotes either a pest or a watering problem. If you are unsure of the cause of any condition, ask your nurseryman for advice.

SELECTING ANNUALS

Almost all flowers are subject to some type of problem, either in the soil or from insects. Watch for any unusual conditions and take steps at once. Details of insect pests and diseases can be found in a later chapter, along with recommended sprays and insecticides.

Many popular flowers are grown in Florida. Your choice should be determined by your artistic preference for color, size and shape, which gets back to your original landscape planning. With flower beds, always place the tallest flowers at the back, such as hollyhocks and larkspurs, to provide a background for the smaller plants in the middle and edge of the flower bed. It is also more appealing to mix flowers (both for color and variety) in the same bed to create interesting patterns of shape and color. A bed with

Young annuals are conveniently available at nurseries in 6-pack containers.

nothing but one variety tends to look too regimented and unimaginative. The only exceptions to this rule might be petunias and roses, both of which are very acceptable without other flowers mixed in. Study the colors of various flowers and the mature size of the plants, then plan the manner in which you will position them in the flower bed for maximum artistic effect.

Building flower beds to have several levels makes for an interesting display and provides the opportunity for more versatile arrangements of flowers. A top level, perhaps six feet above the ground, dropping to a second level four feet high and a third two feet high, held in place by a low stone edging, can be an appealing spot in your garden on which your blooming flowers seem to cascade down like a colorful waterfall of blossoms and foliage.

Blue Puff Ageratums

Ageratums can make a beautiful cluster of flowers.

The following flowers are very popular with Florida gardeners:

Ageratum

This is a low, bushy plant six to twelve inches in height, with clusters of small, fuzzy, ball-shaped flowers of lavender blue (also pink and white). The Ageratum is good for edging flower beds, for use in rock gardens and for patches of contrasting color in a large flower bed. A slow grower from seed, it is better to buy seedlings. Plant in February through April for flowering in April through August. These are tender plants requiring full sun or partial shade, and they like improved, well-drained soil. Spray for aphids, red spiders and leafhoppers.

Alyssum *Sweet Alyssum*

Alyssum is a very small, delicate bush about eight inches high, with rounded clusters of white, lilac and purple fragrant blossoms. Sweet Alyssum is an outstanding winter-flowering annual. It makes a good ground cover for edging flower beds and on rock gardens. Sow seeds where plants

Alyssum grown as a border.

Sweet Alyssum, container grown

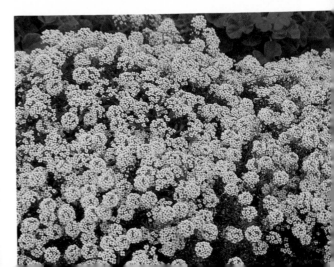

are to grow, or buy seedlings. Plant in September through January for flowering in October through June. These hardy little flowers like moist, good soil and lots of sun in the summer. Keep them somewhat drier in the winter. Spray for aphids.

Amethyst Flower *Browallia*

Growing one to two feet in height, with tubular violet or white blossoms, the Amethyst Flower is easy to grow from seeds or cuttings. It can be used as a house plant or for cut flowers. Plant in September through November for flowering in December through May. The tender plants require pinching to avoid staking the stems. They like rich, moist soil and will grow in sun or partial shade. Slug pellets around the base will ward off slugs.

Annual Chrysanthemum

Growing two to three feet in height, these attractive plants have succulent, aromatic leaves and double or single daisy-like flowers in yellow and white, or yellow with reddish rings. They can be used for cut flowers and border plantings. Producing dense masses of blossoms, chrysanthemums thrive in sun or partial shade. Plant from February to May for flowers in May through July. They prefer moist, well-drained soil and suffer from aphids and nematodes.

Chrysanthemum growing in a greenhouse.

126 *Gypsophila* — Baby's Breath

Baby's Breath has loose branching, bushy foliage, with many tiny white-and-rose flowers on wiry stems. Baby's Breath grows to twenty-four inches and makes attractive floral arrangements when combined with other flowers in a vase. It quickly blooms and goes to seed. For continuous flowering, plant new seeds each month. This hardy plant likes rich, well-drained soil with sun and partial shade. Plant in September through March for flowering in October through May. It suffers from root-knot and aphid, and is available in a perennial variety.

Begonias

Begonias do best during the cooler months, so they should be planted in partial and full shade. These are small, rounded plants suitable for low borders, hanging baskets and patio pots. The foliage varies from bright green to waxy bronze, with variegated types available. Flowers are red, pink and white. You should buy transplants, since begonia seed is very fine and difficult to germinate, even in a greenhouse. This is one of the best flowers for season-long bloom. The wax varieties are a popular plant for Florida. The variety called Non-Stop tends to flower much of the year.

Begonia Viva

Bingo Pink Begonia

Bingo Rose Begonia

Glamour Begonia (salmon picote)

Champion Yellow Begonias

Wax Begonias

Pink Avalanche Begonia

Bells of Ireland

A two-foot-high, thorny plant, Bells of Ireland have small, white flowers encased in a large bell-like green sheath. Used as cut flower, dried arrangements, borders and bedding, this tender plant likes sun and partial shade and needs moist, rich soil. Plant in February through July for blossoms in April through summer. The seeds germinate in cool weather, around 40 degrees. Spray for aphids.

California Poppy

These cup-shaped flowers on tall, gray-green stems make an impressive display in shades of yellow, white, orange pink and red. The hardy plants grow two feet high in well-drained, improved soil and must have full sun. Plant the seed where it is to grow in November through January for a riot of color from March through May. Poppies last only a day on the stem but flower profusely. Spray for aphids.

Calendula dwarf mixture

Calendula

A favorite for cut flowers and bedding plants, calendulas have light-green, slightly sticky leaves and yellow to orange flowers that grow twelve to fifteen inches high. They are hardy and prefer a good moist soil in sun or partial shade. Plant from seeds in September through January for flowers in December through June. Spray for aphids and caterpillars.

Chinese Forget-Me-Not

Blue, white and pink clusters of tiny flowers atop long, sticky stems almost eighteen inches high make the Chinese forget-me-not an interesting addition to any garden. These tender plants withstand light frost and prefer moist soil in sun and partial shade. This is a very satisfactory plant for borders, bedding, cut flowers and rock gardens. Plant from September through April for blooming in December through July. Watch out for root rot.

Candytuft

Candytuft grows beautiful red, pink, lilac, violet and white crowded clusters of flowers atop twenty-inch stems. This flower is a favorite for cut flowers as well as edging and bedding plants. A hardy specimen, candytuft likes moist soil and full sun. Plant seeds in September through February for November-through-April blossoms. For continuous flowering, plant seeds every ten days. Spray for aphids. A perennial candytuft also is available.

Celosia — Cockscomb

The cockscomb is a constant favorite with gardeners. It offers an impressive display of background color in a flower bed. The cockscomb grows two to four feet high, with feathery flower clusters or compact,

Cockscomb, Geisha variety

Celosia, Apricot Brandy

Golden Torch Salvias

velvety heads in red, yellow, white and purple. This tender plant enjoys rich, moist soil in sun or partial shade. The seeds are easy to grow and should be planted in February through April for May-to-September blooming. Dwarf varieties also are available. Watch out for root-knot and caterpillars.

Coleus

An ever-popular plant for indoors or out, coleus has inconspicuous flowers but breathtaking leaves in red, green, yellow, bronze and variegations of these colors. Excellent for pots, planters and mass displays in flower beds, tender coleus needs well-drained, improved soil and does best

Coleus, Wizard mixture

Coleus, Rose Wizard

Saber Pineapple Coleus

Golden Rainbow

in partial shade. Grown from seed or cuttings, it should be planted in February through July. New plants can be started by placing a stem in a glass of water until it roots, then transplant to good potting soil indoors or outdoors. A fast grower, the coleus should be pinched to promote bushy growth. Treat for aphids, mites, mealybugs and nematodes.

Cornflower (Bachelor's Button)

Cornflower produces papery, round blossoms in blue, white, pink, red and dark purple. This hardy plant covers a large area with its grayish foliage and colorful blooms and is excellent for bedding and cut flowers. Tolerant of almost any soil, cornflowers thrive in full sun and grow to thirty inches in height. Plant seeds in September through January for December-to-June flowering. Treat for aphids and root-knot. Cornflowers will re-seed themselves year after year.

Cosmos

Cosmos are easy to grow. In fact, in some parts of the world, they grow wild. Reaching six feet tall in Florida, the cosmos can be found with white, pink, crimson, orange or yellow, daisy-like flowers atop thin, graceful stems. This tender plant likes plenty of moisture and soil that is not too rich. Plant seeds in February through April for a mass of flowers from May through August. Be warned: these tall plants blow over easily and sometimes should be staked. They also suffer from aphids, mites and caterpillars.

Dahlia

An herbaceous plant with large leaf clusters and many branches, the dahlia grows from thick, potato-like roots. These roots should be dug up after the first frost and stored in peat or sawdust through the winter, then set out again six inches deep in February and March for summer flowering. Dahlia blossoms are profuse: large, daisy-like, single and double blossoms in red, white, yellow, pink, bronze and combinations of these colors. Dahlias grow best in improved soil with good moisture and prefer sun to partial shade. Dahlias are tender plants, growing to five feet in height. Treat for nematodes, aphids, stem borers and powdery mildew.

African Daisy

This hardy plant grows almost thirty inches high in Florida, with blue, white, violet, cream, yellow, bronze and red daisies atop long thin stems. The African daisy has few problems and grows easily in full sun, with no particular preference for soil. Plant in August through January for March-to-June blossoms. Excellent for cut flowers or edging a flower bed, the African daisy will re-seed itself year after year. Whether cut or still on the plant, the flowers will close at night.

African Daisy

132 **Tahoka Daisy**

Very similar in appearance to an aster, the Tahoka daisy has long-lasting, frilly blossoms with lush, fern-like foliage. As bedding plants and cut flowers, these daisies are violet-blue, with yellow centers. These hardy plants like moist, good soil and grow to two feet in full sun and partial shade. Plant seeds from February through April for blooming from June through November. Tahoka daisies are easy to grow but suffer from wilt and aphids.

Four O'Clocks

Easily grown from seed, this brightly colored tuberous rooted flower comes in red, pink, white, yellow and variegated varieties that do well in moist soil, with full sun or partial shade. Plant in the spring for a carpet of blooms two feet high from summer to the first frost. Ideal for flower beds and large areas requiring color.

Geranium

The geranium is an herbaceous plant with hairy, aromatic leaves and clusters of white, red and pink blossoms. It is a Florida favorite indoors and out, though geraniums do best in full sun. They thrive in any soil but need little water. In fact, the soil should be on the dry side to prevent root rot. For robust, thick plants, geraniums should be pinched back. Otherwise they will grow tall and spindly to about eighteen inches. Numerous varieties offer a wide range of colors. The flowers last a long time. The Crimson Fire, Cherry Blossom and Sincerity varieties are good for pot plants. For hanging baskets, try Sugar Baby, a pink flower; Yale, a double-lilac white, or Cornell, a lavender flower. There are also fancy leaf and scented types.

Geranium, Orbit Red

Geranium blossom

Gayfeather (Blazing Star)

Actually a perennial, this plant is grown in Florida as an annual. A sparsely branched species, its leaves are threadlike, with a flower spike of small clusters of purple and white. It can be used as a border planting or for cutting. Gayfeather has few problems, is hardy and thrives in moist soil in sun and partial shade, reaching a height from two to three feet. Plant in fall and spring for summer and fall flowering.

Gladiolus

Gladioli grow from corms. They should be dug up six weeks following flowering, before the foliage becomes yellow or brown, and stored in dry peat or sawdust through the winter. Planting should be done after the last frost for future flowering, anytime except midsummer. "Glads" can be planted every week to ensure a continuous display of their impressive flowers, which are multi-colored on a tall, green spike. They prefer full sun and improved, well-drained soil. These tender flowers are subject to thrips, caterpillars, foliage diseases and corm rot, a condition that requires dusting with Captan before planting and after digging up for storage. Often reaching heights of three to four feet, gladioli are an elegant flower, excellent in rows at the back of flower beds to provide a background for shorter flowers. They are also very effective around a patio in small circular beds about a foot across, in which a dozen corms can be planted for a compact display of the flowers. For added strength and growth, a handful of bonemeal should be placed around each corm at the time of planting.

Globe Amaranth

A favorite source of dried flowers, the globe amaranth has stiff branches with dense, clover-like heads in purple, red, pink, white and muted

Vaughn's Trial, Geranium

Red Standard

134 orange. Excellent for borders, cut flowers and dried flowers, this tender plant tolerates poor soil and grows to twenty inches in full sun. Plant seeds from March to April for flowers from May through July. It has few growth or insect problems.

Godetia (Farewell-to-Spring)

This is an upright plant with clusters of satin-like flowers in white, red, rose and purple. The godetia grows to eighteen inches in partial shade. A hardy plant, it likes any well-drained soil and has only one insect problem: plant bugs. Planting from September through January will give you a mass of double and single primrose-like flowers from December through June.

Gaillardia (Indian Blanket)

With soft, hairy leaves and stems and multi-colored flowers in shades of red, orange, yellow and white, the gaillardia is useful as a coastal planting. They are quite salt-tolerant. In fact, they will thrive almost anywhere. This hardy species does well in sandy soil and full sun. In many western states, gaillardia can be seen growing wild. They have few insect problems and are possibly one of the most rewarding flowers to include in your garden. Plant seeds September through January for blossoms from April through August. Pinching off spent heads will prolong the blooming period. There also is a perennial variety. It grows a little taller and offers a slightly different flower formation.

Hollyhock

With large, dark-green, coarse leaves and hairy, thick stems, the hollyhock grows six to seven feet tall. It is ideal against a wall or fence and provides a colorful, stately background to a flower bed. Pink, dark-red and scarlet flowers, both single and double, open from the bottom all the way

Hollyhock

up to the terminal spike. The hollyhock likes good soil and moisture in either sun or partial shade. Hollyhocks should be planted from August through January for flowering in March through June. Plant seeds in fumigated soil and mulch well to prevent root-knot. Placing hollyhocks next to a building allows the roots to grow under the wall. This is a protection against root-knot.

Larkspur

Larkspur is loved for its delicate dark-green leaves and erect branches, where blooms open from the bottom to the terminal spike. Larkspurs are as impressive a background plant as hollyhocks. Growing to four and five feet tall, larkspur spikes come in lavender, blue, white, violet and pink, both single and double. This hardy plant enjoys most soils, adequate water and sun or partial shade. It will reseed itself and grows best if seeded in its growing location. Plant from October through December for flowers from March through May. Particularly tall larkspurs may need to be staked. You should treat for crown rot, mites and caterpillars.

Lobelia

Lobelia grows into a small bush about twelve inches high and wide, covered with tiny, irregular, blue, white and red blossoms. The lobelia is excellent for edging, bedding, pots and planter boxes. This tender plant likes improved soil, adequate moisture and thrives in sun or partial shade. It can be planted from seed or cuttings from September through March for flowers from November through May. Cutting back prolongs the flowering period. The lobelia does well during cool weather but will wither at freezing temperatures.

Molten Fire (Summer Poinsettia)

Like the coleus, molten fire plants are grown for their brightly colored leaves rather than their flowers, which are inconspicuous. Growing to four feet in Florida, molten fire is striking: its leaves are blotched with red, green and yellow. Useful as a background or a bedding plant, molten fire likes fortified, sandy soil and full sun. If the soil is too rich, foliage color will be less brilliant. Too much water causes crown rot. Plant seeds or tip cuttings in February through May for a massive display all summer. Root-knot and caterpillars can be serious problems.

Marvel-of-Peru

A tuberous-rooted, bushy plant with glossy leaves, Marvel-of-Peru has funnel-shaped, red, yellow, white or striped flowers that open late every afternoon and close in the morning. A tender plant, it likes most soil types and sun or partial shade, and grows two feet tall. Plant seeds from Februay to May for April to September flowers. Light frost will damage the plant, but it does recover.

Marigold

Strong-scented foliage, double blossoms in orange, yellow or maroon and a compact, bushy shape make the marigold an ideal addition to any

Diamond Jubliee Marigold

Orange Gitana

Marigold

Spinwheel Marigold

garden. The pyrethrin in the leaves of some varieties may help repel some insects. Plant from seeds, clippings or seedlings in February to May for lush foliage and endless flowers from May to November. Marigolds thrive in moist, good soil and in sun or partial shade. Spray for spider mites and serpentine leaf miner.

Morning Glory

Nothing covers a wire fence quicker than morning glories. Their lush, heart-shaped leaves and delicate, funnel-shaped flowers greet the morning with pink, blue and deep red splashes of color. The blossoms close later in the day, but the leaves form a solid, living wall for privacy. Morning glory vines also can be used over a trellis around the patio for glorious shade and eye-catching beauty in the morning. Soak the seeds in water for a few days, and plant them where they will grow. Planting from February to April will give you a good show from March through November. Morning glories like sun and partial shade and are tolerant of any kind of soil and moisture. Be warned: once planted, morning glories will re-seed themselves prolifically, year after year.

Nasturtium

Known in England as "the poor man's flower," nasturtiums will grow virtually anywhere with very little care. The nasturtium nevertheless is a very rewarding plant that flowers profusely. Coming in dwarf bush

Nasturtium

varieties as well as climbers, nasturtiums are tender plants **preferring** light, moist soil and full sun to partial shade. Nasturtiums provide wonderful color for bordering a flower bed, as well as edging it with its thick, rounded leaves. They are resistant to nematodes but do suffer from aphids and serpentine leaf miner. Plant seeds where you wish them to grow in February and March for April through June flowering. The more flowers you pick, the more will appear. Caution: do not fertilize nasturtiums. This leads to excessive leaf growth and very few flowers. Nasturtiums are the one flower that seems to thrive on neglect, making it a popular item for lazy gardeners!

Nicotiana (Jasmine tobacco)

Nicotiana's coarse, bushy stems form a compact plant over two feet high with many white, crimson and cream flowers at the top. The flowers close during the day but open at night, emitting a heady perfume that is most pleasant. This hardy plant does well in well-drained, improved soil and thrives in sun and partial shade. Use where a dense, thick patch of foliage and flowers is desired. Plant seeds in August through November for blooms from March through June. Spray for aphids.

Large Nicotiana

Nicotiana blossoms

Beconsfield Pansies   Universal Orange Pansies

Hybrid Show Pansy Blossom   Hybrid Show Pansy Blossom

Pansy

These low-growing plants are perennials but are used as annuals. For bedding, borders, patio plantings and cut flowers, pansies have an Old World charm. Their dark green foliage is about eight inches high, and they produce masses of velvety, flat flowers in almost every color of the rainbow, variegated. The flowers look like small, smiling faces staring up from the ground. A cold-weather plant, pansies should be planted from September to December for flowering from January through May. They are hardy. They thrive in rich soil with good moisture and both in sun and partial shade. Mulching is advised, both for protection in cold weather and improved growth and flower protection.

Petunia

For years, the petunia has been one of Florida's most popular flowering annuals. Some outstanding varieties are Old Glory White, White Cascade, Red Baron, El Toro, Blue Flash and, for a bright orchid color, the

Sugar Daddy. Don't plant in the same site three years in a row — rotate to a different annual. For hanging baskets or trailers, try Pink Carousel or Linda. One of the most glorious displays in any garden is a bed of petunias in mixed colors. Pinching the center shoot of these plants promotes dense, bushy foliage from ten to twenty inches in height, with endless single or double funnel-shaped flowers. Petunias are difficult to grow from seed (the seeds are microscopic). Buy seedlings from a nursery and mix up your colors when you plant. August-through-January plantings will flower October through July. Petunias like good soil with adequate moisture and do best in sun, especially in winter. But they also will thrive in shade. They are excellent as a bedding plant, but many people use them in planters and window boxes.

Resisto Rose Petunias

Summer Madness Petunias

Rose Picotee Petunias

Ultra Red Petunias

Periwinkle Blue Blossoms

Periwinkle White Blossoms

Periwinkle (Vinca)

Periwinkles are among the easiest flowers to grow, and survive almost any amount of neglect. They are very salt-tolerant and grow in almost any soil, in full sun or partial shade, to a height of twelve to eighteen inches. They are evergreen but become a little sparse in late fall and winter. Spring growth is bright green, with purple-blue flowers. Periwinkles should be sprayed for leaf rollers in summer. A new dwarf series is available called Magic Carpet. Both require more protection than the regular, green trailing periwinkle.

Phlox

Phlox has smooth-edged leaves and erect branches with clusters of blossoms at the tips. It is an excellent border plant that can be massed in a flower bed. Phlox has few insect problems and responds well to fertilization, growing one to two feet high with profuse blossoms of various colors. Although phlox can be transplanted, it does better if planted from seed where it is meant to grow. Plant from September through February for riotous color from December through May. The plants like dry, sandy soil and do well in sun or partial shade. A hardy plant, phlox will re-seed, but the next germination will have poorer color.

Portulaca (Moss Rose)

A great summer bloomer, portulaca takes hot summer temperature very well. A super bedding plant, the leaves of portulaca are thick, narrow and succulent and grow no higher than six inches. The rose-like flowers open only in sunlight, and flowering time is short, requiring new seeding every six weeks to maintain the carpet of color they create. Use this flower as a border plant or on rock gardens, and plant from February through May for May-to-October blooms. A tender plant, portulaca does best in full sun, in enriched, well-drained soil. Its only problem is damp-off, if planted in a poorly drained area.

Portulaca blossoms

Sunnyside Portulacas

Salvia beds at 1979 trials

Salvia Carabiniere

Blaze of Fire Salvia

Salvia

Salvia does well in full sun or partial shade. This sturdy plant has two-lipped flowers one to one-and-a-half inches long in racemes. The flowers are usually bright scarlet and grow to twenty-four inches. A tender plant, the salvia prefers enriched, moist soil in sun and partial shade. Plant seeds or cuttings from February through June for April-to-September blooming. Excellent for borders, bedding and cut flowers. If cut back, the plant will bloom again. Although scarlet salvias are the predominant favorite, this plant does come in pink, purple and white as well as a blue perennial described in the following chapter. Other varieties you may want to try are Red Hot Sally and St. John's Fire.

Shasta Daisies

Double Shasta Daisy

Shasta Daisy

These attractive large daisies are usually white, some double, other single with contrasting yellow centers. Growing 18 to 24 inches in height, they make a vivid display. A dwarf variety is also available. They should be planted in early spring for summer and fall flowering. Clumps can be divided in the fall for new plantings. Shasta daisies are very hardy but do best in moist, rich soil with full sun.

Snapdragon

For cut flowers and bedding plants, snapdragons are most attractive. They grow in all colors except blue and have tubular flowers growing up a

144   tall spike that can reach thirty-six inches in height. The snapdragon is an excellent choice for backgrounds. Frequent cutting of the flower spikes encourages more blooms. Snapdragons like moist, rich soil and thrive in sun or partial shade. A hardy plant, they have been known to live through a winter and continue blooming a second year. Plant seed from September through December for flowering from January through June. Snapdragons do experience problems with nematodes, wilt, rust and aphids.

Statice (Sea lavender)

A bushy plant with rough, wiry stems, statice has small flowers atop a branching spike in lavender, blue, white, rose and yellow. A hardy plant, statice likes good soil and moisture and full sun. In Florida, it grows to two feet in height and transplants easily. Plant seeds from September through January for flowering from February to August. Statice has problems with foliage diseases.

Spider Flower

A tall, hairy and strong-scented plant, the spider flower produces many white, rose and purplish blossoms with long stamens on short, strong spines. Sow the seeds where they are to grow. In Florida, these flowers will reach four feet in height. They thrive in sandy soil and full sun and are very hardy, with a long flowering season. Plant seeds from September to May for blossoms from April through September. The spider flower has few insect problems.

Strawflower

As its name indicates, the strawflower is crisp and dry-looking. Arrangements of dried strawflowers have been a favorite for years. Coming in yellow, orange, red, pink and white, this tender plant likes good soil and full sun, withstands some drought and has few insect problems. Plant seeds from March to May for May-to-August blooming. In Florida, strawflowers will grow to thirty inches in height.

Sweet Pea

Few vines surpass the sweet pea for impressive appearance and fragrant, frequent flowering. Blooming in white, pink, lavender, blue, orange and red, sweet peas turn any fence or trellis into an expanse of color and heady fragrance. They often grow ten to fifteen feet above the ground, depending on the height of the support. Most gardeners will make a fence six feet high and as long as desired, then prepare a trench at the bottom before planting. Sweet peas are considered difficult to grow, but with good preparation of the soil, including fumigation and frequent fertilizing, they can be no more trouble than any other flower. Although hardy, the flowers will freeze, and the plants do best in full sun or partial shade. Plant seeds where they are to grow, in October through January for January-to-April blooming. The more flowers you pick, the more will grow, and nothing freshens up a room better than a large vase of sweet peas. There also is a dwarf bush sweet pea, as well as a perennial type. But the blossoms on these are not as impressive nor as large as the regular type.

Stock

Stock is even more fragrant than sweet peas. It is a firm, erect plant about two feet high, with single or double flowers in racemes. Stock comes in various colors and is best known and loved for the wonderful scent it gives off. A hardy plant, stock likes rich soil with good moisture and thrives best in full sun. Plant from September to February for winter and spring flowering. Stock is not recommended for south Florida, since it will not flower well during mild temperatures or mild winters.

Impatiens — **Touch-Me-Not**

For borders and planter boxes, impatiens, or touch-me-not, provides a beautiful splash of color. It has dark-green, succulent leaves and clusters of pink, white and scarlet flowers. Easily grown from seed, impatiens also roots from cuttings. Pinching the main stem will produce a stockier, bushier plant. Growing from six to eighteen inches, impatiens is hardy, likes well-drained, improved soil and does best in partial and full shade. For a long time, impatiens has been the most popular plant for shade in Florida. Now some of the new varieties will take a little more sun. This is a blessing for Florida gardeners. Recently the impatiens rival the petunia in popularity. The Super Elfin, Scarlet, and Super Elfin White are excellent varieties. Nothing is more attractive than a hanging basket of double-flowering impatiens. Plant seeds in February through July for flowers from April until frost. Watch out for aphids and leaf-feeding caterpillars.

Impatiens, sherbet mixture

Bigtop Zinnias

Zinnia sp. — Zinnias

Zinnias are one of the most popular annuals in the world and one of the easiest to grow. The zinnia can flood a flower bed with double, semi-double and single blossoms in practically every color of the rainbow except blue. From the dwarf varieties for borders and edging plants to the three-feet-high plants for mass plantings and backgrounds, zinnias are unrivaled. Growing best in full sun, they can tolerate almost any soil and bloom profusely from April through November. Staggered plantings from February through August will ensure an ongoing selection for cut flowers. Zinnias are tender plants, suffering from powdery mildew, spider mites, caterpillars and crown rot. Spraying will take care of these problems, but as a preventive measure, water the soil only around zinnias — not the leaves. Peat moss and organic matter added to the soil will improve growth and flower quality. So will a 6-6-6 or 8-8-8 fertilizer (2 pounds per 100 square feet of bed area).

Zinnias should be planted from seed where they are to grow. In warm soils, zinnias will germinate within one week. After the seedlings send out four leaves, they may be thinned to ten inches apart for the smaller varieties, twelve to eighteen inches apart for the larger types. Delayed thinning will result in stunted growth and few flowers. Zinnias need room to grow tall and bushy.

The main problem afflicting this flower is powdery mildew. If there is the slightest indication of a grayish-white coating on the leaves, treat at once with sulfur dust, Karathan, Acti-dione P.M. or Benomyl (Benlate) — and above all, do not water the plants on the leaves. Some zinnia enthu-

Figaro Zinnias

siasts will cover the budding plants with cheesecloth. The filtered light results in increased insect protection as well as flowers of larger size and crisp, striking color.

Zinnias come in solid colors and in striped and variegated types such as Peppermint Stick and Ortho Polka. There are others, such as Dark Jewel, which have twisted and ruffled petals. The largest blossoms are California Giant and Super Giant, which have mammoth-sized blooms almost six inches in diameter. For patio or porch, try a pot of one of the Short Stuff series.

Annuals for Florida

Common Names	Color	Height	Sun or Shade	Hardy to Tender	Seed to Bloom in Days	Planting Season
Ageratum	Blue, Lavender, White, Pink	8"-12"	Sun to Partial Shade	Tender	75-80	Feb.-April
Alyssum	Violet, Purple, White, Lilac	8"-10"	Sun	Hardy	40-60	Sept.-Jan.
Balsam	Rose, Scarlet, Salmon, Yellow, White	18"-24"	Sun to Partial Shade	Tender	45-60	Feb.-March
Carnation	White, Pink, Red, Yellow	12"-36"	Sun to Partial Shade	Hardy	125-150	Aug.-Jan.
Cockscomb	Purple, White, Yellow, Red, Gold	12"-36"	Sun to Partial Shade	Tender	60-80	Feb.-April
Coleus	Many colored leaves, Blue flowers	12"18"	Partial Shade	Tender	Colorful Leaves	All Year
Geranium	Red, White, Pink	12"-24"	Sun	Hardy	85-100	Feb.-June
Impatien's	Pink, White, Purple, Red	6"-15"	Partial Shade to Shade	Tender	65-90	Feb.-July
Marigold	Yellow, Orange	6"-36"	Sun to Partial Shade	Tender	45-60	Feb.-May
Nasturium	Red, Yellow, Pink, Orange,	10"-18"	Sun to Partial Shade	Tender	60-80	Feb.-Mar

Common Names	Color	Height	Sun or Shade	Hardy to Tender	Seed to Bloom in Days	Planting Season
Periwinkle	White, Pink, Lavender	6"–24"	Sun to Partial Shade	Tender	80-90	Feb.
Petunia	White, Pink, Red, Purple	10"–18"	Sun	Hardy	75-90	Aug.-Jan.
Pansy	White, Yellow, Blue	6"–10"	Sun to Partial Shade	Hardy	90	Sept.-Dec.
Phlox	Red, Pink, Purple, White	12"–24"	Sun	Hardy	75	Aug.-Jan.
Portulaca	White, Pink, Salmon, Red, Yellow	6"–8"	Sun	Tender	45-60	Feb.-May
Pot Marigold	Orange, Yellow	12"–18"	Sun to Partial Shade	Hardy	90-110	Sept.-Dec.
Pink's	Pink, Red, White	10"–12"	Sun to Partial Shade	Hardy	60-75	Sept.-Dec.
Snapdragon	White, Pink, Red, Yellow, Green	6"–36"	Sun to Partial Shade	Hardy	90-120	Sept.-Dec.
Wishbone Flower	Tubular Blue, Yellow Throat	12"–18"	Sun to Partial Shade	Tender	60-75	Feb.-Sept.
Zinnia	Yellow, White, Red, Gold	6"–36"	Sun	Tender	45-60	Feb.-Aug.

CHAPTER SEVEN

Perennials

While annuals submerge a flower bed with eye-catching color, the sight is a passing joy. It lasts only a season and then is gone. Perennials, on the other hand, can provide equally impressive rewards without fading so fast. They can continue to bloom year after year. Gardeners with limited time find perennials a blessing. They only have to be planted once and require considerably less care. In general, perennials are more convenient and adaptable to Florida conditions. Even those that are damaged by frost will emerge the following season, often with larger and more abundant blossoms. Not only do perennials have a variety of appealing flowers, but their foliage can be more interesting in shape, size and color than annuals. To improve the overall appearance of your flower beds and ensure year 'round color, you should include an assortment of perennials in the same location as your annuals.

Separate beds of perennials, however, can become permanent "easy" spots in you garden. Hand weeding, watering and insect and disease control will be less demanding than with annuals. Particularly important with perennials is the preparation of the soil before planting — sterilizing with Vapam to kill nematodes and fungus and adding peat moss, manure and compost to improve the nutritive qualities of the soil.

Perennials, as a rule, should be planted in well-drained areas. If this is not possible on your property, plant in raised beds. By staggering planting times of perennials, you can have flowers blooming year 'round, as well as those with decorative leaves, such as caladium. With both annuals and perennials, you should add more seeds or plants every week or ten days to assure continuous growth and blossoms throughout the season. While perennials may require less care, they still need to be fed. Nutrition and soil enrichment helps build energy for good growth of the plants. A 10-20-20 fertilizer formula is advisable. Fertilizer high in phosphorus and potassium helps generate better bulb growth and vigorous blooms. The best time to fertilize is when a plant is actively growing. And do not use a high-nitrogen fertilizer. This would promote foliage rather than flowers.

Perennials benefit greatly from mulching, which makes a flower bed more attractive, keeps down weeds, inhibits soil erosion and helps con-

BULB PLANTING DEPTH CHART

(LINES REPRESENT DEPTH AT WHICH BULB SHOULD BE PLANTED)

CALADIUM

AMARYLLIS

GRAPE HYACINTH

RAIN LILY

CROCUS

DWARF DAHLIA

CANNA

LILY

GLADIOLUS

RANUNCULUS

ANEMONE

YELLOW FALL CROCUS

HYACINTH

FALL CROCUS

DUTCH IRIS

SPIDER LILLY

JONQUIL

DAFFODIL

TULIP

1"
2"
3"
4"
5"
6"
7"
8"

serve moisture in the soil. Cypress or pine wood chips, or leaves or grass clippings are excellent mulch. For perennials that are dormant in winter, mulching in late October and November is recommended. Some gardeners call this practice "putting the perennials to bed for the winter."

Many gardeners divide their landscaping into specific areas: some areas for perennials that become a permanent part of the layout of the garden; and others for annuals, which can vary and change as the mood strikes you. Perennials, however, should be left where you initially plant them, to grow and mature without interruption, as with trees or shrubs. Moving any plant will set it back and inhibit its overall growth and flowering capabilities.

Alpinia Speciosa **Shell Flower**

Commonly found from Orlando to south Florida, this attractive perennial grows from three to eight feet in height, with unusual, shell-type flowers one on top of the other and pearly white in color. Plant the rhizomes about two inches deep in rich, moist soil, with full sun or partial shade. The plants can be used as backgrounds or as interesting specimens in large pots on the patio.

Aster **Stokes aster**

The perennial aster has purplish stems covered with short, whitish hairs. It grows to twelve inches in height, with three-inch blooms on the end of each branch. The Stokes aster is hardy and likes well-drained soil in sun or partial shade. Flowers come in shades of lavender-blue, pink, white and yellow. Plant seeds or root divisions September through March for a

Aster, Pine Princess mixture

154 mass of delicate flowers all summer long. Like many perennials, nurtured plants from nurseries are preferable to starting from seed. More plants are possible every three years by dividing established roots.

Blue Salvia Blue Sage

One of the most enduring and trouble-free perennials, the blue salvia can be grown easily from seed. The mature plant will bloom year after year, an unending source of exquisite, delicate, violet-blue flowers cascading up thin stems over three feet long. Blue salvia will self-seed, producing many seedlings that can be transplanted to other desired areas of the garden. A hardy plant, the blue salvia likes good, moist soil in sun or partial shade. Plant seeds September through June for mature flowers from March through October. Thrips are about the only problem affecting this plant.

Caladium

Caladiums grow from tubers and produce large, heart-shaped leaves. The leaves show a variety of exotic colors and grow twelve inches high on long petioles. Shades of pink, red, white and green make an unusual and provocative display in mass plantings or in pots and planter boxes. Caladiums prefer rich, moist, acid soil and do best in partial shade. These tender plants do produce flowers, but ones so small that they virtually are inconspicuous. The flower has few diseases or insect problems except for chewing insects. The tubers should be taken up if your winter temperature gets below freezing. In the warmer areas of the state, the tubers can be left in the ground all year.

Canna

Cannas have large, paddle-shaped leaves, green or reddish-green in color, with large, soft-petaled blossoms emerging from the center, very much like gladiolus. Cannas can be used as patio plantings, backgrounds (they grow to five feet) and are wonderful in a damp area, such as around ponds or pools. Planting from December through February will result in a display of beautiful flowers through summer. Plant the rhizomes about two inches deep in an area where they can spread. They will spread prolifically, especially in fertile, moist soil with full sun. As the cannas spread, you can cut off the rhizomes and start new arrangements around the garden. Cannas are particularly effective scattered in clumps on a rock garden, or as a background for flower beds. These tender plants suffer during a frost, but recover. Spray regularly; cannas are favorite targets for leaf-rolling caterpillars. A dwarf variety also is available and will grow to about 24 inches. Both regular and dwarf varieties come in pink, yellow, rose, cream and white, plus mixtures of these colors.

Carnation

Carnations are a hardy, straggly plant with blue-gray, grass-like leaves on long stems. From the top of the stems, flowers emerge in a thimble-like calyx that opens into double blooms, with many ragged-edge petals. Pinching off side shoots will give one large flower at the end of each

Cannas are a standard part of most
Florida gardens.

stem, like those sold in florist shops. Carnations have a distinctive fragrance that makes them a favorite as cut flowers. Grown as borders or in planters, carnations thrive in improved, well-drained soil, in sun and partial shade. Plant seeds or cuttings in August through January for blooms from March through June. Carnations weather low temperatures without damage but suffer from aphids, root rot, mites, rust and wilt.

Chrysanthemum

Coming in many different sizes, shapes and colors, the hardy chrysanthemum is one of the easiest flowers to grow and one of the most popular because of its luxurious display of blossoms. Chrysanthemums grow to four feet in height and are quite bushy. They have aromatic, grayish-green foliage, and their flowers are single, double, semi-double and spider-type, in all colors except blue. Chrysanthemums can be used for cut flowers, bedding plants or patio plants in pots or boxes. Pinching side shoots on a stem will result in one large flower at the top. Pruning will increase the

Connecticut Yankee
Delphiniums

density of the foliage and improve flower production. Plant cuttings from February to March for fall flowering. Chrysanthemums prefer improved, well-drained soil in sun and partial shade. Frost damages the flowers, but not the plant. Problems include nematodes, mites, thrips, aphids, leaf spots, stunt and root rot.

Coreopsis Tick-seed

A very hardy perennial, coreopsis has attractive, apple-green foliage and luxurious single and double, daisy-like flowers in yellow as well as yellow-with-maroon centers. This perennial grows to thirty inches and re-seeds itself prolifically. In many parts of the Southwest it grows wild. Weeding out the seedlings around a coreopsis is essential if you want to keep growth under control in a flower bed. Plant seeds from October through May for a sea of yellow color from April through July. Coreopsis thrives best in any well-drained soil in sun or light shade. The plants suffer from aphids, leaf beetles and mites. An annual variety called Calliopsis is available.

Day Lily

Yellow and orange day lilies provide a handsome splash of color to any garden and can be used for bedding or borders. These hardy perennials like full sun and tolerate almost any soil. They should be purchased when in bloom so you can select your preferred color. After flowering, they can be planted any time for blooming from February through October. As their name implies, they bloom for the day, but sometimes survive two to three days indoors after being picked. They multiply rapidly in the ground, and the divisions can be dug up and used to start new clumps of the flowers in other locations. Apart from its attractive flowers, which rise on single stems two feet high, the day lily's low, sword-shaped foliage makes an attractive edging along flower beds or beside pathways.

Delphinium

This is one of the stateliest plants in any garden. The delphinium has rich, palm-shaped foliage and elegant single and double blossoms growing on a stalk as tall as four feet. For background plantings and cut flowers, delphiniums are outstanding. They come in dark or light blue, white violet and rose colors. A hardy plant, delphinium should be planted from seed from September through November for blooming March through May. This plant needs rich, well-drained soil in sun or partial shade. It is prone to crown rot, mildew, mites and caterpillars.

Gaillardia Indian blanket

Similar to the annual gaillardia, this hardy perennial has few problems and grows in almost any soil in full sun. If left alone, it can cover a field in a few seasons. Ideal for cut flowers and border plantings, gaillardias have hairy, light-green foliage and large red, yellow and orange, daisy-like flowers that grow to thirty inches. Plant seeds or clump divisions from September through January for flowering from April to August. Excellent for splashes of color on a rock garden.

Gazania offers a spec-
tacular burst of color.

Gazania

Like the flowers of the African daisy, gazania blossoms close at night. By day, however, they make a colorful display as a border along flower beds or in planter boxes on a patio. Growing six to twelve inches, the gazania likes moist, rich soil, sun or partial shade and is salt-tolerant. The small, daisy-like blooms are three inches across and come in yellow, brown, red and white. Plant seeds or divide the plant for new growth in early spring for summer flowering.

Gerbera Transvaal Daisy

For cut flowers, bedding and border plantings, and potting, the gerbera is one of the hardiest perennials. It grows in rich soil, good moisture and sun or partial shade. This is an up-and-coming plant. The leaves are dark green and rough-looking, with large, slender-petaled, daisy-like blooms atop a long stem. The blooms come in shades of orange, red, white, pink and violet. Plant seeds or divisions from September to January for continuous flowers all year long. The gerbera flourishes as a wild flower on the veld of South Africa. But it responds to good care. Do not plant too deep, and be careful to keep sand out of the crown. That would rot the plant. Treat for leaf-spot diseases, serpentine leaf miner and nematodes. Gerbera daisies also do well as indoor plants in a sunny location. A popular new variety is called Happy Pot.

Gerbera Daisy

Gerbera, Mardi Gras mixture

Gerbera Transvaal Daisy

Gerbera Daisy

Happy Pot Daisy blossom

***Gloriosa Daisy* Coneflower**

With long, coarse leaves and hairy stalks, the gloriosa has five- to six-inch-wide daisy-like yellow and gold flowers wth dark-red touches. As a border, clumps of color on a rock garden, or for cut flowers, gloriosa daisies are extremely rewarding. Hardy and easily grown, they like enriched, moist soil in sun and partial shade and grow to two to three feet in height. Plant seeds or divisions in late summer and fall for spring and summer blossoms. Watch for crown rot, aphids and caterpillars.

Lisanthus

A new perennial in Florida, this plant comes in blue (about eighteen inches tall), white (about two feet tall) and pink (about three feet tall). Lisanthus grows well in fairly dry soil and should not be over-watered. It flowers well in the hot summer months, apparently has few insect problems and is now becoming very popular. Pinching young plants promotes bushy growth.

Lisanthus

Manaos Beauty

Manaos Beauty is prized for its blue-green, serrated leaves and soft, thistle-like blue flowers. This tender plant is an attractive addition to any garden. Growing about thirty inches tall, the Manaos Beauty can be planted all year, for continuous flowering in all seasons. Tolerant of all soil and moisture conditions as well as sun or shade, it grows well under difficult conditions and has only one problem: leafhoppers. It can be used as a bedding or border plant, as well as around foundations and in pots.

Mexican Tulip-Poppy

The Mexican tulip-poppy has narrow, segmented, bluish-green leaves and tulip-shaped, yellow flowers. It grows to two feet and can be used for cut flowers, borders or bedding. This hardy plant has few problems, and enjoys full sun and good, moist soil. Plant seeds where they are to grow from November to December for April-to-June blossoms.

Periwinkle

Both bush and creeping periwinkles have the same characteristics: glossy, oblong, dark-green leaves with everblooming, small, lavender-pink-and-white flowers that are tubular and flat-faced. The bush type can be used as a substitute for shrubs in landscaping, while the creeping type is an excellent ground cover. Both can be attractive in pots and planters, as well. Seeds or cuttings should be planted in spring for year 'round flowering. This tender plant does well in sun or shade, is tolerant of soil and moisture conditions and has few problems, the main one being blight. Periwinkles are very salt-tolerant and will re-seed.

Periwinkle (Vinca) is a beautiful plant for highlights in the landscape.

162 **Shasta Daisy**

This very hardy plant has long, narrow-toothed leaves. Its stiff stems hold up four-inch white blooms with yellow centers. Excellent for borders and unexcelled as cut flowers, shasta daisies have been a perennial favorite with gardeners all over the world. They enjoy rich, moist soil and take full sun, growing to over two feet in height. Plant seeds or divisions from August through December for January-to-May flowers. The plant is subject to root rot, aphids and caterpillars.

Sweet Alyssum

Although sweet alyssum can be transplanted successfully, it is best to sow its seeds where they will grow. The seedlings are delicate and hard to handle. Growing low to the ground in small clusters, sweet alyssum has tiny lilac, white and violet-purple flowers with a very pleasing fragrance. It is good for borders and as clumps of color on rock gardens. Plant seeds from September through January for blooming October through June. Spray for aphids. Watch for damp-off. Be careful not to over-water.

Verbena

Growing only eight inches long, verbena is excellent as a border plant, on rock gardens and in planter boxes. This sprawling plant has hairy, fragrant, serrated leaves with tiny flowers compacted in globular heads. The red, pink and white flowers often have an eye that makes them an interesting item in the garden. These hardy plants prefer good, moist soil in sun or partial shade. Plant seeds or cuttings from August to December for January-through-July blooming. Spray for red spiders and leafhoppers, a major hazard for verbena.

While the preceding perennials have been listed alphabetically, we have left to last what some gardeners consider the best: the rose. Roses come in so many varieties, with new ones appearing each year, that it would be impossible to list them all. However, a visit to a nursery should help you make the best selection. Here, we will detail the different types of roses and hints on buying, planting and caring for these plants.

ROSES

Improved cultivars have increased the long-standing appreciation of roses. Because Florida has a 12-month gardening climate, the rose is an evergreen shrub that will continue to increase its flower yield for at least 5-10 years; some rose bushes have been known to grow up to 20 years and still produce prize winners.

In central and southern Florida, roses grow and bloom all year. Even in northern Florida they bloom for nine months and keep some of their foliage during the winter. A rose shrub can produce a greater abundance of blooms than other flowering shrubs. You receive five to seven bloom cycles. Roses are moderate to high maintenance plants in Florida and caring for them properly is important. Also, the plants usually grow larger here and therefore should be allowed more space to grow. Banking is not necessary for winter protection, but anchoring, on a trellis for climbers and taller varieties to reduce wind injury, is necessary. Two recommended everblooming varieties are the Fortuniana and the Dr. Huey.

SITE SELECTION AND SOIL PREPARATION

Plant roses where they will receive direct sunlight at least six hours daily. Where shading is sometimes unavoidable, the morning sun is preferred because it will dry the dew on the leaves and lessen the chance of black spot. Open areas are also preferred so the roots of nearby plants will not compete for nutrients. Roses should be planted in well-drained soils, not in marsh areas. Sometimes by ditching or raising the bed levels, minor drainage problems can be improved. Our native sandy soils have low water- and nutrient-holding capacities, and nutrients are easily leached beyond the roots during heavy rains. Such soils can be improved with soil amendments; I recommend peat, dehydrated cow manure, wood shavings or sawdust. Add as much as 4-6 inches of any of these materials, or any combination of two or more, to improve the soil.

Hybrid Tea Roses

When people think of roses, it is the *tea rose* that springs to many minds. The tea rose is very popular and grown throughout the world. Growing from three to five feet in height, hybrid tea roses produce flowers that are large and beautifully proportioned. Many of the flowers have a

Yellow Rose blossom

medium to strong fragrance. Tea rose plants have glossy, dark-green foliage. Literally hundreds of varieties are available, with new hybrids being introduced by major nurseries each year. A circular rose bed from 12 to 20 feet in diameter, located in full sun and in the middle of a lawn, can become the focal point of any garden and a source of joy and admiration for many years. Most tea roses can be spaced three feet apart. This leaves enough room for pruning and picking flowers and to allow the bush to branch out and make a compact, attractive display in your landscape.

Grandiflora

Closely resembling hybrid tea rose, the grandiflora grows five to eight feet, with flowers on long stems, singly or in clusters. These make excellent background plantings in a rose garden.

Floribundas

These are known as "landscaping" roses because of their neat, compact habit. They grow only two to three feet in height. The roses appear in clusters and are ideal for low borders and massed plantings.

Climbing roses

Not actually vines, climbing roses usually are used on fences or a trellis, trained and tied in place for support. All standard rose colors are available as climbers, and most varieties, both standard and small, come as climbers. Don Juan is one of my favorite varieties.

Miniatures

Planted in the ground or in pots around a patio, miniature roses are identical to standard varieties except for their smaller size. If grown in containers, miniatures require protection in sub-freezing weather.

Always buy your roses from a reputable nursery to avoid disappointment and poor-quality bushes. Roses are graded with numbers: 1, 1½ and 2. Number 1 bushes are the best, with sound roots and vigorous canes. Number 1½ will be intermediate, and Number 2 will be weak and slow to produce good blooms. Although No. 1 grade roses cost a little more, they are well worth it.

Packaged bare-root rose bushes can be purchased from nurseries and mail-order houses, as well as from chain stores. Bare-root bushes demand greater care in planting and take longer to start than roses already in containers. Bare-root roses are cheaper, but you will have to wait longer before you can pick your first rose.

Container-grown roses are the best buy. Not only can you see the rose in flower when you buy it, but you are assured of a healthy and vigorous bush. For best root development, select a bush in a five-gallon container. Two-gallon containers also are good, though not as advanced as those in five-gallon pots.

The tag on the rose bush may read "All America Rose Selection." This is your assurance of a good rose bush. The designation means the rose has been tested and has outperformed other varieties under an assortment of

Rose blossom

Rose blossom

Rose blossom

Rose blossom

Rose blossom

soils and climates. Generally, AARS winners are good investments for your rose garden.

The best planting season for roses is winter and spring, four to six weeks before the truly cold weather ends or the last freeze occurs. Position the plants in full sun. Shady locations promote lanky growth, poor flowering and disease. If your garden suffers from poor drainage, plant your roses in raised beds. Use masonry or railroad ties as an edging to allow a rise of six to eight inches above surrounding soil. Soil for a rose garden should be loose and well-drained, preferably a sandy loam. Add a four- to six-inch layer of peat moss, shredded bark, compost or other organic matter and mix with a rotor-tiller to a depth of 10 to 15 inches. Rake out rocks and debris and Vapam the soil to kill nematodes and weeds. Be sure to wait at least three weeks after using Vapam to allow the fumigant to dissipate. Otherwise, you will kill your roses.

Rose blossom

Rose blossom

SPACING YOUR PLANTS

The spacing between roses should be determined by the variety. Your nurseryman can advise you on this. In general, floribundas can be spaced 30 to 36 inches apart. Other varieties may need four to five feet of space between each plant. Roses are a very selfish plant and do well on their own. Do not mix other types of flowers in your rose bed; you'll only be asking for trouble!

Plant bushes so their bud unions are slightly out of the soil. This usually is the same height at which they were growing in the nursery. Duplicate the same planting depth that is present in the container. Remove any damaged roots and limbs and apply a root-stimulating fertilizer with plenty of water immediately after planting. To ensure that there are no air pockets in the hole you dig, fill the hole first with water, then sink the rose bush into it carefully and pack the soil in solidly. This will set your rose bush firmly in the ground and enable it to get a good start.

Roses should be watered well all season long. Spring and fall waterings ensure good blooming. Summer watering is essential to keep the plants alive, and mid-winter watering protects the roots against cold-weather injury. Rose bushes should be well mulched. When watering, concentrate on the soil, *not* on the foliage. Moisture on the leaves promotes disease, especially blackspot, for which you will need to spray with a good fungicide. Soaker hoses or trickle irrigation methods are excellent for watering roses.

Roses, like all plants, need regular feeding. Apply a good rose fertilizer when the plants begin growing in the spring, and continue feeding every four to six weeks through late summer. A balanced formula such as 12-12-12, or one that is slightly richer in phosphorus, such as 12-10-20, is recommended. Apply one half to one pound of fertilizer per 100 square feet of bed space, applying in four-to-six-week intervals except in the heat of mid-summer. A systemic fertilizer-insecticide such as Orthene is highly recommended. It can prevent many of the numerous problems that afflict rose bushes.

While fungicides control blackspot, prevention is easier than cure. Providing good air circulation and keeping water off the leaves are two ways to minimize blackspot, a major problem in Florida.

Many roses develop powdery mildew, a white, crusty fungal organism that looks like flour dusted on the leaf surface. Some fungicides may help with powdery mildew. Consult your nurseryman for latest recommendations. It is best to change fungicides from time to time. Some suggestions: Karathane, Zineb and Maneb.

Cooler weather can bring insect damage from aphids. In summer, leaf-cutting bees attack. Regular spraying with a good insecticide such as Malathion can control these pests. Always spray in the evenings to minimize any possible "burned" foliage.

PRUNING ROSE BUSHES

Roses demand constant vigilance and pruning. The pruning should be done several times during the year. Most bush roses are pruned in mid-to-late winter, four to six weeks after the last frost. Climbing roses should be pruned immediately after their flush-of-spring blooms.

Prune hybrid tea and grandiflora roses (1) by removing all weak, spindly stems, or canes, and (2) by reducing the overall height of the bushes to 18 to 24 inches. Always cut right above a bud that faces away from the center of the plant, so the branching that develops will spread away from the crown of the rose bush. Seal the cut ends with clear shellac or with white wood glue. You also should prune during the growing season, keeping old flower heads and weak growth off the plant.

Floribundas should be pruned less severely. Remove weak growth and prune the entire plant down to a uniform height for better landscape appearance.

Climbing roses demand a different technique. Remove weak, spindly twigs that develop along the stems and prune back the most vigorous canes to about four or five feet. Climbers should be pruned only *after* they begin flowering. Pruning in winter before they flower will remove the flowering wood, and your climbers will not blossom.

Perennials

Name	Planting Time	Sun or Shade	Hardy or Tender	Colors	Problems
Alpinia (Shell Flower)	Any	Partial Shade	T	Pink	Caterpillars
Amaryllis	Oct.-Feb.	Partial Shade	H	White, Pink, Red	Red Blotch Caterpillars
Beloperone	Any	Sun to Partial Shade	Semi	Red, White, Yellow	Caterpillars, Aphids
Caladium	March-June	Sun to Partial Shade	T	White, Green, Red, Pink stripes	Aphids, Nematodes
Canna	Nov.-Feb.	Sun	T	Red, Orange, Rose, Yellow, White	Caterpillars
Carnation	June-Jan.	Sun to Partial Shade	H	Red, Orange, Rose, Yellow, White	Aphids, Mites

Perennials

Name	Planting Time	Sun or Shade	Hardy or Tender	Colors	Problems
Chrysanthemum	Feb.-April	Sun to Partial Shade	H	Red, Orange, Rose, Yellow, White	Mites, Aphids, Nematodes, Thrips
Dahlia	Feb.-April	Sun to Partial Shade	T	White, Yellow, Red, Pink	Powdery Mildew, Nematodes
Day-Lily	Any	Sun to Partial Shade	H	Yellow, Orange	Nematodes
Calla	Feb.-April	Partial Shade	T	White, Yellow, Pink	Thrips, Red Spider Mites
Coleus	Any	Partial Shade	T	Lilac, Blue	Mites, Mealy Bugs, Aphids
Gillardia	Nov.-Jan.	Sun	H	Orange, Yellow, Red	Aphids

* All perennials need an improved soil.

Perennials

Name	Planting Time	Sun or Shade	Hardy or Tender	Colors	Problems
Gazania	Feb.-Sept.	Sun to Partial Shade	T	White, Red, Yellow, Brown	Mites, Aphids
Gerberia	Sept.-Jan.	Sun to Partial Shade	H	Red, Orange, Pink, White, Violet	Leaf Miner, Crown Rot, Nematodes
Mexican Tulip Poppy	Nov.-Dec.	Sun	H	Gold, Yellow	Aphids
Sweet Alyssum	Sept.-Jan.	Sun	H	White, Lilac, Violet	Aphids
Amazon-Lily	Feb.-March	Partial Shade	T	White	Leaf Spot Fungus
Gloriosa	July-Oct.	Sun to Partial Shade	H	Gold, Yellow	Aphids, Caterpillars

Perennials

Name	Planting Time	Sun or Shade	Hardy or Tender	Colors	Problems
Blue Sage	Sept.-July	Sun to Partial Shade	H	White, Violet	Aphids, Thrips
Verbena	July-Dec.	Sun to Partial Shade	H	Pink, White, Red	Red Spider Mites
Periwinkle	Feb.-Aug.	Sun to Partial Shade	T	White, Pink, Lavender	Few
Crinum	Feb.-Oct.	Sun	H	White, Rose	Red Spider Mites, Red Blotch
Zephyr-Lily	Feb.-Oct.	Sun to Partial Shade	H	Red, Yellow, Pink, White	Lubber grasshoppers
Society Garlic	Feb.-Oct.	Sun to Partial Shade	H	Lavender	Aphids

* All perennials need an improved soil.

CHAPTER EIGHT

Orchids

The most exotic flower in the world is the orchid. It is unique in the way it grows and breathtakingly impressive in the delicate texture of its petals and limitless variety of shapes and color combinations. Orchids are the second-largest family of plants on Earth, exceeded only by grains and grasses in the number of varieties.

Orchids grow in almost every size, shape and color but still maintain certain common botanical characteristics. The orchid has a six-part flower with three sepals and three petals. One petal is always different in shape and color from the other two and is frequently the lower part of the flower, or the "lip."

Both stem and pistil are found in a fused column. The column produces very tiny, dust-like seeds in a three-part seed capsule that contains as many as two million seeds. Essentially a tropical plant growing in jungles from South America to Hawaii to Africa, the orchid is as tough as many succulents and cacti. Still, it needs certain conditions to flourish and produce its prized flowers.

Orchids are divided into *Sympodial* and *Monopodial* types. The *Sympodial* group normally grows on a rhizome or creeping stem. From these aerial branches will emerge both leaf and flower. The *Monopodial* group has a swollen, bulb-like tissue called a "pseudobulb." *Monopodial* orchids grow from one erect stem that will lengthen each year, adding more flowers and leaves in erect clusters.

Most of the showier orchids grown in Florida are classified as *Epiphytic*. This means they grow elevated above the ground in trees, baskets, pots and other containers, without the use of soil. Instead, they are planted in a combination of organic materials, such as a tree fern, shreds or chunks of bark and osmundine fiber or mixtures of bark, coconut husks, styrofoam chips and porous rock. Most orchids grow rather slowly and do not need a lot of fertilizer. But these plants do need *some* enrichment on a regular basis. *Epiphytic* orchids grow naturally in trees in tropical jungles, where they receive plenty of rain, which dries rapidly on the branches. Domestic growing methods should approximate these conditions. For this reason, orchids require regular watering followed by a partial dryout period before watering again.

The Orchid is an exotic plant which thrives in many Florida gardens. Although most of the Orchids we see are commercially grown, with a little planning and care most gardeners can grow Orchids successfully.

The colors and varieties of Orchids shown on these pages indicate some of the glamour and spectacle these tropical plants can add to your landscape.

Some Orchids come in speckled as well as solid-color varieties.

Another variety grown in Florida is the *Terrestrial* orchid, which will grow in a well-drained mixture of soil and peat.

ORCHID VARIETIES

With our climate, orchids can be grown easily in Florida. Major varieties include *Cattleya*, the most commonly grown orchid for the hobbyist; *Dendrobium*, with showy sprays of flowers that often last for weeks; *Epidendrum*, which has a wide array of beautiful colors; *Oncidium*, an American genus; *Phaius*, a terrestrial orchid that is easily grown; and *Phalaenopsis*, sometimes known as the moth orchid.

In addition to Phaius (also called the nuns' orchid), other terrestrial orchids include *Cymbidium, Calanthe, Terete* types of *Vanda* orchids, some *Epidendrums* and several others with exquisite combinations of color and shape.

It takes five to seven years for an orchid to bloom from seed. Most orchid hobbyists start their collections with plants from nurseries. The blooms vary; it is best to buy a mature plant in bloom. That way, you can select the variety and coloration you prefer. A developed plant bought at a nursery will yield flowers the following year.

In the central and southern half of Florida, good shade trees are all that you need to grow orchids. *Cattleyas, Dendrobium, Oncidiums* and most of the *Vandaceous* group will thrive in the protection of oaks, citrus or other shade trees around the house. Some of the *Vandaceous* orchids even will do well in full sunlight.

On nights when temperatures drop to frost or freezing, you must bring your orchids inside. Almost all orchids can withstand temperatures into the low 30s without damage, unless they are fully exposed to frost under the unprotected sky. But they cannot withstand freezing.

In northern Florida, orchids can be grown outside most of the year, but permanent cold protection will be needed during the winter. Some orchid hobbyists in the state's north leave their orchids outdoors all year, bringing them into the house only when temperatures drop to freezing.

USING A GREENHOUSE

Some hobbyists build greenhouses for their orchids. But even though these plants are tropical, they cannot survive the high heat and light that often builds up in enclosed glass or plastic-covered greenhouses. Proper use of shade and ventilation is essential. Most of the better-known orchids will thrive on only 25-30 percent direct or filtered sun. A greenhouse therefore should have the capacity to provide shade for 70 percent of daylight hours, with adequate ventilation on the sides and top of the structure.

Commercially built greenhouses usually come equipped with exhaust fans and radiator-like pads. Water dripping through the pads cools and humidifies the air as it enters. Humidity is very important for proper orchid growth, and misting your orchids is recommended. All orchids should be fertilized lightly once a month with a liquid plant food.

Dozens of organized orchid societies in Florida have members willing to help and guide newcomers into the fascinating hobby of growing orchids. A nursery is a good source not only for advice on cultivating orchids, but for information on an orchid society in your area.

You should increase your orchid collection by buying new plants. Trying to grow new plants yourself is slow and tedious. Orchids are propagated three ways only: (1) by dividing mature plants into two or more divisions; (2) by seed germination in sterile bottles containing nutrients; (3) by tissue culture, a new reproductive technique also known as "cloning." Cloning involves stimulation of a tiny propagation "eye" or "tip" in a sterile bottle and dividing it regularly as it grows in this artificial, hospital-like sealed atmosphere. If this last method sounds complicated, it is!

CHAPTER NINE

Vegetables

Many people think of a garden as a space that is beautified with flowers. But to just as many the word "garden" means "vegetables." While the aesthetics are detachable, there is no reason why you cannot combine flowers and vegetables into an attractive picture that will please not only the eye, but the palate, as well. There can be just as much beauty in a well-laid-out array of plants that produce food instead of flowers, and, from an economics standpoint, a vegetable garden can contribute a great savings to your food bill, something not to be overlooked in today's society. For every dollar spent on a vegetable garden, you will reap a five- to six-dollar return in value. Not only do fresh, home-grown vegetables save you money, they contain the optimum in health-giving nutrients. Plus, there are fringe fitness benefits to the gardener in the exercise necessary to prepare, weed and care for a vegetable garden.

Your first consideration should be the site. It will be determined by the quantity of vegetables you want to grow, and the type. Of primary importance is exposure. You need at least six hours of full sunlight daily for a productive vegetable garden. Determine which part of your property receives the most sun, then decide how to landscape the rest of the area around this spot. If the appearance of a vegetable patch offends the eye of a flower fancier, you can install a four-foot chain-link fence (or chicken wire). On the fence, vines may be grown to conceal the area behind it, thus maintaining the aesthetic integrity of your flower garden. A row of ligustrum bushes can serve the same purpose.

On the other hand, if your vegetable needs are minimal, you can intersperse flowers with certain types of vegetables, combining both types of plants into an appealing display that fills both your vases and your pantry.

The space allocated for vegetables should be gauged by the preferences of your family. Ask the members of your household which vegetables they prefer. There is no sense in growing bushels of eggplant if only one person likes to eat this vegetable! Once you have made a list of your family's preferences, do a little arithmetic to work out how many plants you will need to produce a sufficient amount of product over a season. This 181

Grow boxes, built above ground level from a few to several inches, are an ideal environment for raising vegetables in properly enriched soil.

Vegetable gardens make good sense in today's economy.

will help you decide whether you need two tomato plants or twelve, one row of corn or ten, a dozen summer squash plants, or none at all.

PLANNING YOUR GARDEN

Having decided on the number and type of vegetables you will plant, continue your arithmetic and work out the amount of space you need to raise your desired crop. Small as it may sound, an area six feet wide and twenty feet long can produce a remarkable amount of food. You do not have to give over half your yard to vegetables. For example, one tomato plant grown in a tub on the patio can produce enough tomatoes for two people for two months or more. A relatively small-sized bed, tucked away at the back of your property, often can be ample space for growing all the vegetables you desire. Make sure the area you select has easy access to water and is far enough away from trees to avoid problems from roots. Be particularly careful to position your vegetable garden away from living fences, such as honeysuckle, whose roots can extend six to ten feet from the hedge and sap the soil of nutrients.

To grow vegetables successfully Florida soil needs dramatic improvement.

A good rototiller can make your gardening tasks easier.

A fumigant, such as Vapam, will help rid the soil of unwanted weeds and insects.

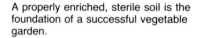

A properly enriched, sterile soil is the foundation of a successful vegetable garden.

If you are going to grow vegetables for the first time, start modestly with a small space. A compact, well-maintained, thriving vegetable garden will be far more rewarding and less frustrating than a large, sprawling area that winds up being a backbreaker and produces far more than you need.

Once you know where you will start your vegetable garden, the next step is to prepare the soil. Remember: to grow *anything*, flowers or vegetables, the results always depend on the quality of the soil.

Check the pH of your soil and take whatever corrective measures may be necessary to achieve the proper balance for your intended crops. Clear out any rocks and debris, then begin rotor-tilling the soil, adding the following mixture: 25 pounds of peat moss, 25 pounds of cow manure, 25 pounds of colloidal phosphate, three pounds of super phosphate and three pounds of quality fertilizer for every hundred square feet of ground space.

After tilling, rake the surface smooth and apply Vapam at the rate of one quart for every hundred square feet. Use either a hose-end sprayer or a watering can, applying one inch of water over the entire area, then covering with heavy plastic or visqueen. Leave the ground covered for at least 48 hours, then remove the plastic and allow the fumigant to dissipate for at least three weeks before planting.

Once you are ready to plant, your ultimate needs will determine how many plants to start, either from seed or seedlings obtained from your nursery or garden shop. Seeds are most useful if large quantities are desired. Otherwise, purchase plants and position them the right distance apart in the soil. Most nurseries carry six-packs of vegetable seedlings. These often are more than enough for the average family.

For tomatoes and certain other plants, sprinklers may be a suitable means of watering.

VEGETABLE PLANTING

Careful planting will help get the vegetables off to a good start. Make a hole just large enough to take a seedling, fill it with water to which you have added liquid fertilizer, such as Nutri-Sol, and sink the seedling in, packing soil gently around the edge until the plant is firmly set in the ground. The liquid fertilizer lessens the possibility of transplant shock.

Once planted, your garden will need watering, fertilizing and weeding, plus spraying for insects and diseases if and when they appear.

Sixteen essential elements are needed for optimum growth of any living plant. Some fertilizers contain only nitrogen, phosphorus and potassium, which are the three most important feeding elements. For vegetables, use a fertilizer that contains the minor elements, as well, with a 12-10-20 formula. Fertilize every two weeks when your seedlings are small, then taper off as the plants grow. Mature plants need to be fertilized every three to four weeks unless the particular vegetable calls for heavier feeding.

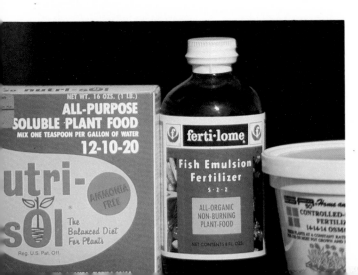

Many specialized fertilizers and plant foods are available for the vegetable garden.

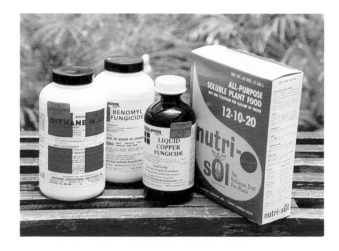

Products such as fungicides, minerals and plant food are specially formulated for specific vegetables.

Several common insect pests undoubtedly will attack your garden, including the mole cricket and cutworm. Mole cricket bait should be applied on the soil before planting. Aphids, stink bugs and leafhoppers succumb to spraying with Diazinon or Malathion. Dipel (Thuricide) and Sevin also will control caterpillars, aphids and worms. Many insect problems appear only after the plants are growing because, obviously, these pests are not going to attack if there is nothing for them to eat! However, sterilizing the soil before planting usually gets any garden off to a disease-free, insect-free start.

With all insecticides, be sure to follow label directions. Most of these sophisticated chemicals do a wonderful job eliminating unwanted insect pests. But if they are mixed too generously, they can set back growth and even kill a plant or harm the leaves.

Weeding your vegetable garden is necessary not merely for looks, but to avoid wasting soil nutrients on unwanted growth. Watch for weeds between your plants and remove them as soon as they appear.

Once your plants are growing, check the calendar and keep a record of the recommended harvest times for each vegetable. Any edible plant should be harvested just when it reaches the height of maturity, except those vegetables where earlier picking is advised. Remember, however, that if crops are allowed to remain on the plant after full maturity, the plant will stop producing and die. To keep a plant producing, you must pick the crop and not let it linger on the stalk. Your seed-to-harvest times, therefore, are very important if you want your vegetable garden to continue producing all through the season. If you have more vegetables than you can eat, continue picking and give them away rather than leave them on the plants. If not, your plants will wither away.

USING GROW-BOXES

Growing your vegetables in the ground is not the only way to raise fresh food. For instance, you might enjoy trying a "grow-box." This is a vegetable bed enclosed by one-by-eight boards, concrete blocks or railroad ties and filled with near-perfect soil. Ideally, a grow-box should contain one-fourth water, one-fourth air, one-fourth mineral and one-fourth organic material.

Grow-boxes provide the opportunity to develop the best possible soil in a small area.

Because a grow-box does not fit tightly on the ground, excess water easily can drain from beneath the frame. The soil inside remains airy and easy-to-work, since you do not walk between the plants and compact the ground above plant roots, as usually happens with ground-level gardens. In addition, plants can extend their root systems below the depth of the soil in the grow-box. And grow-box soil will hold more moisture because of its texture, thereby reducing your watering needs. Building and filling a grow-box adds to the initial cost of your vegetable garden, but in the long run, it is well worth it.

The grow box will allow you to raise vegetables in a controlled environment without the weeding problems of the typical garden.

A trellis can be built at one end of the grow-box and attached to the frame, for climbing vegetables such as beans, pole lima beans, cucumbers and some melons. A grow-box should be placed where it receives at least six hours of full sun daily. Preferably, it should run north and south. Place the trellis, if you build one, at the north end to receive the best light.

Grow-boxes are compact gardens, but do not fall into the trap of placing your grow-box plants too close together. Stunted growth and intensified insect problems can result. A regular program of feeding is necessary. Raising vegetables in a grow-box is exactly the same as if you plant them in the ground, with the added advantage of having superior soil and better drainage.

As with regular vegetable beds, you can *interplant* crops in a grow-box. This refers to placing faster-growing plants between slower-growing varieties. The faster-growing plants can be harvested while the slow crop is still half-grown. Also, planting every two weeks gives you mature vegetables for picking over a longer period of harvest.

RAISED BEDS

A minor variation of the grow-box is the "raised bed." The raised bed has an extra layer of porous rubble beneath the soil, raising the bed even higher off the ground and ensuring good drainage. Some gardeners who dislike bending over because of possible back problems find the raised beds a great convenience.

Container growing is an alternative for apartment and condominium gardeners who lack outdoor space. Five- or ten-gallon containers can be filled with an appropriate soil mixture and planted with vegetables of your choice for growing on balconies or porches. Make sure there is adequate drainage at the bottom of the soil inside the container, maintain a regular watering and feeding schedule and allow your plant to get at least six hours of sun each day.

Some ambitious vegetable gardeners build a "Japanese Ring," ideal if growing space is limited. Two concentric rings of construction-gauge wire are placed in position, making a low circle of soil on the outside like a bundt pan. The inside circle is higher, from four to six feet, and used as a compost pile. Plant your vegetables in the soil and organic material in the lower outside ring. Cucumbers or beans are perfect for this type of planting. They climb the wire on the inside cage for support. Lower-growing vegetables, such as broccoli, cabbage, radishes and lettuce, can be grown on top of the inside ring containing the compost. As the compost breaks down, it provides valuable nutrients to feed the root systems of the lower outside ring.

GROWING ORGANICALLY

Organic gardening has received much publicity in recent years. The term refers to raising crops without the use of certain chemical insecticides or fertilizers. For the avid environmentalist, this method is laudable, but it involves far more work and dedication. Only pesticides considered safe for the environment are used, such as Dipel (Thuricide), Biotrol or Pyrethrins

— all products containing items found in nature that repel insects. Pyrethrin, for example, is found in the foliage of marigolds, giving them their distinctive odor. Many gardeners plant marigolds between their tomato plants as a natural deterrent to certain insects. Pyrethrin sometimes is used as a commercial insecticide.

Organic gardeners feed the soil exclusively with organic substances rather than chemical fertilizers. Compost made from grass clippings, coffee grounds, potato peelings, leaves, small twigs, wood ashes, egg shells and almost anything organic is combined to provide the needed nutrition for the soil. The problem with this method is the time involved: vegetables need nutrients right away for growth, and unless a compost pile has been planned well in advance, growth will be retarded due to insufficient feeding. Cow or sheep manure provides faster feeding, but horse manure is slow in releasing its nutrients and should be used mainly as a soil builder. Many conflicting statements have been made regarding the relative merits of organic versus chemical fertilizing of gardens. But any living plant will utilize whatever is available, breaking it down naturally just as the human body uses its metabolism to extract the various elements needed for growth and sustenance.

Another unusual method of gardening is called *hydroponics*, a newer form of raising vegetables. As the name implies, plants are grown totally in water. Roots never touch soil, but grow in water enriched with chemical nutrients. This method involves a great deal of initial expense and effort, such as building the necessary frames, containers, wire mesh and aeration equipment. For the home gardener, it is much easier and just as effective to grow vegetables in the traditional manner.

A variation of hydroponics is "aggregate culture." A container is filled with some type of mixed aggregate, such as sand, wood shavings, sawdust, pebbles and similar items, then filled with water and liquid fertilizer. Again, this is for the esoteric-minded hobbyist rather than the practical gardener who has the land, sufficient space and time to grow a vegetable garden.

HERBS

Herbs have been grown since biblical times. Not only are the leaves used, stems and roots often make flavorful additions to food. Some seeds and flowers go into perfumes and dyes. Some herbs like a semi-sunny spot, but most should be protected from the hot Florida summer sun. Many do well in flower beds and as hanging baskets and border plants. Fresh parsley is a favorite herb grown in the vegetable garden for garnishes and for flavoring. Nothing beats fresh mint in iced tea as a flavoring.

Herbs are similar to vegetables in that they require well-draining soil, one that has been improved with organic matter such as peat moss, builder's sand, perlite or dehydrated cow manure. To get your herbs off to a good start, fumigate the soil with Vapam before planting. Fertilize with a good liquid plant food, lightly, once a month. Many of Florida's favorite herbs may be purchased in seed packages at your local nursery and garden supply.

190 CONTAINER GROWN FLORIDA HERBS

Small Pots (six inches in diameter or less)

Catnip	Parsley	Summer Savory
Chives	Rosemary	Sweet Marjoram
Nasturtium	Sage	Thyme
Oregano		

Larger Pots

Ambrosia	Chamomile	Lavender
Angelica	Chervil	Lovage
Anise	Comfrey	Mint
Balm	Coriander	Rue
Basil	Dill	Saffron
Borage	Fennel	Tarragon
Caraway	Horehound	

What follows is a selection of popular vegetables that can be grown successfully in Florida, plus a chart listing varieties and planting dates.

Beans (Snap beans)

Grown as bushes, or pole beans, which need support, snap beans also come in wax-podded varieties. Pole beans are considered to have a better taste, and they freeze very well.

Beans need a fertile soil with ample organic matter, good moisture and lime. Bush beans require fifty to sixty days from planting to harvest. Pole beans take a little longer. Both varieties can be grown in most of Florida if planted in September or early October. Pole beans often are planted in the spring as soon as the danger of frost is past. More than one planting is suggested to extend the harvest season. Beans are a tender crop and suffer from bean leafhoppers, bean leafrollers, Mexican bean beetles and bean rust.

Bush Beans

Beans (Lima or butter beans)

Lima beans need a rich soil and prefer a warmer and more humid climate than snap beans. They are fairly drought-resistant, but they suffer from insect damage.

Beets (Common, or red beets)

Although beet leaves and stalks make excellent cooking greens, this vegetable is grown for its enlarged tap root, a favorite cooked, cooled and sliced up in salads.

Beets are hardy and need fertile soil with good moisture. They need very moist soil for good seed germination and are a cool-weather crop. They suffer from nematodes, caterpillars and, occasionally, fungus on the leaves.

Broccoli

A highly nutritious vegetable, broccoli is easy to grow and prepare for cooking. It is a shallow-rooted plant needing a steady supply of moisture and good soil. Broccoli culture is the same as for its relative, the cabbage. Seeds take four to six weeks to grow large enough to transplant, then sixty to seventy days to harvest. Several crops are possible from one plant, though the first harvest is the best. It is the unopened flower buds that are eaten, together with the stems and some of the smaller leaves near the buds. Never allow flowers to develop. Buy the plant in October, and at the same time, plant seeds for a further supply after the first crop is harvested. Broccoli is attacked by caterpillars and other insects and suffers from several diseases.

Brussels sprouts

Another relative of the cabbage, brussels sprouts are rather like a tiny cabbage, growing in clusters up a stem. As the heads begin to get crowded,

Growing Brussels Sprouts

An abundant Cabbage crop

break off the lower leaves to give them more room. Rather sensitive to environmental conditions, brussels sprouts develop best during cooler weather and do not always yield satisfactorily. They are targets for aphids, caterpillars, plant bugs and several diseases.

Cabbage

High in Vitamin C, very hardy and easy to grow, cabbage comes recommended for the home gardener. Good soil, abundant moisture and lots of fertilizer are needed, and cabbage does best during cooler periods. A hardy vegetable, cabbage is best grown in a seedbed. When transplanting, always plant it deeper than it has been growing before. Spray for caterpillars and plant bugs. Cabbage also is prone to several diseases.

Cantaloupes (Musk melon)

The smooth honeydew and the netted honeydew are fairly difficult to grow in Florida. Preferring a warm, dry climate, they do best in the spring before the humid weather begins, which also can bring on foliage diseases.

Cantaloupe is an all-time Florida favorite.

Tender to cold, cantaloupes are heavy feeders and need sandy soil rich in organic matter. Be sure to plant only those varieties recommended for Florida, and watch for foliage diseases such as downy mildew and gummy stem blight.

Carrots

Carrots are an excellent source of Vitamin A. They are hardy, require a rich, deep, well-prepared soil and should be grown in the cooler time of the year. Slow-growing, carrot seeds take about 14 days to sprout and 80 to 110 days to grow to harvest. Thinning out small carrots will allow the remaining plants to grow larger and longer. Several plantings are recommended for a longer harvest season. Carrots suffer from some foliage diseases and nematodes.

Cauliflower

Very similar in culture and problems to the cabbage, the cauliflower is hard to grow and needs a cool season to thrive best. To make the head (the curd) white, wait until it has developed two or three inches in diameter, then tie the leaves over the head. This will result in the bleached-white color familiar to us all. Cauliflower suffers from several diseases and is attacked by caterpillars and other insects.

Celery

Celery first was used as a medicine. Now it is popular chopped up in salads as well as cooked as a vegetable. Almost a swamp plant, celery germinates in wet soil and grows only in very moist ground that is rich in organic matter. A hungry feeder, it needs several applications of nitrogen fertilizer to thrive, and the soil *must* be kept very moist throughout the

Cauliflower is an excellent Florida crop but is subject to insect and disease problems.

194 entire growing cycle. A hardy plant, celery should be grown during the cool periods of the year. A slow grower, it takes from eight to twelve weeks from seeds to plants, and from plants to harvesting takes 100 to 120 days longer. This vegetable suffers from several diseases, and caterpillars eat the tender stalks.

Chinese Cabbage

For salads or as a cooked vegetable (especially in Chinese dishes), Chinese cabbage is a pleasant change from the ordinary. A very productive, hardy plant, Chinese cabbage prefers moist soil with plenty of organic matter and grows best in the cooler seasons. If planted in dry soil, it will become tough and will bolt (flower) during hot weather. From seed to harvest takes 75 to 85 days. The young seedlings will transplant easily. The only problem, like with most cabbage-type vegetables, is leaf-eating caterpillars.

Collards

Collards are a cabbage that does not form a head. Their taste is very distinctive and is enjoyed by many people. Collards are hardy and grow best during the winter months, requiring a fertile soil with good moisture. For improved succulence and taste, fertilize liberally. Collards are ready for harvest 50 to 60 days after the plants are set. The tops can be cut off or only the larger leaves, leaving the younger, upper leaves to develop. Collards suffer from several diseases and are plagued by caterpillars and plant bugs.

Chinese Cabbage is an unusual but tasty garden crop.

Sweet Corn is a staple for many Florida gardeners.

Salad vegetables such as Cucumbers are an excellent addition to any garden.

Corn (Sweet Corn)

Though tender to cold, corn is easy to grow and enjoys warm weather, a rich soil with moderate, continuous moisture, and heavy fertilization. It should be planted in a series of two or three parallel rows to ensure pollination. Two or more plantings per season are recommended for continuous harvesting. Although corn freezes well, it is best when cooked straight from the garden.

Caution: Corn earworm usually is present, as well as budworm. An insecticide such as Sevin must be sprayed on the cornsilk every other day after it appears, until it turns black. For budworm, place a small pinch of cutworm bait in each bud of the small corn plants. Corn also suffers from fungus and bacterial diseases.

Cucumbers

Cucumbers are used for salads or for pickles. They need soil high in organic matter and moisture. Fast-growing, cucumbers do not transplant easily. Plant the seeds where the vines are to grow. They are sensitive to cold. Never allow a cucumber to mature on the vine; otherwise, the vine will stop producing. To avoid disease problems, plant cucumbers resistant to downy mildew. This plant also suffers from nematodes, virus and pickleworms.

196   Eggplant

Eggplant fruit must be harvested while still immature, or about two-thirds its full size. Good fruit has a glossy purple skin. This vegetable requires rich, moist soil. The plant is sensitive to cold but, if not frozen, will live for several years. Culture is similar to tomatoes, though eggplants require higher temperatures, need to be fed heavily and given plenty of water. They require 80 to 85 days from plants to picking. Care should be taken in transplanting. A serious problem with eggplant is the continuing battle with red spiders and nematodes, as well as the tomato pinworm.

Endive (Also: Escarole)

This plant is a warm-weather substitute for lettuce, with frilled, deep-cut leaves. It is more popular than escarole, which is very similar. To eliminate the slightly bitter flavor, the outer leaves should be tied at the top of the plant with string or a rubber band. In two to three weeks, the leaves will be blanched and the bitter flavor removed.

Endive and escarole take 90 to 95 days from seed to harvest. They have few problems, and the culture is identical to lettuce.

Kale

Kale's culture is the same as for cabbage. Kale is one of the better-tasting cooked greens, a hardy pot herb that is a welcome change as a vegetable. It suffers from several diseases and is attacked by caterpillars and plant bugs.

Kale can be grown as a garden plant or pot herb.

Kohlrabi is a sturdy vegetable much like the Turnip.

Kohlrabi

The enlarged stem of kohlrabi is eaten as a vegetable. Similar to the turnip, it has a milder flavor. Kohlrabi is cold-hardy and needs a fertile, moist soil and cold weather. This is a fast-maturing plant, taking only 50 to 55 days from seed to harvest. It should be picked young, when about one to three inches in diameter, and will need spraying for caterpillars.

Lettuce

Head lettuce is difficult to grow in Florida. Instead try Bibb lettuce, which has more vitamins and a better flavor. Lettuce is hardy and needs rich soil with plenty of organic matter. It grows well in sun or partial shade. Since lettuce has short roots, it needs a continuous supply of moisture. Drought and hot weather induce bolting (flowering). Bibb lettuce takes from 50 to 60 days to mature, and prefers cooler weather.

Leaf lettuce requires less care and is more tolerant of heat than other types of lettuce. There are many varieties, with Cos or Romaine the easiest to cultivate. All lettuce suffers from bolting, aphids, foliage diseases and virus.

Lettuce is a delicious and inviting vegetable crop but must be protected from insect and disease damage.

Mustard (Leaf)

Several varieties of mustard are popular as cooking greens, all easy to grow and ready for picking 40 to 45 days from seed. Mustard greens can be grown all year, but do best during the cool season. They suffer from caterpillars, cabbage looper and several diseases.

Okra

Okra will grow on most well-drained soils provided there is plenty of moisture. These are hungry plants and should be fertilized generously every two weeks. Okra is a warm-weather crop that matures in about 50 to 55 days from seed. Planting a second crop 50 days after the first will double your harvest. Pick the pods daily while they are immature; otherwise, they will become woody. Okra suffers from stink bugs and is devastated by nematodes.

Onions

Onions can be grown from seeds, plants and sets, with most home gardeners choosing sets. This hardy vegetable is available in three types: green, multiplier and bulbing.

Green onions can be planted anytime sets are available, usually from September through March. This simple and easy way to grow green onions will give you a harvest in about fifty days.

Multipliers usually are sold in bunches. They do not form a bulb and continue to produce more plants throughout the season. At harvest time, simply remove a group, replant two or three and use the rest. Multiplier also can be grown from seed.

Bulbing onions can be bought in trays as young plants or started from seeds or sets. Set these out as soon as they are available, but no later than

Onions, grown from seed or sets, are not difficult to grow but require water and high nitrogen for best results.

A cool weather plant, Garden Peas are most commonly grown from seed.

November. Bulbs will be ready in late spring and early summer. **Tropicana Red and Granex varieties produce bulbs shortly after winter and can be grown from seed quite easily.**

Onions must have nitrogen available throughout their growing season. Otherwise, fertilize this plant the same as most other crops. Lack of moisture inhibits growth, so keep your onion plants well watered. They have few problems and are one of the easiest vegetable to grow.

Peas (English garden)

Wait until November to plant peas in Florida, because they only thrive in the coolest months. Peas need improved soil and good moisture. They are ready for harvest 50 to 55 days after seed. Dwarf varieties are the simplest to grow. Peas must be picked often before they get a chance to mature and become hard. They can suffer from leaf diseases.

Peas (Southern cowpeas)

Vigorous, tender to cold, Southern peas come in many varieties and grow on bushes or vining plants, doing best early in the season. Plant as soon as danger of frost is over. After they become established, these plants are drought-resistant, like hot weather and will flourish in almost any soil. They need a low-nitrogen fertilizer, moderately applied. Several plantings will extend your harvest. Treat for cowpea curculio, caterpillars, plant bugs and nematodes.

Sugar Snap Peas grow best above ground on a fence or trellis.

Golden Bell Peppers

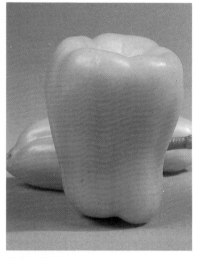

Yellow Belle

Pepper (Bell or sweet)

Fertile soil rich in organic matter and plenty of water and fertilizer are necessary for a good crop of bell peppers. These plants are tender, but if protected, will live for several years. Usually grown as an annual, they will produce usable peppers in about 65 to 80 days from planting. Pick the peppers when they reach their largest size, before they turn red; however, the red peppers also are good to eat. Problems include nematodes, fungus, bacterial and virus diseases. Thrips can cause young fruit and flowers to drop.

Pepper (Bird)

Bird peppers are easily grown and can be found growing wild in many parts of Florida. They are *very* hot and used in cooking and making pepper sauce.

Banana Peppers (Butterfingers) are a sweet and flavorful crop and a pretty plant in the garden.

Potatoes (White or Irish)

To plant potatoes, take a seed potato and cut at least one eye in a piece of the flesh, and plant it to grow into a fresh bush. The larger the seed piece, the more vigorous the plant will be. Do not plant table potatoes bought at the store — these have been treated with sprout inhibitors. Potatoes should be sewn as soon as seed potatoes are available. This vegetable needs good soil and constant moisture. Fertilize the same as for other crops. Potatoes are hardy, but a hard freeze will kill them. When the vines mature and die down, you may harvest your new potatoes. Late blight and other diseases make it necessary to spray weekly. Nematodes and caterpillars also are a problem.

Potatoes (Sweet)

Sweet potatoes (sometimes wrongly called "yams") like a light-to-medium soil that is not too high in nitrogen. If you fertilize too heavily, you will wind up with enormous vines and few sweet potatoes. These are tender plants, susceptible to cold, and take from 120 to 140 days to mature.

Plant portions of the vine about six to nine inches long, burying four inches of stem into the soil. Sweet potatoes are prone to weevils and caterpillars. A sweet potato placed in water will sprout vines, which then can be cut and planted for growing new sweet potatoes.

White potatoes are best started from seed potatoes and need protection from insects and diseases.

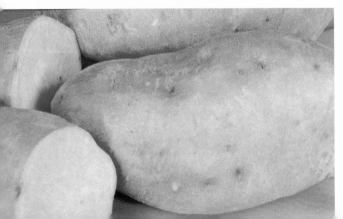

Sweet Potatoes are slow-growing plants which require good moisture and sunshine to grow well.

202

Spinach (Summer, New Zealand)

Summer spinach has a better, milder flavor than the regular spinach, and is easy to grow. Once established, it is fairly drought-resistant and grows all summer. Cut three inches of foliage from the ends of branches for cooking. Be warned: the large seeds are slow to germinate, and the plants suffer from caterpillars.

Squash (Summer, includes Yellow Crookneck, Yellow Straightneck, Patty Pan and Zuchini)

A bush type with small runners, summer squash is easy to grow in any good soil. Tender to cold, summer squash are fast growers, taking 45 to 60 days from seed to maturity. Plant in spring after danger of frost has passed. Plant where they are to grow; the seedlings do not transplant well. A late summer planting will give you a fall crop. Summer squash are subject to nematodes, pumpkin bugs, pickleworms, virus and downy and powdery mildews.

Squash grows rapidly in good soil in spring or fall.

There are many popular Squash varieties in Florida, but all need protection from insects and diseases.

Pumpkins, related to
Squash and Gourds, grow
well in enriched soil but
need plenty of water and
insect/disease protection.

Squash (Winter running, includes Butternut, Acorn and Buttercup)

Picked when the skin has hardened and the vegetable is mature, winter squash grow on long, aggressive vines in any good soil. The recommended varieties for Florida take from 90 to 105 days to mature and can be picked and stored in any cool, dry place for future use. They suffer from the same problems as summer squash, except virus.

Swiss Chard

Swiss chard is a beet grown for its fleshy stems and leaves. One of the best-cooking greens, it will produce for a long time if only the outside leaves are picked as needed. A rich, moist soil is needed for best growth. Swiss chard can be grown all year but does best in cooler weather, with a hardy, quick crop that takes 55 to 60 days from seed to harvest. It has problems with caterpillars.

Tomatoes

Before you plant tomatoes, you should treat with Vapam first, then follow with organic materials, peat moss and manure, as well as hydrated lime or dolomite. All of this is necessary because Florida's predominantly sandy soil lacks nutritive elements. But do not overfeed with nitrogen fertilizer, as this will promote foliage and few fruit. Once the fruit appears, however, nitrogen and other fertilizer elements are needed generously. Full sun and plenty of water are essential for healthy tomatoes, which need the right soil, feeding and sun possibly more than any other vegetable. Most of the cherry-type tomatoes do well in Florida. But the larger varieties fruit poorly when the night temperatures get above 68 degrees.

Tomatoes can be grown from seed. For the average home owner who only needs enough fruit for home use, however, it is more convenient to purchase the plant at a nursery. Before planting, mix a cupful of hydrated lime or two cupfuls of dolomite into each two cubic feet of planting media.

Tomatoes, a universal favorite, need frequent spraying.

Better Boy Tomatoes

Bonus VFN Tomatoes

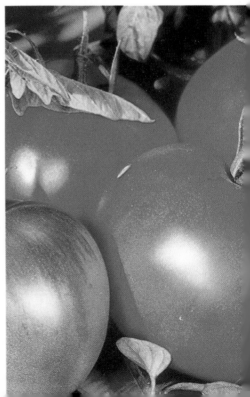

This will prevent "blossom-end rot," which is caused primarily by a lack of calcium in the soil. Too much nitrogen and uneven watering also can cause "blossom-end rot." Using an all-purpose fertilizer will provide your tomatoes with the needed nutrients for healthy plants and good fruit. Once the plants start growing, be sure to stake the branches. This way, they take up less room and are easier to spray for insect and disease control. Also this keeps the fruit off the ground and prevents soil rot.

One of the worst pests for tomatoes is the leaf miner. One species is a small maggot, the immature stage of a fly, that makes a winding tunnel in the tomato leaves, causing them to die. Leaf miners do not attack the fruit itself, but the southern armyworm and hornworm attack and eat everything, often overnight. Diazinon, Sevin, Dipel or Thuricide will control armyworms, but hornworms barely are affected. Because of their enormous size, they can be picked off by hand. A watchful eye should be kept for the hornworms (often six to eight inches long). They can strip a tomato plant in a matter of hours.

When buying tomato plants, ask a nurseryman about the best varieties for your area, as well as the recommended spray for insect pests and diseases. Regular spraying is essential to maintain good, healthy tomato plants throughout a season.

Turnips

Both the roots and tops of turnips are eaten. The Shogoin foliage turnip does especially well in Florida. It is a hardy, cool-weather vegetable that grows rapidly in rich, moist soil. A preventive spray program for aphids will be necessary, because once aphids get established between the leaves, they cannot be eradicated. Seed to harvest takes 35 to 50 days. Watch for aphids and leaf spot diseases.

Watermelons

Watermelons do well in well-drained soil with good moisture content. This plant is tender to cold, and seeds should be sown after danger of frost has passed. Seed to harvest is 85 to 100 days. Do not plant seeds in soil that previously has been growing watermelons because of a soil-borne disease known as "wilt" (Fusarium). A weekly spray program is advisable to control such fungus diseases as gummy stem blight, downy mildew and anthracnose. Other problems with watermelons include virus, aphids, rindworms and nematodes.

Florida Vegetable Planting Guide

Crop	Varieties	Spacing in Inches		Seed Depth Inches	Planting Dates in Florida		
		Rows	Plants		North	Central	South
Beans, snap	Extender, Contender, Harvester Wade, Cherokee (wax)	18-30	2-3	1½-2	Mar.-Apr. Aug.-Sept.	Feb. Mar. Sept.	Sept. Apr.
Beans, pole	Dade, McCaslan, Kentucky Wonder, 191 Blue Lake	40-48	15-18	1½-2	Mar.-June	Feb.-Apr.	Jan.-Feb.
Beans, Lima	Fordhock 242, Concentrated, Henderson, Jackson Wonder, Dixie Butterpea, Florida Butter (Pole)	26-48	12-15	1½-2	Mar.-June	Feb.-Apr.	Sept.-Apr.
Beets	Early Wonder, Detroit Dark Red	14-24	3-5	½-1	Sept.-Mar.	Oct.-Mar.	Oct.-Feb.
Broccoli	Early Green Sprouting, Waltham 29, Atlantic	30-36	16-22	½-1	Aug.-Feb.	Aug.-Jan.	Sept.-Jan.
Cabbage	Copenhagen Market, Marion Market, Badger Market, Glory of Enkhuizen, Red Acre, Chieftan Spray	24-36	14-24	½	Sept.-Feb.	Sept.-Jan.	Sept.-Jan.
Carrots	Imperator, Gold Spike, Chantenay, Nantes	16-24	1-3	½	Sept.-Mar.	Oct.-May	Oct.-Feb.
Cauliflower	Snowball Strains	24-30	20-24	½	Jan.-Feb. Aug.-Oct.	Oct.-Jan.	Oct.-Jan.
Celery	Utah 52-70, Florida Pascal	24-36	6-10	¼-½	Jan.-Mar.	Aug.-Feb.	Oct.-Jan.
Chinese Cabbage	Michihli, Wong Bok	24-36	8-12	¼-½	Oct.-Jan	Oct.-Jan.	Nov.-Jan.
Collards	Georgia, Vates	24-30	14-18	½	Feb.-Mar.	Jan.-Apr. Sept.-Nov.	Sept.-Jan. Aug.-Nov.

Crop	Varieties	Spacing in Inches		Seed Depth Inches	Planting Dates in Florida		
		Rows	Plants		North	Central	South
Corn, Sweet	Silver Queen (white), Gold Cup, Golden Security, Seneca Chief, many others	34-42	12-18	½	Mar.-Apr.	Feb.-Mar.	Jan.-Feb.
Cantaloupes	Smith's Perfect, Seminole, Edisto 47, Gulfstream	70-80	48-60	¾	Mar.-Apr.	Feb.-Apr.	Feb.-Mar.
Cucumbers	Poinsett, Ashley (slicers), Wisconsin SMR 18, Pixie (picklers)	48-60	15-24	½ - ¾	Feb.-Apr.	Feb.-Mar. Sept.	Jan.-Feb.
Eggplant	Florida Market	36-42	36-48	½	Feb.-Mar. July	Jan.-Feb. Aug.-Sept.	Dec.-Feb.
Endive-Escarole	Deep Heart Fringed, Full Heart Batavian	18-24	8-12	¾	Feb.-Mar. Sept.	Jan.-Feb. Sept.	Sept.-Jan.
Kohlrabi	Early White Vienna	24-30	3-5	½	Mar.-Apr. Oct.-Nov.	Feb.-Mar. Oct.-Nov.	Nov.-Feb.
Lettuce (Crisp) (Butterhead) (Leaf) (Romaine)	Premier, Great Lakes types, Bibb, Matchless, Sweetheart, Prize Head, Ruby, Salad Bowl, Parris Island Cos, Dark Green Cos	12-18	12-18	¾	Feb.-Mar. Sept.	Jan.-Feb. Sept.	Sept.-Jan.
Mustard	Southern Giant Curled, Florida Broadleaf	14-24	4-8	½	Jan.-Mar. Sept.-May	Jan.-Mar. Sept.-Nov.	Sept.-Mar.
Okra	Clemson Spineless, Perkins Long Green	24-40	18-24	1-2	Mar.-May Aug.	Mar.-May Aug.	Feb.-Mar. Aug.-Sept.
Onions (Bulbing) (Green)	Excel, Texas Grano Granex, White Granex, Tropicana Red White Portugal or White types, Shallots (Multipliers)	12-24 12-24 18-24	3-4 1½-2 6-8	¾ ¾ ¾	Jan.-Mar. Aug.-Nov. Aug.-Mar. Aug.-Jan.	Jan.-Mar. Aug.-Nov. Aug.-Mar. Aug.-Jan.	Jan.-Mar. Sept.-Nov. Sept.-Mar. Sept.-Dec.
Parsley	Moss Curled, Perfection	12-20	8-12	¾	Feb.-Mar.	Dec.-Jan.	Sept.-Jan.
Peas	Little Marvel, Dark Skinned Perfection, Laxton's Progress	24-36	2-3	1-2	Jan.-Feb.	Sept.-Mar.	Sept.-Feb.

+H — Hardy, can stand frost and some freezing (32° F) without injury.
SH — Slightly hardy, will not be injured by light frosts.
T — Tender, will be injured by light frost.
+ — Tomatoe varieties best adapted to staking.

Florida Vegetable Planting Guide (continuation)

Crop	Varieties	Spacing in Inches		Seed Depth Inches	Planting Dates in Florida		
		Rows	Plants		North	Central	South
Peas, Southern	Blackeye, Brown Crowder, Bush Conch, Producer, Floricream, Snaps, Zipper Cream	30-36	2-3	1-2	Mar.-May	Mar.-May	Feb.-Apr.
Pepper (Sweet) (Hot)	Calif. Wonder, Yolo wonder, World Beater Hungarian Wax, Anaheim Chili	20-36	2-3	1-2	Feb.-Apr.	Jan.-Mar.	Jan.-Feb. Aug.-Oct.
Potatoes	Sebago, Red Pontiac, Kennebec, Red LaSoda	36-42	12-15	4-8	Jan.-Feb.	Jan.	Sept.-Jan.
Potatoes, Sweet	U.S. No. 1, Porto Rico, Georgia Red Goldrush, Nugget, Centennial	48-54	18-24		Mar.-June	Feb.-June	Feb.-June
Radish	Cherry Belle, Comet, Early Scarlet Globe, White Icicle, Sparkler (white tipped)	12-18	1-2	¾	Oct.-Mar.	Oct.-Mar.	Oct.-Mar.
Spinach	Virginia Savoy, Dixie Market, Hybrid 7	14-18	3-5	¾	Oct.-Nov.	Oct.-Nov.	Oct.-Jan.
Spinach, Summer	New Zealand	30-36	18-24	¾	Mar.-Apr.	Mar.-Apr.	Jan.-Apr.
Squash (Summer)	Early Prolific Straightneck, Early Summer Crookneck, Cocozelle, Zucchini, Patty Pan	42-48	42-48	½	Feb.-Mar. Aug.	Feb.-Mar. Aug.	Jan.-Mar. Sept.-Oct.
(Winter)	Alagold, Table Queen, Butternut	90-120	48-72	2	Feb.-Mar.	Feb.-Mar.	Jan.-Feb.
Strawberry	Florida 90, Tioga, Sequoia	36-40	10-14		Sept.-Oct.	Sept.-Oct.	Oct.-Nov.
Tomatoes (Large Fruited)	Manalucie, +Homestead-24, Indian River, Floradel, +Tropired, Big Boy+, Walter	40-60	36-40	½	Feb.-Apr. Aug	Feb.-Mar. Sept.	Aug.-Mar.
(Small Fruited)	Large Cherry, Roma (Paste)	36-48	18-24	½	Feb.-Apr. Aug.	Feb.-Mar. Sept.	Aug.-Mar.
Turnips	Japanese Foilage (Shogoin) Purple Top White Globe	12-20	4-6	½-¾	Jan.-Mar. Aug.-Oct.	Jan.-Mar. Sept.-Nov.	Oct.-Feb.
Watermelon (Large) (Seedless) (Small)	Charleston Gray, Congo, Jubilee, Crimson Sweet Tri-X 317 New Hampshire Midget, Sugar Baby	90-120	60-84	2	Mar.-Apr.	Jan.-Apr.	Feb.-Mar.

Florida Vegetable Planting Guide (continuation)

Crop	Plant Hardiness +	Days to Harvest
Beans, snap	T	50-60
Beans, pole	T	60-65
Beans, Lima	T	65-75
Beets	H	60-70
Broccoli	H	60-70
Cabbage	H	70-90
Carrots	H	70-75
Cauliflower	H	55-60
Celery	H	115-125
Chinese Cabbage	H	75-85
Collards	H	50-55
Corn, Sweet	T	80-85
Cantaloupes	T	75-90
Cucumbers	T	50-55
Eggplant	T	80-85
Endive-Escarole	H	90-95
Kohlrabi	H	50-55
Lettuce	H	50-80
Mustard	H	40-45
Okra	T	50-55
Onions	H H H	100-130 50-75 75-105
Parsley	H	90-95
Peas	H	50-55
Peas, Southern	T	70-80
Pepper (Sweet) (Hot)	T	70-80

Florida Vegetable Planting Guide (continuation)

Crop	Plant Hardiness +	Days to Harvest
Potatoes	SH	80-95
Potatoes (Sweet)	T	120-140
Radish	H	20-25
Spinach	H	40-45
Spinach, Summer	T	55-65
Squash (Summer) (Winter)	T T	45-60 95-105
Strawberry	H	90-110
Tomatoes (Large Fruited) (Small Fruited)	T T	75-85 75-85
Turnips	H	40-50
Watermelons (Large) (Seedless) (Small)	T	80-100

Wax Scale

CHAPTER TEN

Insects and Diseases

Florida has one of the most appealing climates in the world. It is a sub-tropical paradise that has brought people from all over the world to live and enjoy the balmy ambience, especially in the coastal regions. But no paradise is perfect, and because we have no extended freezing periods in most of the state, insects flourish year 'round without being killed off as they are in colder climates. Insects constitute five-sixths of all living creatures on Earth, so it is understandable that almost every temperate region in the world has its share of insect problems. Fortunately, modern chemical science has produced many products that help keep insect populations at a tolerable level. But every gardener must keep a watchful eye for signs of infestation. Unless recognized and treated early, insects and plant diseases can decimate a garden very quickly.

Chewed leaves, nips from flower buds, squiggly lines on leaves, black soot and sooty mold are all positive indications that your garden has been invaded. Other problems, such as root fungi, virus and nematodes, need closer inspection to determine their presence.

You can not raise flowers or vegetables, or have a healthy lawn or beautiful shrubs and trees, without taking some steps to control the insects and diseases that are present in Florida. Early treatment with the proper pesticide is necessary to help you keep one step ahead of any crawling pests and insidious plant diseases. All these gardening hazards are diverse in their habits and effect, requiring the right means of controlling them.

Nematodes exist everywhere in varying degrees. Some soil samples contain only a few; others are packed with these destructive organisms. For this reason, Vapaming the soil in your flower or vegetable garden on a seasonal basis is vital. For lawns, it is advisable to have the area treated professionally with Mocap or Oftonal for maximum protection. Nematodes — microscopic pests that can ruin almost everything that grows — are the major soil problem in Florida. They are sometimes referred to as round worms, eel worms or thread worms. Angry gardeners discovering damage have called them a lot of other names, too!

Affected plants become weakened and die. If you observe a sick plant, examine it at once. Absence of feeder roots, a stubby root system or a 213

214 darkened root system indicate nematode infestation. You can obtain a nematode soil testing kit for a small fee from your local County Extension Service. Better still, send about a pint of moistened soil dug from two to six inches below the surface to the Nematology Department at the University of Florida in Gainesville. The university staff will only test for nematodes. For a full soil analysis to help you determine elements you need to add for arriving at the right pH balance and establishing proper nutritional content, send a dry sample to the Soil Science Department. There is a small fee for each test. The County Extension Service can supply a box and form for shipping samples.

INSECT CONTROLS

With so many insects and diseases able to plague Florida gardens, you must learn the proper methods of control. Most of the remedies are highly sophisticated chemical compounds that cure certain problems. Unwisely applied, they can kill plants as well as become dangerous for animals, birds and humans. Be sure to read label directions on any product you use and do not exceed the recommended amounts.

Insect baits can be applied from shaker cans; others need spreaders. But be careful to keep birds away from treated areas. Powdered insecticides and fungicides can be applied with dusters on a calm day. Other products can be applied with atomizers, though this type of application mainly is confined to house plants.

PARAPHERNALIA FOR THE GARDEN

There are many conveniences for applying fertilizer, insecticides and herbicides in the lawn and garden. The following run-down covers those most readily available:

Hose-end sprayers are inexpensive and easy to handle. They mix prescribed amounts of material to the flow of water and spray either a fine mist, for plants and lawns, or a stream of water for trees and hard to reach foliage.

Compression sprayers are versatile and convenient for almost any garden use. They can be heavy when full, but spray either mist or stream uniformly and are handy for getting to hard-to-reach spots. They employ a pump device, have adjustable nozzle, and vary in price according to the material from which they are constructed.

Dusters spray powder materials such as *Sevin* or sulphur evenly and without weight or transport problems. They are inexpensive and most are adjustable for fine or heavy dusting. Dust only on calm days.

Trombone sprayers act on a compression system drawing material from a pail or other container. Their greatest advantage is the ability to spray long distances and into tree foliage.

Atomizers are best for houseplants and small, delicate plants. The principle is the same as the compression sprayer.

For heavy jobs, you may want to use a powder sprayer, as shown on the next page. You may also broadcast material with spreaders, or apply insect bait, fertilizer, or herbicides with a variety of simple self-application packages available on the market.

Hose-end Sprayer

Compression Sprayer

Duster

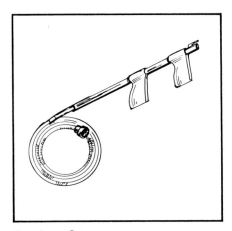

Trombone Sprayer

Atomizer Sprayer

Bait

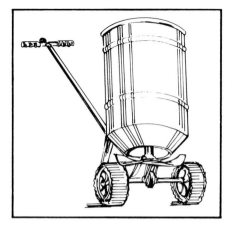

Spreader

Power Spreader

Spreaders are used in applying certain granular products, both ferti- lizers and insecticides; either a drop spreader or the rotary type is effective. If you want to use a hose-adaptor spread for liquid fertilizer or insecticide, get the type with the calibrated dial settings. These are more accurate and help you guard against over-applying. This is especially important when spraying products such as Malathion, a highly effective insecticide that kills the majority of garden pests. Malathion can be fatal to flowers, shrubs and trees if too strong a mixture is applied.

Pump-type compression sprayers, either hand-operated or power, are excellent not only for saturating soil but reaching tops of trees. These are good for spot weed killing, too. However, sprayers used for weed killers should not be used for anything else, because of possible contamination. As the name implies, weed *killers* do just that — not only to weeds but other plants. The tools we use, the chemicals we apply in a routine fashion, are potentially dangerous if caution and restraint are not used. Chemical insecticides and fertilizers are formulated to be used in certain prescribed dilutions. To ignore the directions can endanger not only your plants, but animals, birds and yourself. For example: never spray on a windy day, because the liquid chemicals can burn skin and eyes. Inhaling sprays (such as Malathion) can cause grave internal damage, too. After use, insecticides should be stored in a safe place in the original containers, out of reach of children or animals.

SAFETY PRECAUTIONS

If you do get chemicals on your skin while spraying, wash with warm, soapy water as soon as possible. Wearing rubber gloves and a respirator is a good preventive measure against contamination. Long-sleeved shirts and trousers also are recommended to prevent any spray from touching the body and possibly causing an adverse reaction.

All insecticides are *poison* — they have to be to do their intended job — and great care must be taken in handling, mixing and applying.

Later in the chapter, you will find a listing of the most common insects and plant diseases prevalent in Florida. Studying the descriptions will enable you to identify and control the particular problem in your garden. Once a week, you should examine all of your plants for signs of insect damage or disease. Look at the flowers, leaves, stems and, if necessary, the roots as well. Keep an eye out for evidence of insect infestation or disease. Turn over leaves, because many problems start on the underside. Pull mulch away from the plant's base to check for insects. Most are nocturnal, so they will hide during the day from the hot Florida sunshine.

A cupping or curling of a leaf can indicate a fungus, virus or weed killer. To determine the exact cause, you should be familiar with the variety, culture and characteristics of a plant before making a diagnosis. Small annual seedlings can be healthy and dark-green one day and wilted the next, a sure sign of a fungus disease known as "damping off." Other fungus diseases include wilt, canker, leaf spots, root rot and stem problems. Bacterial diseases often are identified from breakdown of the plant tissue.

Do not mistake deficiency diseases for fungus problems. For example: *frizzle top* on Queen palms may *look* like a disease but is caused by insufficient watering. Newly planted flowers and shrubs that are inadequately watered can exhibit symptoms that look suspiciously like an infection. But the cause may be transplant shock combined with lack of water.

Another common disease-like condition is fertilizer burn, easily recognized by the brown, burned edges of leaves.

FLORIDA'S MOST COMMON INSECTS:

Hymenoptera — Ants

There are many varieties of ants, ranging in color from red to brown to black. The large carpenter ant, sometimes called the wood ant, grows to three-eighths of an inch in length, with a black abdomen and red thorax and head. This insect often will build tunnels in dead trees, logs and

Fire Ant Mound

218 sometimes houses. The most dangerous ant, however, is the fire ant, which will build a large, porous mound above the ground. Its bite is painful and results in pustular, itching bumps on the skin. Dursban or Diazinon will control most ants, and for fire ants, Amdro bait is very effective.

Aphis spiraecola — Aphids

Aphids are one-sixth of an inch long and vary in color depending on the foliage they feed on. They may be green, blue, white, yellow, red or black. Aphids insert their stylet (their needle-like mouth) into plant tissue and feed on the juice, resulting in deformed, tightly curled new leaves. Aphids particularly are prone to attack ornamentals in a garden. Spraying with Diazinon, Sevin and Malathion will control these pests. Also very effective is the systemic insecticide known as Orthene.

Trichoplusia — Cabbage Looper

Broccoli, cauliflower, brussels sprouts and kale are very susceptible to attack from this insect. The cabbage looper is a large caterpillar from one to three inches in length. It gets its name from the way it pulls itself forward like an inchworm, "looping" its body as it moves. Loopers normally appear in spring and early fall and are dark-green to lime in color. They are best controlled by spraying with organic insecticides like Dipel, Biotrol and Thuricide.

Aphids, which are sucking insects, will attack most garden plants, but can be controlled with regular spraying. Fortunately, other insects also prey on Aphids. One of them is the Ladybug.

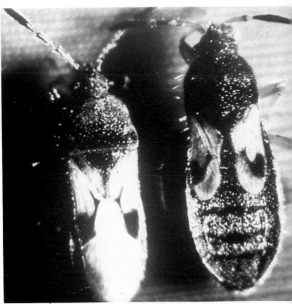

Chinch Bugs are the biggest threat to St. Augustine lawns.

The Chinch Bug thrives in lawn grasses, but can be controlled with spraying.

Blissus insularis — **Chinch Bugs**

The chinch bug can do serious damage to St. Augustine grass by injecting its saliva into the stems and blades of grass. The chinch bug ranges from one-sixteenth to one-fifth of an inch in length and is orange-red in color, changing to brown when mature. One application of Diazinon, Dursban, Ethion or other chinch bug spray usually controls this pest.

Spodoptera ornithogalli — **Cutworm**

This large caterpillar, which is about two inches long and a quarter-of-an-inch wide, literally cuts off plants at ground level. Cutworms feed at night and are particularly fond of tomatoes, peppers and practically all vegetables and annuals. Spraying with Diazinon or Sevin will help control these pests. Sprinkling mole cricket bait on the ground before planting also is effective. A non-chemical means of protecting plants is to cut the bottoms from paper cups and encircle the base of each plant with the cylinders, keeping the cutworm away from the stem. Similarly, a toothpick placed next to the plant stem will prevent the worm from encircling and killing it.

Ctenocephalides — **Fleas**

Fleas attack warm-blooded animals rather than plants. Any dog or cat owner will need no introduction to this pest, which lays its eggs in animal fur. These eggs then are carried into a house, where they fall on carpets and in furniture. The eggs develop into a tiny worm-like larvae that then pupate into adult fleas. Very tenacious, fleas have been known to live for eighteen months without a host animal to feed on. Initially, any animals should be treated with Sevin or any other pet spray fatal to fleas. Indoor areas should be sprayed with Precor to stop development of the flea larvae. All outside areas should be sprayed with Diazinon or Malathion. If your property is badly infested, you will have to repeat this program every ten days until you are rid of the problem.

Errinnysis — Hornworm

A menacing-looking monster, the hornworm is harmless to humans but devastating to tomatoes and poinsettias. Growing to four inches or more in length, with a horn-like projection on its head, this ravenous eater can strip a tomato bush in a matter of hours, eating only the leaves and leaving the stems. Spraying with Sevin or *Bacillus thuringrensis* (Dipel, Thuricide or Biotrol) will control the hornworm. Because of its size, however, many people prefer to keep a watchful eye out and pick the worms off the plant by hand. This is often the best way once they have gained a foothold in the garden. A sure sign of impending infestation is the appearance of the adult moth, sometimes called the Phoenix or Hawk moth, which is quite large.

Corythucha ciliata — Lace Bugs

Only one fourth to one third of an inch long, the lace bug is light-colored and appears to have lacy wings. Its favorite foliage includes pyracantha, azaleas, oaks, avocados, sycamores and elms. It feeds on the leaves and deposits a silvery residue that ultimately turns brown. Two applications of Malathion, Diazinon, Cygon or Orthene usually will control this pest.

Pseudococcus longispinus — Mealy Bug

Mealy bugs are a quarter of an inch in length, with a waxy covering on their bodies. These insects are a common problem on crotons, citrus trees, mangoes, ivy and many other indoor and outdoor ornamentals. They are easily controlled by spraying with Malathion, Diazinon, Cygon or Orthene.

Mealy Bug

Gryllotalpa hexadactyla — Mole Cricket   221

A particular problem in Bahia, Bermuda and similar Florida lawns, the mole cricket tunnels and feeds on the roots of the grass as well as attacking vegetables and young seedlings. From one to one-and-a-half inches in length, mole crickets are able to move easily through sandy soil due to their powerful front legs that act somewhat like bulldozers beneath the ground. In winter they hibernate three to five feet down, emerging in summer to mate, at which time they are often seen in great quantities near street lights and other brightly lit areas.

From early June through mid-August, mole cricket bait can be effective, spread evenly over moistened ground. Diazinon and Spectricide can be sprayed with good results, but with severe infestations in a garden, you should call in professional exterminators who use Oftonal or Mocap.

Scales

There are several types of scale, almost all of which can be controlled by spraying with an oil emulsion or a systemic such as Cygon or Orthene. A few of the more common scales include wax, red, round, cottony cushion, snow and tea scale.

Ceroplastes ceriferus (Fabricius) — **The wax scale** is a creamy white scale one-eighth to one quarter of an inch in size. It looks like a small drop of wax. Very common on podocarpus, it also attacks hibiscus, camellias and mangoes.

Chrysomphalus aonidum — **The Florida red scale** is a tenth to a twelfth of an inch in diameter, dark-red to black in color, with the center slightly raised. It attacks many Florida plants, including citrus and hibiscus.

Saissetia coffeae — **The round or hemispherical scale** is one eighth of an inch wide and about a tenth of an inch high, ranging from light to dark brown in color. It often is found on ixoras, gardenias, roses and cycads.

Icerya purchasi — **The cottony cushion scale** grows one eighth to a quarter of an inch long. It is brownish-red in color, with a small, cottony

Cottony Cushion Scale

222   white mass about a half inch long. This scale is found on many ornamentals, as well as pittosporum and citrus.

***Pinnaspis strachani* — Snow scale** is a twelfth of an inch long. The female scale is dark-brown and difficult to see. The male scale is one-twenty-fourth of an inch and snow white, giving the appearance of confectioners' sugar sprinkled on twigs and branches. Snow scale is a serious problem on citrus, hibiscus and many ornamentals.

***Fiorinia theae* — Tea scale** can devastate camellias, often infesting them so heavily that the leaves look as if they are painted white. The white color indicates the very tiny, male scales. Female scales are one-twentieth of an inch across and brown.

Veronicellidae — Slugs

Slugs look like snails without shells and leave a slimy trail behind them. From one to three inches long, slugs feed at night, attacking tender foliage on most plants, then hide during the day. Although not insects, slugs nevertheless are a serious garden pest and should be treated with slug and snail bait containing Mesurol or Methaldehyde. For the organic gardener who prefers not to use chemical insecticides, a flat saucer can be sunk into the soil and filled with beer, which will attract slugs in great numbers. The beer does not kill the slugs but enables them to be swept up and disposed of early in the morning.

Slugs feed on tender foliage but are difficult to trace. Slug and snail bait gives most effective control.

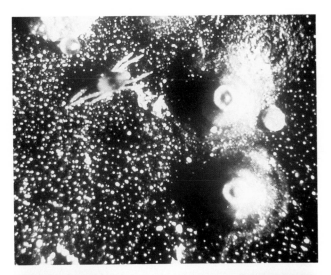

Spider Mites with Scale

Spider Mites, resistant to
natural pyrethrins of plants
such as Marigolds, can
spread webs quickly and
destroy healthy plants.

Tetranychus sp. — **Spider Mites**

Spider mites are not true insects, but they, too, are a serious garden pest. They are difficult to see without the aid of a magnifying glass. A stippled, white-dot pattern with a brownish cast to the leaves is evidence of spider mites. They suck the juice from a plant. Some gardeners plant marigolds to keep spider mites away, only to find these flowers covered with a shiny, silky web — evidence that the mites have destroyed the plant. Spider mites are a major problem in summer and in areas that do not get good airflow, such as porches or entranceways. The pests are very prolific and hatch a new generation every five days. Regular spraying with a miticide is essential. Trithion, Tedion, Kelthane or Chlorobenzilate are some recommended products.

Webworms are a particu-
lar danger to Florida trees.

Nezara viridula — Stink Bug

A large, green insect almost an inch long, the stink bug gets its name from the offensive odor present after it is crushed. These pests attack citrus fruit trees, blackberries, tomatoes and many other vegetables and ornamentals. Spray with Malathion, Diazinon or Dursban for good control.

Hyphantria cunea — Webworms

In the fall, these pale, creamy-white worms spin large webs over trees, destroying the foliage. They drop off trees and attack any other leafy shrubs in the area. The webs have to be removed by hand, but the insects are destroyed by spraying with Malathion or Diazinon. Advance spraying during the summer is recommended to prevent damage to any foliage in the fall.

Dialeurodes citrifolii — White Fly

The white fly really is closely related to the scale. It causes black sooty mold on ornamentals. Most of the damage is done during the larval stage, when citrus, gardenias and ornamentals usually are attacked. For

White Fly   White Fly on Citrus

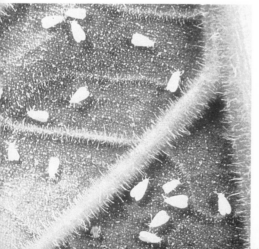

ornamentals, use a systemic insecticide such as Cygon or Orthene. For fruit trees, Malathion or Diazinon are strongly recommended.

FLORIDA'S MOST COMMON PLANT DISEASES:

Diplocarpon rosae — Black Spot

Black, circular spots on leaves, often surrounded by a yellow halo, are signs of this disease. If not treated, black spot can cause peristent defoliation and weaken the plant. Water remaining on the leaves for several hours will aggravate this disease and cause it to spread. Susceptible plants, such as roses, should not be watered before nightfall, but in the early morning when the sun has a chance to dry the leaves and lessen chances of black spot. Raking up black-spotted leaves will minimize the chance of further infection in your garden.

A persistent disease, black spot needs spraying every two weeks to keep it under control, especially during rainy seasons. Daconil, Fore, Benlate and Funginex are recommended to cure black spot and keep it from reappearing.

Rhizoctonia solani — Brown Patch

During warm, humid weather, this disease appears as a small, brown, circular area in a lawn. If the infection spreads, large areas of turf can be destroyed. Spray with Daconil, Fore or Benomyl.

Agrobacterium tumefaciens — Crown Gall

Crown gall starts out as round knots or blisters on shrubs and trees. On larger plants with light infection, the diseased areas can be trimmed out, cutting behind the gall into good wood. But on small plants, it is best to remove and destroy the infected plant. The only preventive is to buy gall-free plants. There is no cure.

Damping Off (Numerous fungi)

A number of fungi attack small plants before they emerge from the soil, or shortly thereafter. Stems have the appearance of being pinched. Sterilizing the garden soil with Vapam or drenching young plants with Captan, Dithane M-45 and other approved fungicides will control damping off.

Erwinia Amylovora — Fire Blight

Plants damaged by this disease appear badly burned, with leaves turning brown and hanging on the limbs for months. Roses are the main victim, as well as pears, loquats and pyracantha. Loquats can be treated for this disease by spraying with streptomycin twice a year, a method that also is effective with other plants. Fire blight can be controlled manually by trimming two or three inches below the infected wood with clippers that have been sterilized in physan (a hospital sterilizer) or a 10-percent chlorine solution. This is very important to avoid spreading the blight. Be moderate in fertilizing a fire-blighted plant. Over-fertilization aggravates the problem.

Leaf Spot Fungus

Leaf Spot Fungus (Numerous Fungi)

Spraying with Benlate, dithane M-45 or Zineb can control leaf spot fungus, which causes small spots at first. Later, large brown areas may appear on leaves. The dead spots will fall out, leaving large holes. This type of damage often is wrongly attributed to caterpillars. As with most fungal infections, sanitation is important. Rake up fallen leaves for disposal. This will help prevent spread of the infection to other plants.

Lethal Yellowing (Mycoplasma-like organism)

Mycoplasma has a true cellular structure, containing RNA, RNR, DNA, protein and enzymes. It is thought to be transmitted by leaf hoppers. In coconut palms affected with this disease, the coconuts drop and the fronds yellow, blacken and die. Tetracycline injections every three months give temporary relief, but replacement of an infected plant is the best solution. In south Florida, Jamaican coconut palms are susceptible to lethal yellowing and usually are replaced with resistant varieties such as the Malayan dwarf palm.

Mushroom Root Rot

Ornamentals and trees that die suddenly often are victims of this disease. It can be identified by peeling the bark back near the base for the telltale white film that is the mycellium, or fruiting body, of this fungus. Replace with a different variety after destroying the infected plant, and be sure to sterilize the soil with Vapam before replanting in the same area.

Powdery Mildew

Powdery Mildew (Numerous fungi)

Spraying with Karathane, Acti-dione, Benomyl or other approved fungicides will control powdery mildew, a silvery-white fungus that grows over the top and bottom leaf surfaces of many plants, especially crape myrtle, roses, cucumbers, watermelon and zinnias. Sulfur is another remedy, though care should be taken because sulfur can burn certain plants.

Pythium sp. — Pythium

Starting at the root tips and moving up the root system, pythium deteriorates the plant tissue, causing the outer layer of the root to soften and slide off when pressed between thumb and forefinger. Soil sterilization before planting is the best way to prevent this disease, which can be controlled by spraying with Subdue or Truban *(Terragole)*. Like most fungal infections, pythium is better handled through prevention than cure.

Sooty Mold

Not really harmful to plants, sooty mold is an indication that aphids, white flies or scales are attacking your garden. This fungus growth does, however, cut down on the plant's ability to produce food, and grows on the secretion (honeydew) left by feeding insects. Getting rid of the insects will help cure the mold problem. The mold can be washed off plants with a mild, soapy solution or a strong stream of water.

228 Virus (Numerous viruses)

A virus is a disease caused by atoms of nucleic acid with a coat of protein. Viruses must invade other living cells to survive, since they have no cellular structure of their own. Only an electron microscope is able to single out the presence of a virus, which can cause mottling, curling and twisting of leaves, as well as a mosaic pattern. Infected trees should be destroyed. As a preventive measure, always buy healthy plants and trees with certified bud wood.

MR. GREEN THUMB RULE

Malathion and Diazinon will control the majority of insect infestations, and using Vapam on the soil prior to planting will eliminate most fungal diseases in the garden. Keep these three chemical aids to good gardening on hand at all times, to maintain the healthiest growing conditions for your plants.

***Rhizoctonia solani* — Brown Patch** — This is a cool-weather fungal disease that affects St. Augustine, Rye, Zoysia, Centipede, Bermuda and Bahia grasses. It is more common when the temperature is above 70 degrees with high humidity. Grass turns brown quickly and leaves pull loose from runners easily. This fungus is not fatal but can damage a lawn and weaken the turf. Spray with any good fungicide labeled for "brown patch," including Fore, Daconil, Tersan, Benomyl, Maneb or Terrachlor.

***Piricularia grisea* — Gray Leaf Spot** — Gray leaf spot causes brown and gray lesions on stems and leaves, with a dark-brown margin around the infected areas. It usually affects Rye and St. Augustine grasses in the hot, humid, summer months. Spray with Thiram, Fore or Daconil for control of this fungus.

Brown Patch

Sclerotinia homoeocarpa — **Dollar Spot** — An easy fungus to identify, dollar spot starts by turning the grass a pale yellow in areas two to three inches in diameter, spreading to form larger diseased areas. Often seen in fall and spring when fog and dew are present, dollar spot is a major problem with Bermuda and Zoysia and occasionally Bahia, but can sometimes attack St. Augustine and Centipede lawns, as well. Two applications of Daconil, plus complete fertilization, usually will take care of this problem.

Helminthosporium sp. — **Leaf Spot** — Ultimately fatal, leaf spot begins as brown, purple or yellow areas with a dark border and a black spore center. Blades of grass turn yellow and die. A serious problem with Bermuda grass, leaf spot also can attack Zoysia and St. Augustine lawns. This disease attacks throughout the year and is best controlled with Daconil, Tersan or Fore.

Nematodes

These microscopic eel worms or roundworms, also called thread worms, are a major problem in Florida. They exist in the soil in every area of the state. Nematode damage is identified by lack of feeder roots, blackening of root systems or thickening of the roots with the galls or raised knots caused by these pests. Should you choose to sterilize your entire lawn area, you have to wait two to three weeks before replanting, and be sure to keep the sterilant (Vapam) at least two to three feet away from the root zone of existing trees or shrubs. Nematode control in lawns is best handled by a certified pest control operator, as there is no easy way to exterminate nematodes other than by sterilizing the soil, preferably before planting a lawn. With nematodes, prevention is easier, cheaper and better than cure.

Three more fungus diseases that attack Florida lawns include:

1. *Phythium*, associated with newly planted grass and prevalent in poorly drained areas. Control with Subdue.
2. *Fairy Ring*, a circle of mushrooms inside which the grass will die. In severe cases, soil fumigation may be necesssary, but usually, hand-picking the mushrooms, fertilizing and increasing the watering will eliminate this problem. *Caution:* Do not attempt to eat any mushrooms picked from a fairy ring. They are poisonous.
3. *Slime Mold*, an unattractive black mold, sometimes gray or yellow. It is harmless and can be washed off with the hose. Proper mowing usually takes care of this minor problem.

When spraying for fungal diseases, it is best to spray an entire area rather than to try spot treatments. When examining your turf for possible fungus disease, take a magnifying glass. Most of the fungal organisms are too small to be seen with the naked eye.

CHAPTER ELEVEN

Vines

One of the many joys of Florida living is the large number of vines that can be grown here. Their leafy, green runners climb over walls, fences, trellises and planters. Not only in residential areas but in the wilds, these persistent, ever-spreading plants add eye-catching color to the landscape. Their attractive foliage intermingles with blossoms of almost every color.

Vines add to the beauty of any garden, but they also can serve a very practical purpose: blocking out the fierce summer sun and screening windows, walls and patios from excessive heat. Vines grow quickly and provide welcome shade with a minimum of care and effort. The majority of vines are flowering plants. But many home owners enjoy vines that do more than beautify. These include the grape vine or vines such as cucumbers, melons and climbing figs, which also produce food for the table.

To select the right vine for your particular needs, you should study the characteristics of each variety, learn its growing habits and requirements and its resistance to cold. Vines are among the easiest plants to grow, and with their sheer mass and moisture content, they create a distinct cooling effect, both physically and psychologically.

For outdoor plantings, March through October is the best time to start a vine in the ground. For container-held vines, planting can be done any time except the dead of winter. Like most plants, vines do best in good, improved soil consisting of one-third peat, one-third dehydrated cow manure and one-third natural, existing soil. Since vines eventually will grow together, it is best not to place them too close to each other. Three to four feet apart is a good rule of thumb. Daily watering is essential after planting, then cut back to about an inch a week once the plant takes hold and begins to mature. Vines planted in full sun require more water than those growing in shade. Test the soil with your finger if you are unsure about watering; if it has dried out, step up your watering. Vines must have moist soil to maintain healthy foliage and satisfactory growth. Letting the soil dry out is the quickest way to kill any plant, especially one that has to endure Florida's scorching sunshine.

Vines are climbers, so they need support. A fence, trellis or rough wall is necessary for all vines. If you do not wish a vine to spread out of control, 231 keep it trimmed. The more often you trim a vine, the bushier it will become. Most vines have tendrils that wrap around any available support. But some, such as the climbing rose, have to be tied to a fence or trellis.

LANDSCAPING WITH VINES

Vines are particularly useful for covering unattractive fences. A chain-link fence is practical but not very aesthetically appealing. Yet it provides perfect support for the Passion Vine, Honeysuckle, Confederate Jasmines and Morning Glories. Honeysuckle is ideal particularly for growing on a chain-link fence. It will wind in and out of the mesh, creating a solid base from which other branches emerge. It will cover the fence totally (and usually in one season), providing privacy for the garden and a cool, soothing background for the rest of the landscaping.

For shady areas, plants such as Algerian Ivy, English Ivy, Philodendron, Fatshedera and Jasmines can be used successfully. The ivy family is suited for climbing up rough, outside walls of houses, where it not only provides a dense screen against the sun, but enhances the beauty of the home.

Compared with flowering annuals and perennials and vegetables, vines could be called trouble-free. But despite their hardiness and fast-growth characteristics, they cannot be planted and forgotten. But once they are established, they require very little care and will become an admired and useful part of your landscape.

ALPHABETICAL LISTING OF VINES:

Algerian Ivy
Allamanda
Bauhinia
Bleeding Heart
Bougainvillea
Cape Honeysuckle
Carolina Jasmine
Climbing Fig
Confederate Jasmine
Coral Vine
Cydista

English Ivy
Fatshedera
Golden Chalice
Grapes
Mexican Flame Vine
Morning Glory
Night Bloomng Cereus
Ornamental Gourds
Passion Fruit Vine
Trumpet Honeysuckle
Wisteria
Wood Rose

THE BEST VINES FOR FLORIDA

Hedera canarensis — Algerian Ivy

A vigorous grower reaching 25 feet in length, this plant resembles English ivy but with much larger leaves. It is good for covering tree trunks and walls. Plant 12 to 18 inches apart in sheltered locations where winter temperatures do not drop far below freezing for extended periods.

Allamanda cathartica — Allamanda

Producing trumpet-shaped, yellow, waxy flowers almost four inches across, this vine is a fast-grower, blooms ten months out of the year and can extend to twenty feet in length. Sensitive to temperatures in the twenties, it is used more extensively in central and south Florida. Shoots should be trimmed, and the plant should be pruned before new growth starts in the spring. Grows well in sun or light shade. As its botanical name implies, all parts of this plant are cathartic.

Bauhinia kalapini — Bauhinia

Similar to the more-familiar Bauhinia trees, this vine has to be trained along a trellis. But it grows quite easily from seed and produces exquisite, dark-red flowers. This plant is injured by frost but grows back. Ideal for central and southern Florida.

Clerodendrum thomsoniae — Bleeding Heart

Sometimes called Glory Bower, this West African vine grows well in Florida, producing white flowers enclosed in heart-shaped calyces that bloom most of the year. The vines should be supported on a trellis or fence. Bleeding heart survives in all parts of the state, but can be injured in colder areas. As long-lasting cut flowers, clerodendrums are very popular for floral arrangements indoors.

Bougainvillea sp. — Bougainvillea

Available in brilliant shades of deep pink, almost-red, orange and yellow, this vine has been known to climb to the top of 50-foot trees. Frost will injure bougainvillea, but it grows back again. A truly impressive grower, bougainvillea can be used in hanging baskets and patio plants or allowed to bush into a tall, very thick shrub that can form a remarkably dense hedge blessed with flowers and dark-green foliage. This plant flourishes in most areas of Florida but needs regular feeding with fertilizer high in phosphorus and potassium.

Bougainvillea

Bougainvillea Blossoms

Cape Honeysuckle

Tecomia

Tecomaria capensis — Cape Honeysuckle

This South African vine is beautiful, shrubby and blooms most of the year with brilliant, orange-red flowers. A very aggressive vine, it can be propagated easily from soft wood cuttings.

Gelsemium sempervirens — Carolina Jessamine, Carolina Jasmine

Best suited to north and central Florida, this plant grows well in full sun or partial shade. It reaches 20 to 25 feet and offers a delightful scent from its bright-yellow flowers that bloom in early spring. The foliage is bright green but shows iron chlorosis when grown in alkaline soil.

Ficus pumila — Climbing Fig

Tolerating heat as well as semi-shade, the climbing fig has dark, evergreen leaves almost four inches long. It is a good climber, often reaching a height of 30 feet. This vine does well against walls but has to be staked. Plant every two feet for an eventual mass of very attractive foliage. The foliage is popular and used extensively in public places such as Disneyworld in Orlando.

Trachaelospermum jasminoides — Confederate Jasmine, Star Jasmine

This vine is a profuse bloom in early summer. The vines should be planted 24 to 36 inches apart, since they grow rapidly. This vine works either as a ground cover or over fences, trellises and patios. Its foliage is dark green, and the brilliant white flowers, resembling pinwheels, have a strong, delightful fragrance. Planted around an entranceway, this vine can fill the house with its perfume. Susceptible to damage from lower temperatures, it does best in central and south Florida. It can be started from tip cuttings or air-layering.

Atigonon leptopus — Coral Vine

A prolific grower, the coral vine is covered with delicate pink flowers most of the year and has tendrils that enable it to climb almost any porous or semi-porous surface, such as a low wall or fence. It has unusually heavy growth and should be trimmed back after blooming. Otherwise it can get out of control.

This vine can be planted from seed very easily, and during summer and fall, self-sown small plants can be found underneath the mature foliage. In north Florida, frost can injure this vine, but it will grow back again.

Coral Vine spreads its clinging tendrils to any porous surface.

236 Cydista

A South American plant that does well in Florida, cydista has beautiful pink flowers, sometimes veined with rose or purple coloration. It can be grown from seed and should be protected from severe cold. Best planting time is in the spring, with flowers summer through fall.

Hedera helix — English Ivy

This ivy is evergreen, with dark, leathery leaves. English ivy is excellent for covering masonry walls and will grow 30 to 35 feet. Plant the vines 12 to 18 inches apart, as close to a wall as possible. However, do not use them for covering hot, reflective walls that receive the afternoon sunlight. English ivy grows best in rich, improved soil with adequate moisture.

Fatshedera lizei — Fatshedera

This vine is a cross between Japanese aralia and English ivy. This evergreen botanical wonder is a leaning vine-shrub growing to ten feet, with star-studded, dark-green foliage. It needs support for climbing and is subject to damage from low temperatures. Against a wall, in a protected corner, or as an indoor or outdoor accent, the fatshedera is most impressive. Plant in good, rich soil with adequate moisture.

Solandra guttata — Golden Chalice

Grown from seed and soft wood cuttings, the golden chalice does well in fertilized soil with adequate moisture. This vine needs a trellis to climb and has exquisite, tubular, golden flowers almost ten inches long, which open white and slowly darken to their ultimate rich, golden yellow. At night, the blossoms give off a light, pleasant fragrance.

GRAPES

A grape vine not only enhances the beauty of any garden, but provides luscious fruit for the table. Used most frequently on arbors and fences, a grape vine will wrap its tendrils around posts, wire or wooden supports. Several varieties do well in Florida, but you should check with your nurseryman on the best grape vines for your area.

One of the best and easiest to grow is the *Muscadine* grape. It offers tough-skinned, purple, round berries of excellent flavor. Muscadines should be planted in full sun and in soil with good drainage. Bare root stock is planted while dormant, from November 15 through April. Grapes bought in containers can be planted at any time. These vines must be pruned each winter during their dormant stage. Suckers should be cut off, and tendrils should not be permitted to wrap around and girdle the vine. Muscadines are vigorous, hungry plants and should be well fertilized once a month after planting. Use a quarter of a pound of general-purpose or citrus fertilizer, scattered 12 inches from the base of the vine. The second year, use a pound of fertilizer for each plant, applied in March, May and just after harvest. For the third year, and every year thereafter, use two and a half pounds per plant. Vines should not be fertilized after September

15. Keep the area around the base of each plant free of weeds, but be careful to cultivate lightly. Grape roots grow near the surface.

Muscadines are easier to grow than bunch grapes. They are native to the southeastern sections of the U.S. and Florida, and many varieties are resistant to Pierce's disease, which renders the growing of European or Northern bunch grapes impossible in Florida. However, muscadines must be protected against pests. Spray with a good fungicide such as Manzate D, Diathane M-22 or neutral copper every two weeks from the time the flowers appear until the fruit begins to ripen. This will prevent fruit rots and leaf spots. Spraying is very important during the rainy season, and it should be continued every two weeks until the wet season ends. Spraying with a regular insecticide, such as Malathion or Sevin, also is advised, except when the vines are in bloom. Spraying then would kill pollinating insects.

GRAPE VARIETIES

Three varieties of *bunch grapes*, however, can do well in all parts of the state except the southeast coastal regions. *Lake Emerald, Norris* and *Stover* are resistant to Pierce's disease.

Norris is the largest of these varieties, with deep-purple grapes and skins that are easy to separate from the pulp. A high-yielding, vigorous vine, *Norris* does well from cuttings, but being self-sterile, it must be planted close to one of the other two varieties to fruit satisfactorily. Susceptible to anthracnose, it must be sprayed five or six times with a fungicide, from the time bud growth begins until fruit reaches full size. Be sure to spray when it is in full bloom. Like most grapes, *Norris* has poor salt tolerance. But it adapts well to most soils.

Grape vines suffer from several other diseases that must be controlled to ensure good, healthy vines and a fruitful harvest. The most common problem, *downy mildew*, causes gray patches to appear in spots that eventually turn brown. *Black rot* shows up as dark brown lesions on leaves, usually round in shape. If untreated, this disease causes the grapes to rot. *Anthracnose* causes deformed leaves and lesions. Leafhoppers, aphids and the grape leaf folder are three insects that attack grape vines.

All of these problems can be controlled with a fungicide such as Zineb or dithane M-45. Spray when the first green shoots are about three inches long, then every two weeks thereafter for four or five times. Adding Malathion and Sevin to the spray will take care of many insect infestations.

Senecio confusus — Mexican Flame Vine

Salt-tolerant, easy to start from cuttings and growing back quickly after frost damage, this popular vine produces very large, orange-red, daisy-shaped flowers all year. A fast-grower, it does well in most soils and should be shaped to keep it from growing out of control.

Ipomoea sp. — Morning Glory

Growing 10 to 15 feet in length, morning glory vines do best in full sun, but also flourish in partial shade. They produce blue, pink or white flowers abundantly that open in the morning and close later in the day. Plant seeds where they are to grow. Soaking seeds in water several days before planting will hasten germination. Blooming six to eight months of the year, morning glories do very well on fences and trellises and cover any area very quickly. This vine self-seeds prolifically; in fact, once introduced into a garden, it is difficult to eradicate, which makes this plant a favorite with lazy gardeners!

Hylocereus undatus — Night Blooming Cereus

This flowering, climbing cactus does well in central and south Florida, producing delicate, fragrant, white blossoms all summer. This plant will extend its dark-green, ridged branches up to 20 feet, with aerial roots that cling to walls.

ORNAMENTAL GOURDS

These climbing plants are very popular. Their leaves resemble pumpkin or squash foliage. They climb and produce a variety of unusual gourds that can be dried and used for interior decoration.

Passiflora edulis — Passion Fruit Vine

A rampant, woody vine, the passion fruit has three-lobed, serrated leaves and climbs with tendrils. The fruit is slightly oval, with a purple, shell-like rind. The pulp is juicy and aromatic, with many seeds. The juice is particularly tasty, and both juice and seeds can be added to fruit salads for interesting flavor. This vine likes full sun, needs a strong support to climb on (chain-link fence is recommended) and requires good, moist soil. Seeds take two weeks to three months to germinate, and the vine can be grown from cuttings or air-layering. The plants need heavy mulching, and new plants should be started every three years. The passion fruit has poor salt tolerance and suffers from nematodes, caterpillars and crown rot.

This vine gets its name from its unusual flowers, purple and white with a configuration resembling a crucifix, or "the passion of Christ." Another variety, *Passiflora edulis favicarpa*, has yellow fruit and is very vigorous and productive.

Lonicera sempervirens — Trumpet Honeysuckle

A native of Florida, the trumpet honeysuckle grows well in good organic soil, producing red, tubular flowers tinged with yellow on the inside. This plant is grown mainly for its dense foliage. It does well in north and central parts of the state and can be started from seed or cuttings.

Wisteria sinensis — Wisteria

Wisteria is a very vigorous vine growing 30 to 40 feet in length. Over fences and patios, wisteria does best in full or partial sun and can be trained as a small flowering tree. The blossoms are blue-white, pea-shaped flowers hanging in clusters like grapes, and appear in the spring. The foliage is dark-green but yellows badly from iron deficiency in alkaline soil. Wisteria can be pruned back after flowering. It is an exquisitely showy vine in spring, with plenty of foliage through summer and fall. But it loses its leaves during the winter.

Ipomoea tuberosa — Wood Rose

This unusual vine does well in south and lower-central Florida and gets its name from its seed pods that resemble carved wooden roses. It will grow from seed and suffers injury below freezing, but will grow back unless killed to the ground.

Ornamental Gourds make nice decorations for the home, and the vines will cling to trellises, fences, or growing frames.

Vines For Florida

Name	Flower Color	Perennial or Annual	Deciduous or Evergreen	Blooming Season
Allamanda Cathartica	Golden Yellow	P**	E	Nearly All Year
Queens Wreath Coral Vine — Antigonon	Pink	P*	D	Summer, Early Fall
Beaumontia — Grandiflora (Heralds — Trumpet)	Large White	P***	E	Summer
Bougainvillea	Purple, Red, Orange, Gold, White	P**	E	Spring, Winter, Fall
Trumpet Vine (Campsis)	Red, Orange, Yellow	P	D	Summer, Fall
Clerodendrum (Bleeding Heart)	Crimson Corollas White Calyces	P**	E	Spring, Summer
Clytostoma Callistegioides (Painted Trumpet)	Lavender	P	E	Early Summer
Carolina Jessamine Gelsemium	Yellow	P	E	Spring
Cydista Aequinectialis	Pink	P**	E	Summer
Ficus Pumila (Creeping Fig)	Incon	P	E	None
Impomoea Tuberosa (Wooden Rose)	Yellow	P	semi-E	Fall

* Tops die to ground with first freeze. Plants grow back following spring.

Vines For Florida

Name	Flower Color	Perennial or Annual	Deciduous or Evergreen	Blooming Season
Jasinum	White	P	E	Spring, Winter, Summer, Fall
Honeysuckle (Lonicera) Semperuirens	Red, Yellow	P	E	Nearly All Year
Black Eyed Susan Clock Vine (Thumbergia)	White, Yellow	A		Fall, Summer
Petrea Volubilis (Queen's Wreath)	Bluish-purple	P**	E	Spring, Summer
Pyrostegia Ignea Flame Vine	Orange	P**	E	Nearly All Year
Hedera English Ivy	Incon	P	E	None
Trachelospermum Jasminoides (Confederate Jasmine)	White	P	E	Spring, Summer
Stephanotisi Floribundia	White	P**	E	Summer
Tecomaria Capensis Cape Honeysuckle	Reddish-orange	P**	E	Nearly All Year
Wisteria Sinensis Chinese Wisteria	Purple — Blue White	P	D	Spring

* Tops die to ground with first freeze. Plants grow back following spring.
** Damaged or killed for use in central and south Florida.
*** Requires winter protection.

CHAPTER TWELVE

Florida Lawns

Having a beautiful lawn is like having a nice frame around a work of art. It adds beauty to your home. Selecting the right grass for your lawn is important. Factors such as the pH of your soil and determining the amount of money, time and care you want to put into your lawn should all be taken into consideration. I often make the analogy, when teaching, it's better to have an old Chevy with the engine running and properly maintained than to have a Cadillac you can't afford to keep up. The suitability and maintenance demands of your lawn can be just as exacting as with your car.

Most newcomers to Florida face the problem of selecting the right lawn. The fescues and blue grasses of the North are not adaptable to Florida. Many have tried to grow them, but without success. In Rome, do as the Romans do; in Florida, grow the grass or lawn that is best adapted for Florida. The following discussion will provide some basic guidelines for establishment and care of your Florida lawn.

A lawn pays a special dividend in Florida. Compared with concrete, it can reduce garden temperatures from three to six degrees, an appealing aspect during hot, humid summers. Above all, lawns provide the background against which the colors and textures of your other plants are displayed to their optimum aesthetic potential.

The type of lawn that should be grown depends in large measure on the size of your property, on the amount you wish to spend and on the time you can devote to its upkeep. Those who have semi-rural property on several acres possibly can get by with fertilizing and mowing the grasses already in the soil. This will provide an orderly expanse of green that looks neat and attractive. But for the majority of homeowners with homes on normal-sized city lots, a lawn should be planned and started from scratch. This means total preparation of the soil, careful selection of the type of grass to plant and proper upkeep of the lawn to maintain its appearance and keep it free of insects and disease.

A lawn should serve the particular needs of the property owner. Few people have the time or inclination to care for a "putting green" lawn. Those are best left to professional landscapers. The bent grasses needed for this type of lawn are difficult to raise and are prone to disease. In addition,

Florida lawn and turf grasses are a very important part of the landscape and help to create a green living environment but need regular care, a regular feeding program, and frequent watering.

they require constant and frequent mowing, often three or four times a week. Golf course greens usually are mowed daily, which is beyond the capabilities of the average household.

Many newcomers to Florida encounter problems with lawns because they do not always realize that the Fescues and Blue grasses grown in the northern states are not adaptable to our climate. The heat, the humidity and the ever-present problems of insects and disease make the selection of lawn grass a vital consideration.

No single species of grass can qualify for all the uses to which a lawn is put. Only tough, coarse grass will survive in a high-traffic area. Grass with fine leaves makes a beautiful display but requires more care and attention to fertilizing and control of pests and fungus.

ST. AUGUSTINE LAWNS

The grasses most widely used in Florida lawns are the St. Augustine varieties. These are easy to maintain and tolerate shade well. In fact, St. Augustine is the most shade-tolerant grass grown in our state, and it is excellent for coastal areas because of its high salt tolerance.

St. Augustine grass has much to commend it: rich, blue-green color; adaptability to shade or sun; and rapid, healthy growth. Its major weaknesses are its lack of resistance to brown-patch disease and chinch bugs, but both these problems are relatively easy to handle with the proper sprays. There are St. Augustine special fertilizers for Florida lawns. St. Augustine also can develop thatch problems due to overfeeding and mowing the lawn too low. Even though this grass is coarser than other varieties, it tolerates almost any type of soil, from sand to muck-type soil, and is highly resistant to wear and foot traffic. St. Augustine needs heavy watering, but it has fair drought resistance.

The most common types of St. Augustine used in Florida are hybrids of an older, seldom-used variety that gives today's grasses their hardiness.

Bitter Blue has dark, blue-green leaves that do well in shade. An improved variety, *Floratine*, has closer nodes at the beginning of each leaf blade.

Floratam is another good variety, developed by the University of Florida and Texas A&M. It is an extremely vigorous grass with larger inner nodes, and is resistant to SAD (St. Augustine decline) virus and chinch bugs. Floratam is not as shade-resistant as the other varieties and should not be planted in shady areas.

Another variety is *Seville*, which makes a beautiful, low carpet-like lawn. Seville often is sold in plug form rather than flats.

For greater cold-hardiness, the *Raleigh* variety of St. Augustine was developed for areas where temperatures drop to uncomfortable levels.

Unlike other grasses, St. Augustine does not grow from seed but from plugs or sod. It usually is sold in flats a yard square, which can be placed edge-to-edge to fill in the desired lawn area or cut into smaller squares and arranged in a checkerboard pattern to grow together to form the lawn. Once established, St. Augustine puts out vigorous growth in the form of long runners which can be cut off and replanted to fill in other areas. Do

Proper mowing helps protect the beauty and life of the lawn

De-thatching will help to improve growing conditions for thick, mature, St. Augustine lawns.

Tifway Bermuda

Seville St. Augustine

not make the mistake of mowing St. Augustine grass too low. Set your mower at three inches for most types, including Floratam. Dwarf types such as Seville must be kept at two inches. These heights are better for the health and growth of the grass, as well as for giving a lush, rich look to your lawn. While it is an aggressive, vigorous grower, St. Augustine does not tolerate heavy-traffic areas.

BERMUDA LAWNS

If St. Augustine is considered the most elegant of all the grasses, the true aristocrat would be *Bermuda*, a fine-bladed grass with a rich appearance, often used on golf course greens and fairways. A Bermuda lawn can be most spectacular but requires frequent mowing and a lot of care, plus frequent fertilizing, to maintain its deep, rich, green color. Planted from seed or sod, Bermuda is a vigorous grower and can take over flower beds or unwanted areas unless these are edged with some type of impenetrable border such as metal strips, wood or brick. In some parts of the world,

Bermuda lawn grass

Bermuda grass is known as "Devil grass" because of its tenacious growth habits. Once introduced into a garden, it is almost impossible to eradicate. This characteristic makes it a most desirable lawn grass, but it has to be kept under control. Bermuda can be cut very low, preferably with a reel-type mower. The best varieties for Florida are *Tifway* and *Ormond*.

ZOYSIA

Very similar in appearance to Bermuda is *Zoysia* grass, which has been advertised extensively in recent years by mail-order nurseries. An attractive grass, Zoysia is very slow-growing, taking as long as two years to cover a desired area. In Florida, it suffers very badly from nematode problems. Despite its ultimate good appearance, Zoysia is expensive and cannot compete with existing grasses. It requires heavy feeding. Zoysia adds up to higher initial cost, costly upkeep and debatable results in the long run. In Florida, *Emerald Zoysia* and *Mayer Zoysia* are preferred varieties. Many grasses are better buys, but if you do decide to plant Zoysia, buy your plugs locally and not through the mail. Zoysia can be started from sprigs, plugs or sod.

BAHIA

The most drought-tolerant grass available is *Bahia*, with two recommended varieties: *Argentine* and *Pensacola*. The Argentine, which is the more popular, is a flatter-growing grass without the long seed stalks typical of *Pensacola*. Both varieties can be started from seed or sod. *Argentine* mows into a very attractive lawn, but *Pensacola* will put out tall seed heads two or three days after mowing, giving the lawn an untidy appear-

Bahia, seeded out

Bahia, ready to plant

ance. Plant five to ten pounds of Bahia seed per thousand square feet of ground, tilling the seed in lightly. Scarified seeds, which are prepared for easier germination, will sprout faster and make a more successful lawn planting. Bahia grass is tough and looks better if cut with a rotary mower, though the blade will have to be very sharp. Bahia grass can dull a mower blade faster than most grasses.

CENTIPEDE

In northern Florida, *Centipede* grass is recommended. Its lack of salt tolerance makes it unsuitable for the coastal areas. Centipede looks like a dwarf St. Augustine. It needs ample moisture, though it can tolerate dry

Winter Rye Grass

spells. In high alkaline soils, it tends to look yellow, or iron-deficient, and it will brown out after a harsh winter. Plant Centipede grass in full sun, either from seed, at the rate of four ounces per thousand square feet, or from sprigs.

RYE GRASS

For winter color in any lawn, *Rye* is a good, temporary grass. Plant from seed (five pounds per thousand square feet) from October through November for a lush, rich, green spread until May, when it dies off. Rye grass must be fertilized in December and January and replanted every year.

PLANNING AND PREPARING YOUR LAWN

Putting in a lawn takes more than merely filling up the open spaces between trees, shrubs and flower beds. You have to determine how much of each open area gets full sun or partial sun and which is fully shaded all day. These factors are crucial in your choice of the type of grass to plant. Soil analysis also will help you choose a variety that will do well. For example, in south Florida, St. Augustine does best in a high pH soil while Bahia grass tends to turn yellow. The chart on page 265 can help you determine the best grass for your area of the state, and the conditions existing in your garden.

Weeds are like a red flag that signals you have a turf problem. If the pH of the soil is unbalanced, weeds are more likely to invade your property. Check your pH and make sure you have the proper balance for your type of grass. The presence of Spurge weed may indicate a nematode problem. Dead spots and brown patches may indicate that feeder roots have been damaged by mole crickets or fungus diseases. Lawns that have been thrown on top of old lawns without adequate sterilization often succumb to nematodes. Watering should also be checked: too much water can encourage Dollar weeds; too little water and the grass will weaken, allowing Beggar weed or Creeping Charlie to take over. Lawns that are overly compacted are also more susceptible to weed infestation. Again, a healthy lawn is the best defense against weeds; but if you have the problem, here are some tips for getting rid of these uninvited guests.

GRASSY WEEDS

Grassy weeds are the most difficult to control. It is hard to kill a grassy weed because of the possiblity of damaging the lawn. One control for grassy type weeds, however, is glyphosate, sold under the name of Round-Up or Kleen-Up. This material is non-selective, meaning that it kills any green plant it comes in contact with. It is translocated from the green leaf to the root system where it kills the plant.

Match Weed creeps into lawn grasses.

Dollar Weed, or Pennywort, thrives in wet areas, but can be killed out with a broadleaf spray.

False Dandelion, a broadleaf weed

One of the most obnoxious weeds is the sand bur. Not only does it stick you, but it is hard to remove from the skin. One way to pick up the sand bur seed is to use a broom covered with an old piece of burlap. Sweep this over the lawn, allowing the material to pick up the burs. When you have collected all the burs, you can simply throw the burlap away. Crab grass is another troublesome weed; to get rid of it completely you may have to dig it out by hand, but you can kill the weed with a local application of glyphosate.

BROADLEAF WEEDS

Clover is often very attractive with its tiny white flowers, but it is, nevertheless, a weed that can be treated in Bahia with 2,4-D or in St. Augustine lawns with Atrazine.

Creeping Beggar weed is sometimes called "stick tight." Its tiny jointed seed pods will stick to almost anything they touch. This wood vine weaves its way through your lawn. Repeated applications of 2,4-D or Atrazine should give control.

The Shamrock is a variety of the Oxalis weed. It is often sold in nurseries, but remember that the definition of a weed is a plant out of place. Having Yellow Wood Sorrels growing through your yard probably will not bring good luck. Repeated applications of Atrazine in St. Augustine or 2,4-D with Dicamba in Bahia should give control.

Dollar weed is sometimes called Pennywort. This round-leafed weed is attached to a stem in the center of the leaf. It grows in wet areas and can be controlled partly by reducing the amount of water. Spraying with Atrazine in St. Augustine and 2,4-D in Bahia will control the weed.

Chickweed tends to be a problem during the winter season. This vining weed is a succulent and prefers moist soil. Again, spraying with Atrazine in St. Augustine and 2,4-D in Bahia will control the weed..

TYPES OF WEED KILLERS FOR FLORIDA LAWNS

Selective weed killers are designed to kill the weed and not injure the lawn. Of these types, the most common are 2,4-D, or dicamba, which are considered hormone weed killers. They are often sold as Weedone, Weed-Be-Gone or just 2,4-D. 2,4-D can be very damaging to tomato plants, poinsettias and papayas. Spraying should be done on a day with little or no wind. Most weed killers are more effective when the weeds are young, tender and actively growing. It is better to use a light application more than once than to spray heavily and risk burning the surrounding grass. Atrazine is a good herbicide to use on St. Augustine. Use caution when applying, and, as with any herbicide use according to label directions. Atrazine is sometimes sold under the trade name Purge. It is different from most herbicides in that it gives you some pre-emergent weed control, which stops the germination of weed seeds. Some of the common brand names for pre-emergents are Balan, Dacthal, Balfin and Atrazine.

Non-selective herbicides, such as glyphosate, will kill any plant they come into contact with. This chemical is absorbed through green foliage. Cacodylic acid is also absorbed through the foliage. It differs from glyphosate in that it burns the foliage back and does not have the long-lasting or deep effectiveness.

MR. GREEN THUMB RULE

Never use a sprayer for weed killer and then reuse it for insecticides or fungicides. Mark the weed-killer sprayer for WEED KILLER ONLY! Even thorough washing may not get rid of these potent chemicals, so don't risk contamination. Each chemical has its own special purpose; use them all accordingly.

MOWERS AND MOWING

Many gardeners spend considerable money, time and effort on putting in a lawn, then attack it with a mower that does little more than lacerate the grass instead of cutting it. Then they wonder why the turf deteriorates after a few weeks with rough brown tips to the leaves.

Every lawn deserves care and consideration when it is being mowed, just as attention should be given the type of mower being used and its condition.

Mowers come in two types: rotary and reel. The rotary mower is the more widely used because of its versatility. The rotating blade can cut not only grass, but small shrubs and vines. It can be used to level wild ground before tilling, as the blade is, in actuality, a lethal weapon that slices off almost anything in its path. Despite warnings, many people lose fingers and toes that foolishly have found their way beneath the protective housing. Rotary mowers also will hurl debris, stones and small twigs at frightening speed from the chute, a potential danger that has caused serious

WAYS TO KEEP WEEDS IN CHECK

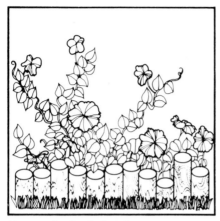

Preservative-treated posts

Weed killer spray

Bark or gravel mulches

Brick

injury to people and pets. When mowing with a rotary mower, always check the surface of the lawn for foreign objects and remove them before mowing is being done.

Rotary mowers often have an attachable bag fastened to the chute to collect the clippings. But letting the cut grass sink back into the sod is good for the soil. It provides natural nourishment to supplement applied fertilizers.

A lawn need not consist of one variety only. For example, St. Augustine may well fill any large, shady areas, but you still can plant Bermuda in portions that receive full sun. As a general rule, plant the grass best suited to the soil and sun/shade ratio in the various areas of your property. Remember, no grass will grow in dense shade.

Before you begin building your lawn, determine the pH of the soil. The pH will have a bearing upon your choice of grass and whether you will need to add chemicals.

Next, rotor-till the soil to a depth of six or eight inches. Apply Florida, Canadian or Michigan peat three inches thick over the surface, together with 10-20-10 fertilizer, which is high in phosphorus to promote root growth. Rotor-till again to blend the peat and fertilizer into the soil, turning this over to a depth of six inches. Rake and smooth soil, removing any debris, roots or stones. If this intended lawn area adjoins your home, slope the soil gently away from the house to ensure good drainage. This need not be a perceptible incline, which might spoil the aesthetics of your lawn. But the grade should be enough to allow water to drain off and not lay stagnant after a heavy rain. Poorly drained lawns soon develop disease and root rot.

HOW TO PREPARE A PROPER LAWN

Step 1: Determine the pH of the soil, which will be an important factor in the selection of your lawn.

Step 2: Evaluate the amount of light your lawn will receive. If you have dense shade your choice may be St. Augustine. For a bright sunny area where watering may be less frequent, Bahia is a possible choice.

Step 3: Add Florida, Canadian or Michigan peat. Till this in to a depth of six inches. The peat should be 2 to 3 inches thick over the surface area. Also, till in a 10-10-10 or 20-10-10 fertilizer, one high in phosphorus to promote good growth.

Step 4: Roll or rake the soil smooth, going as close to the final grade as possible.

Step 5: Decide which process you want for putting in your lawn, such as seeding, sodding (the easiest way), sprigging or plugging.

SEEDING

Seeding is the way most people from the North are used to starting their lawns. It can be done here, but not as quickly or with the same success. Our sandy soils dry out rapidly. Seeds must be kept moist, if any success is expected. A sprinkler system is almost a necessity when seeding.

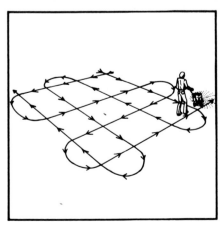

Sow seed and spread fertilizer by applying half in a north-south direction and half in an east-west direction, or lengthwise then crosswise over the entire lawn.

Checkerboard sod plugs across the lawn area for best coverage and spreading potential.

SODDING

Sodding is the easiest way to an instant lawn, but it is also the most expensive. Sod should be laid on the final grade, on an evenly raked surface. One piece of sod should butt up against the next piece. Rolling is desirable for an even turf. You will need frequent waterings until the root base is established.

SPRIGGING

Sprigging is a time-consuming method for starting a lawn. The sprigs must be kept moist, like seeds, or they will die. A sprig is one strand of grass that has nodes, leaves and roots. Commercially, some sod farms have large tractors called sprig spreaders. The workers use this equipment to chop up sprigs, spread them over the sod field and roll it level. Then they apply water on a daily basis and produce sod. Many people do not cover their sprigs deep enough with soil; consequently, they don't often get the quality lawns the commercial growers produce. For the average homeowner, plugging or sodding is generally a more efficient method.

PLUGGING

Plugging is another relatively easy way to start your lawn. Plugs are normally sold in 2- to 4-inch squares which are planted 12 to 18 inches apart. Often a checkerboard pattern is used.

Step 6: Water ... Water ... Water ...

WATER: THE KEY TO A GOOD LAWN

Some people only water their lawns during drought periods, and some won't water for some time after it has rained, thinking the rain took care of it. Lawns use an abundance of water, especially during the warm, humid season. As discussed in Chapter 1, water is one of the most important

Open cans, such as tuna cans, can be used as rain gauges to check the amount of water reaching the lawn. As a basic standard, each watering should deliver from one-half inch to an inch of water to the lawn.

factors in growing plants of any kind. Lawn grasses are constantly giving off moisture; it is part of their respiration process. That moisture has to be replaced, which means your lawn will need either frequent rain or frequent deep watering. Watering is, of course, the most reliable means. The average lawn grass will be up to 85% water. This high percentage should help us realize how important water is to a healthy lawn.

WHEN TO WATER

Whatever watering system you use, check to make sure you are getting adequate coverage. Sprinkler systems are designed to overlap and to avoid leaving brown spots, but even the best sometimes miss a few patches. Check out your system and find ways to compensate. A healthy lawn will demand a reliable deep-watering system.

Your lawn will get some additional moisture from rain, normal condensation and even morning dew; but you can't really rely on these. Nor can you rely on occasional short waterings. It is better to water once or twice a week with ½ to 1 inch per application than to sprinkle lightly every day. This develops a stronger and deeper root system as opposed to a shallow one. After watering for 15 minutes, I check the level of water in a tuna can sitting on my lawn. By multiplying the amount by 4, I have a good idea how many inches per hour my sprinkler system is putting out.

By and large, the best time to water is in the early morning when the temperature is moderate and the water can do the most good. However, if this time is a problem, afternoon or mid-day waterings are better than no watering at all.

LAWN CARE AND FEEDING

Many gardeners are under the impression that normal condensation, occasional rain or early-morning dew is sufficient moisture for a lawn. Not so! Without adequate watering, any plant will die. But a lawn is too great an investment of time, labor and money to lose through infrequent or insufficient watering.

Your grass also will need feeding — not merely to promote health but to help it choke out weeds that inevitably invade any lawn. Healthy grass will fight for its own space in the ground, and this battle should be reinforced with fertilizer to enable the grass to hold its own. Many horticulturists believe in fertilizing only once or twice a year. But more frequent, lighter fertilizings seem to be the secret to continuing the good growth of turf.

Two very efficient methods will distribute granular fertilizer over a lawn. The first method is the drop spreader. It must be pushed back and forth across the lawn in parallel paths until the entire turf is covered. Set the spreader according to the recommendations on the bag of fertilizer. This will ensure that the proper amount of fertilizer is dispensed. The second mechanical means is the rotary spreader, which broadcasts fertilizer granules over a wider area than the drop spreader and provides good coverage with less chance of missing any sections of the lawn.

A method of fertilizing that has become quite popular in recent years involves adding a liquid fertilizer dispenser to the hose line leading to your sprinkler. This is very reliable and provides an easy way to water and fertilize lightly at the same time.

All lawns need NPK — nitrogen, phosphorus and potassium — but other minor elements, such as iron, also are advisable for optimum turf growth. Check the label on your fertilizer to make sure you are feeding your lawn all the elements needed for the best results.

Fertilizing, adequate watering and a good soil base usually will ensure a good lawn. But a weed-free lawn seldom is achieved without taking additional steps to kill and keep out unwanted growth. Weeds are more likely to invade a lawn if the pH balance is not right for the type of grass you are growing. And too much water tends to encourage Dollar weeds, while too little moisture allows Beggar weed or Creeping Charlie to take over. If the soil is heavily compacted, your lawn will be more susceptible to weed infestation.

The blades on a rotary mower should be kept sharp. Next to nematodes and insect infestation, a dull blade is probably the most common killer of lawns. Mowing is meant to cut grass evenly and smoothly, not beat it to death. Professional gardeners sharpen their mower blades daily. But once a month during mowing season should be sufficient for the average home owner. Otherwise, sharpen every two or three months, depending on the amount of mowing being done.

LAWNMOWER MAINTENANCE

Sharpening a mower blade is relatively simple, with a file or a grinder. Be sure to take off equal amounts of metal on both sides of the blade to maintain proper balance. As a safety precaution, always disconnect the spark plug before working on a mower. An accidental start or a sudden release of compression can throw the blade into motion, causing serious injury. For foolproof safety, the spark plug can be removed totally to ensure the motor does not start.

Standard maintenance on a mower includes checking and changing the oil, the spark plug and, if needed, the air filter. Generally, a full crankcase of oil will last a season, but like your automobile, your mower will operate at peak performance only if the oil is clean. Replacing a worn spark plug will eliminate difficult starts and conserve gasoline. The air filter seldom needs replacing, but it does require regular cleaning. Squeezing a warm solution of detergent through the filter will remove most dirt. Before replacing, dry the filter between layers of paper towels, then spray with WD-40 or a similar thin lubricant, which will improve the filter's capability to trap dust particles. Before putting up the mower for the winter, be sure to drain the gasoline from the fuel tank. If left standing over long periods, gasoline tends to separate, producing a gummy residue that will clog the fuel line. After every use, hose the underside of the mower to remove finely packed grass clippings from the housing, as well as any impacted soil. Allow the motor to cool before this washing, otherwise the cold water from the hose may crack the engine block. Occasional oiling of the wheels and crankshaft also will help maintain your mower in peak condition for years of good service.

ALTERNATE MOWER TYPES

The reel mower was popular years ago before the rotary mower was invented. Still used for certain applications, the reel mower has one basic advantage: for tender-leaved grass such as Bermuda and Zoysia, a reel mower does the best job. Its mechanism actually *cuts* the grass in the same way scissors cut, rather than *slicing* the grass off, which is what a rotary mower does. For reel mowers equipped with gasoline motors, the maintenance tips given above will apply. A manual reel-type mower does require a little more muscle, because in addition to pushing it across the lawn, you are producing the power to turn the wheels, which in turn rotate the blades.

Unless you have a relatively small expanse of lawn consisting of Bermuda or Zoysia, a rotary mower is the better investment.

Reel mowers are best for fine grasses such as Bermuda or Zoysia.

For small lawns, some people prefer an electric mower, which is a rotary type, powered by electricity rather than a gasoline motor. Electric mowers are somewhat quieter and give off no fumes. But they do require a very long extension cord, and that demands careful planning of your mowing pattern to avoid running over the cord.

The height at which you should set your mower depends upon the type of grass you have. St. Augustine should be kept at three inches and the dwarf variety at two inches. Bermuda and Zoysia look best when cut to two inches, as do most other lawn grasses.

After you have planted a lawn, allow it to grow fairly high before mowing, then mow once at a setting of about five or six inches. Then make another pass to cut it down to the final, desired height. Place your mower on level concrete to make the height adjustment, measuring from the blade to the ground for accuracy. Never try to mow very high grass down to two inches as this may result in damage to the grass. Mowing grass is like having a haircut at the barber: gradual shortening will achieve the desired results better than a heavy-handed attack!

SOD CUTTING AND THATCHING

To remove old sod, you can rent a sod cutter. Set the depth at two inches and move the machine in parallel lines in order to scoop out the soil evenly. A sod cutter is a great time-saver over digging up old sod by hand, and it is neater.

Thatching is not the undesirable condition some gardeners believe, because this layering of lawn clippings can create a natural foundation over which new growth can flourish. Thatch also allows a cultivated lawn to grow over and replace an older lawn or other grasses, as often happens with St. Augustine and Bermuda. And thatch is a vital element for providing a solid base for a lawn, for walking or for mowing. Without a solid thatch base, it is difficult to run a mower across a lawn.

However, thatch sometimes can become too thick and compact, providing a breeding ground for insects and disease. When this occurs, you need to loosen the thatch and remove some of it to allow air and moisture to circulate down to the soil.

You can rent a verti-cutter, which should be set at a half-inch into the soil, allowing the teeth to reach down into the thatch and pull it out without damaging the lawn itself. A power rake is another method of dethatching Bahia lawns. It slices through the layers of rhizomes and stolons, allowing air and water to flow through. However, a power rake is liable to remove almost one-third of your grass, and using one is, quite truthfully, a major job for the average gardener. Many home owners hire a professional landscape company to handle dethatching.

COMMON LAWN PROBLEMS IN FLORIDA

Contrary to popular belief, a general-purpose insecticide is *not* the total answer to the varied problems that can affect lawns in Florida. Certainly it will help, just as Malathion and Diazinon will take care of the majority of insect pests that affect flowers and vegetables. But proper diagnosis of any condition is the key to learning the cause and the cure.

A wise gardener gives his lawn a regular checkup and takes notes of anything that appears out of order, such as dry-looking areas, brown patches, poor growth and unhealthy turf. You must take into consideration the type of grass in which any unwanted condition is present. Is your Bermuda fading away while the St. Augustine is flourishing? Has the Bahia lost its fresh, sparkling-green appearance? Is the Zoysia simply not spreading?

Note *where* the problem exists — in sun or in shade? Is the unusual patch circular? Does it perhaps follow a clearly defined line through the turf?

Often, an odd-looking section denotes a simple lack of water. Perhaps your sprinkler system heads are clogged and not dispensing water properly. You may have spilled some gasoline on the grass when refilling your mower. Gasoline and oil will affect grass very quickly, causing a growth setback and poor appearance. A handful of granular fertilizer carelessly dropped similarly will burn out a patch of grass.

Check for insects by parting the grass and examining the soil. Look for raised tunnels or trails, or a yellow, mottled look that usually follows an attack by juice-sucking insects. A distinctive patch of dead grass two to three feet in diameter can indicate a fungus infection.

Once you have found the problem, you can go about diagnosing the cause. Do not allow any unusual condition to persist, thinking that it will go away. Uncontrolled insects or disease can wipe out an entire lawn in a single season. For this reason, a regular program of insect and disease control is a valuable insurance policy against loss of your total investment in your lawn.

If you are uncertain as to the cause and what to do, consult your nurseryman. He can recognize and prescribe suitable treatment.

The following are the problems that most often afflict lawns in Florida:

Sod webworms — No lawn is safe from these predators. Watch for large moths at dusk, usually one half to three quarters of an inch long, fluttering about the grass, then disappearing into the turf. The moths lay tiny eggs,

Sod Webworms are a serious threat to any Florida lawn but can be controlled easily with regular spraying.

Grubs will destroy root systems in short order if left unchecked.

evidenced by fine webbing over the turf. The webbing is best seen in the early morning when the dew is still present. Unchecked, these eggs hatch into tiny worms that chew the grass steadily, destroying the turf. During the day, the worms stay curled up under the thatch. Quick and easy control of sod webworms is possible by spraying with Dipel, Thuricide, Diazinon, Dursban or Sevin.

White grubworms — Like sod webworms, white grubworms attack all grasses, eating away at the root system, sometimes so severely (especially with St. Augustine) that the turf is left like a loose carpet on the ground. To check for white grubworms, cut a one-foot square of sod a few inches deep, lift it up and check the root system. If present, the grubs will stand out starkly against the soil, curled up in thick, white little balls, about an inch to an inch and a half long and a half inch wide. Dangerous as they can become, white grubworms can be controlled by thoroughly drenching the soil with Diazinon, Dursban or Spectracide. Apply the granular insecticide, followed by a deep watering. Control is most effective when applied about six weeks after the main emergence of June beetles, which appear after the grubs have pupated. Regular annual application will help keep your lawn free of these pests, which are most evident in spring and fall.

Armyworms — Laying from fifty to a hundred eggs at a time, the armyworm moth is another plague that attacks all types of grasses. Upon hatching, the worms start eating the grass, crawling across the lawn somewhat like an army — hence the name. Armyworms are very heavy feeders and, if not checked, can completely destroy a lawn. Spray with Diazinon, Dursban, Sevin, Dipel or Thuricide for good control.

Mole Crickets — A major cause of damage to Bahia and Bermuda lawns, the mole cricket is easily detectable by its tunnel trails on the soil surface: raised mounds about a half-inch high, spreading in all directions. A soft sponginess, along with five-inch-wide holes, are another indication of mole crickets. This annoying pest can be controlled by spraying with Dursban, Diazinon or Baygon. Oftonal, formerly only used by professional extermi-

Mole Crickets

nators, is now available for home owners and provides a longer residual effect than other products. Both Oftonal and Mocap are used by certified pest control operators. Both these insecticides have an offensive odor. Special masks, boots and gloves usually are worn by the professionals when they apply these toxic insecticides.

One preventive measure that can be taken safely by any gardener is to sprinkle mole cricket bait throughout the lawn in May through late August. Use mole cricket bait *after* you have watered the lawn thoroughly. Watering (or an unexpected rain shower) will diminish its effectiveness.

Chinch bugs — Chinch bugs are the primary problem with St. Augustine grass. These tiny, heat-loving insects attack the leaves and stems, sucking the life fluids from the grass, which then turns yellowish-brown and looks as though it has been burned. Chinch bugs can be detected in the hottest parts of the lawn and along sidewalks and patios. Spray with Diazinon, Spectricide, Dursban, Ethion, Aspon or Baygon.

Chinch Bug damage in a once-healthy lawn

PLANNING AND PREPARING YOUR LAWN

Putting in a lawn takes more than merely filling up the open spaces between trees, shrubs and flower beds. You have to determine how much of each open area gets full sun or partial sun and which is fully shaded all day. These factors are crucial in your choice of the type of grass to plant. Soil analysis also will help you choose a variety that will do well. For example, in south Florida, St. Augustine does best in a high pH soil while Bahia grass tends to turn yellow. The following chart can help you determine the best grass for your area of the state, and the conditions existing in your garden:

VARIETY OF GRASS	BEST AREA			SUN	SHADE	SALT-TOLERANT		COMMENTS
	NORTH	CENTRAL	SOUTH			YES	NO	
St. Augustine	X	X	X	X	X	X		Does best in wet salt-free areas
Bermuda	X	X	X	X		X		Dies without ample sun. Needs wet, salt-free soil
Zoysia	X	X	X	X	Partial Shade		X	
Bahia		X		X			X	Does not thrive in shade
Centipede	X						X	

CHAPTER THIRTEEN

Houseplants

For centuries, man has brought plants indoors to brighten his home and add year 'round color. But there are *no* house plants, in reality. Anything grown indoors has its origins in nature. For this reason, the indoor gardener should try to duplicate as closely as possible the conditions under which plants grow in their outdoor environment. Water, light and soil are as important in the home as they are in the garden, because all plants rely on these elements for nourishment, growth and healthy foliage and flowers.

Many people are misled by the lush appearance of house plants in stores and florist shops, not realizing that the healthy condition comes from ideal greenhouse environment, proper feeding and the right amount of light. These folks buy a plant, take it home and then wonder why it droops, yellows and dies after a few weeks. They blame the store when *they* are to blame for not taking proper care of the plant. You must discover the specific needs of every plant grown indoors. Some need more sun than others. Many can survive with a cup of water once a week; others need daily watering. Each house plant has individual requirements. You cannot expect any plant to flourish when it is dumped in a corner and neglected. Take care of your plants as you would any member of your household. Check them daily, testing the soil with your finger to make sure there is sufficient moisture, and position them so they receive enough direct or filtered sunlight.

The more common types of indoor plants, such as ivy, can be bought at supermarkets and dime stores. But for more esoteric varieties, go to a reputable garden shop where you can get advice and instructions on establishing the proper conditions for continued growth and healthy appearance.

Knowledge is power — and learning all you can about the plants in your home will give you the capacity to keep your indoor garden in the best possible shape.

Indoor plants are not immune to disease and insect problems. A rich, sterile potting soil is the only guarantee of avoiding such hazards from the outset. Never use soil from your garden for indoor plantings, because you run the risk of bringing in fungal disease and insects. If you notice a plant

For indoor plants, always start with a good quality sterile potting soil.

showing symptoms of wilting or poor growth, it may be infected and will need treatment just like outdoor plants.

One of the biggest mistakes made by indoor gardeners is over-watering. Many plants should be allowed to dry out between waterings; others need light daily watering. Knowing what a particular plant needs will enable you to gauge the amount and frequency of water.

SOIL FOR INDOOR PLANTS

Good commercial soil mixes are available at a garden shop. Most are sterilized and adaptable for indoor gardening needs. Soil is the basic material in which every plant has to grow, but certain additives are useful in adapting soil for certain plants or for a particular purpose. These include:

Vermiculite: A very light, mica-like mineral which has been expanded by extremely high heat. Its porosity allows it to hold water like a sponge, and it also improves the drainage of heavy soils. A sterile medium, it can be used to start seeds or root cuttings.

Perlite: A white, sterile medium which has been produced from the heat explosion of volcanic rock. Its rough edges will hold water, though not as long as vermiculite. Perlite is recommended as a good addition to a soil mix for plants that prefer to be kept on the dry side. Perlite is a good rooting medium for succulent stems that tend to rot if given too much moisture.

Sand: Finely ground particles of stone, mostly quartz. Coast sand will improve the drainage of any soil and is a necessary component of a soil mix for growing cactus. Sand also is one of the best mediums for rooting clippings.

Leaf Mold: Partially decayed leaves, usually oak leaves. Leaf mold improves the quality and fertility of any soil and is one of the best sources of organic material.

Humus: Decayed vegetation that aids in the soil's ability to absorb water. Humus also improves the quality and fertility of soil.

Peat Moss: The decomposing remains of plants. Sphagnum peat moss is by far the best type of peat, since it resists further decomposition. Peat has good water-retaining properties and helps lighten soil texture.

FERTILIZING INDOOR PLANTS

No aspect of gardening is more misunderstood than fertilizing. Most people presume that a sick-looking plant needs feeding. Actually, lack of plant food seldom is the cause. More often than not, problems with indoor plants stem from inadequate light, improper watering or an insect or disease that has attacked the plant.

Many good house plant fertilizers are on the market. Two of them — Peters and Nutri-sol — are excellent both for indoor and outdoor plants.

Plants that actively grow during spring and summer will benefit from a monthly feeding. Fertilization should be discontinued or lessened during winter, when many plants slow down and even become dormant.

It can be confusing to examine the great variety of plant foods available: powders, liquids and tablets; fast-release and slow-release compounds; organic and inorganic nutrients; fertilizers to be used only once a month; others to be given with each watering. The best method is to follow the directions for each particular plant and feed accordingly rather than to fertilize everything you have. The only exception to this would be to add a little Nutri-sol every time you water, thereby ensuring your plants not only get moisture but a little "shot in the arm" as well. However, major feeding should only be done at the recommended intervals for each plant.

Choice of fertilizer *is* important, however, with acid-loving plants such as azaleas, gardenias, camellias and all citrus plants. Select an acid-type fertilizer from your garden shop for use with these plants.

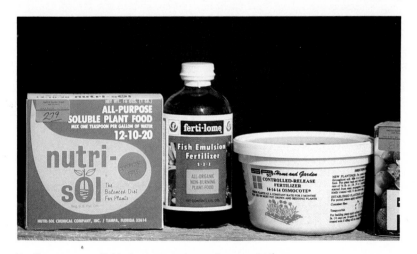

Fertilizers are available in many types and concentrations.

INDOOR PLANT DISEASE AND PEST PROBLEMS

Warm temperatures and low humidity are the general rule in a house, and these conditions are ideal for many pests that plague indoor plants. Without the presence of their natural enemies, insect pests can multiply rapidly and destroy a plant quickly. For the indoor gardener, therefore, pest control is a continuing process.

Before adding a new plant to your indoor garden, it should be isolated for a two-week period — put in quarantine. Check the underside of the leaves thoroughly for any signs of insects. The younger leaves at the growing tips of plants are especially vulnerable to attack. If you find no trace of insect infestation, place your new plant with the rest of your indoor garden, but still maintain a watchful eye. Prevention is the best possible method of pest control, because once insects or disease get a hold, it is often a losing battle to try to cure the condition.

For example: a chemical spray is effective in controlling the adult fungus gnat, but there are six other stages in the gnat's life cycle which may not be affected at all. It would take over a month of proper spraying to eradicate this pest completely, using an insecticide that only kills the adult. Consult a garden shop for the proper compounds to use to handle *all* stages of insects as they develop among your plants.

The most common indoor plant insect problems include:

Fungus gnat: Generally considered harmless, the fungus gnat is a familiar indoor plant pest. With black bodies and grayish-brown abdomens, the adult gnats are smaller than fruit flies, for which they are sometimes mistaken. The female lays from a hundred to three hundred eggs in the soil. At the usual household temperature of 72 degrees, the eggs hatch in only four days. Th emerging maggot feeds on the root hairs of young seedlings. The larvae are seen easily when the plant is watered. They look like white "bugs" floating on the surface. A severe fungus gnat infestation will cause a plant to droop and look unhealthy with yellowing leaves. The plant also will get root rot because of the damaged root hairs. Fungus gnat is a sure sign of over-watering. Use only sterile soil, and if you notice a fungus gnat infestation, spray weekly to control the adults. Use a soil insecticide to destroy the larvae.

White Flies: These are some of the most difficult of all indoor pests. Brushing the leaves of an infected plant will send these small insects scattering. White flies lay their eggs on the underside of leaves. The larvae feed on plant sap, causing leaves to turn yellow. If unchecked, white flies eventually will kill a plant. Control of white flies is not easy, but it can be done by scraping the eggs from the underside of leaves with your finger and thumb and washing the leaves with a mild solution of warm water and household detergent, followed by spraying every four days. Undersides of leaves should be checked often for evidence of eggs, larvae or adult white fly.

Red-Spider Mite: Although red-spider mites are hard to see with the naked eye, the damage caused by them is very obvious. Yellow or brown speckles on new foliage indicate an infestation. So do fine webs on the leaves, especially on the undersides. An infested plant slowly will stop growing and die. Treat in the same manner as for white flies, described above. If a plant is severely infected, it is often wiser to discard the plant, to avoid the red-spider mites infecting other indoor plants.

Mealy Bug: This insect resembles a small cluster of cotton. Attacking all parts of a plant, mealy bugs usually are found in leaf axils. Mealy bugs suck sap, eventually killing the plant. They are especially fond of cacti and succulents. To kill individual bugs, take a swab of cotton or a Q-tip, dip it into rubbing alcohol and touch the mealy bug. Next, spray with an outdoor insecticide — a fine, enveloping spray from about eighteen inches away from the plant — and follow up the next day with a total washing of the plant. Use warm water and a mild household detergent. Quarantine the plant for several weeks after treatment to ensure the problem does not reoccur.

Scale: Scale insects are the most annoying of all household plant pests, because they often go unnoticed until the infestation has become severe. Overall yellowing or yellowing in circular spots can be clues to these insects, which appear as brown blisters or white scales. Spraying is ineffective; the insects have hard shells. Washing with warm water plus detergent can help, but in many cases, it may be necessary to destroy plants infected with scale. Regularly washing your plants with warm water and detergent can serve as a preventive measure against scale, as well as many other plant problems.

Aphids: Although aphids are the most common insect problem, they are the easiest to handle. Adult aphids are green in color and large enough to be seen easily and removed by hand. Aphids reproduce rapidly and quickly can disfigure a plant if allowed to breed unchecked. Any indoor plant spray will destroy aphids effectively.

Plant Diseases

Fortunately, few diseases cause indoor plants major problems. Using a systemic fungicide usually takes care of most fungi. But many problems such as *Rhizoctonia, Pythium* and *Phythophthora* (which cause root and stem rot) usually are the result of improper watering and cause "damping off" in seedlings.

LIGHTING CONDITIONS FOR INDOOR PLANTS

There is a difference between an indoor plant *surviving* and *thriving*, a factor that can be traced directly to the amount of light it receives. Plants that demand a sunny location should be placed where they get the maximum amount of light entering the room, preferably near a window with southern or western exposure. For plants needing filtered light, an east window is preferred, though light filtering through sheer drapes against a south window is acceptable. If a plant is described as tolerating low light conditions, it will continue to grow in any room where there is a natural light source, including a northern exposure window.

If natural light is limited in a room, you might want to install sup-

Begonias are among the best and most colorful plants for hanging baskets.

plemental electric lights such as "grow-lamps." These valuable light sources come in round or tubular forms and provide the ultraviolet light essential for good plant growth and health. While these lamps do give out a light that is harsh on the eyes and aesthetically unappealing, they can be turned on during periods when a room is not being used. Many indoor gardeners switch on their grow-lamps after their families have gone to bed, giving plants six to eight hours of artificial sunshine while everyone else is asleep.

If plants are placed near a window, you may need to turn their pots every few days to maintain straight, upright growth. Plants bend naturally towards their light source. This is why many indoor plants bend towards a window, causing disfigured stems and an unbalanced look.

The most desirable light levels will vary from one plant to the next. But all plants *must* have light to complete the process of photosynthesis, which enables them to take in sufficient nutrients for growth. Matching the right plant to the light level is very important. Hardy, light-loving plants will favor an east window. Plants thriving in partial shade will do well by a north window. Check with your garden shop on the light needs of any plant you decide to purchase.

DIFFERENT TYPES OF INDOOR PLANTS

Hanging Baskets

Hanging baskets provide interesting focal points in any room decor. Plants suspended in the air always seem to hold a greater appeal than those merely placed on a shelf or on a coffee table. For plants with long, trailing vines, a hanging basket is the only practical way to give near-natural conditions for growth.

Many people place hanging baskets in stairwells, but no plant will survive in an area without windows, unless it receives fourteen to sixteen hours of artificial light daily.

As a general rule, one two-inch, pot-size plant can be used for every two inches of basket diameter. Three plants of this size could fill a six-inch-diameter basket, with four plants to an eight-inch basket, and so on. Hanging wire baskets are very popular but should only be used outdoors where dripping does not constitute a problem. Indoor baskets should be plastic with attached saucers to catch excess water draining through. Do not use ceramic baskets. They lack drain holes in the bottom.

Here are five easy steps for making a moss-lined hanging basket:

1. Pack moistened, long-fibered sphagnum moss tightly against the sides of the basket.
2. Mix equal parts of loam, vermiculite and peat moss and fill the basket to within one inch of the top.
3. Pot your plants in the basket — as many as the size will take.
4. If the basket is wire, hang it in a suitable spot from a tree, making sure that light filters through in sufficient quantity. If the basket is plastic, hang it in any desired spot where it will get enough light from a nearby window or grow-light suspended above it.
5. Check the moisture content daily. Indoor baskets may need only weekly watering, but outdoors, you may need to water twice a day during the heat of summer.

Hanging baskets are very attractive, and ideal for displaying asparagus fern, English baby tears, ivy and pothos, as well as the very popular airplane plants and piggyback plants.

FERNS AND FOLIAGE PLANTS

From the elegant stateliness of the Australian tree fern to the dainty maidenhair, ferns are unrivaled in variation and versatility. They do not flower, but the delicacy of their foliage is more than sufficiently attractive.

Most ferns are not difficult to grow, but the low humidity in most houses in winter can create a problem. Ferns then require daily misting with distilled water. A dry atmosphere also may encourage mealy bug and scale, which has to be treated manually because many ferns are too sensitive to stand chemical sprays.

Apart from true ferns, there are popular fern-like plants, such as the asparagus fern, the peacock ferns and the "air-fern," which is really not a plant at all, but the dyed skeletal remains of a moss animal living in the sea.

Indoor and outdoor Ferns add a special touch to the home.

The Bird's Nest Fern grows well inside and outside with good soil and regular misting.

Like ferns, foliage plants are grown for their attractive leaves. Although these plants bloom, their flowering indoors is rare or insignificant. These various species are used as indoor trees, in dish gardens and terrariums, and are especially attractive when combined with other indoor plants to form a lush, miniature jungle.

CACTI AND SUCCULENTS

Cacti and other succulents are a most intriguing group of plants. In addition to their unique appearance, they can produce some of the showiest and most unusual flowers. This group can withstand extreme climatic conditions and, as a result, are ideal for indoor use. If their basic needs are met, these plants can grow indefinitely.

Contrary to popular belief, cacti do not grow in sand. Their native soils usually are quite rich in organic matter, and these plants only fail to produce lush vegetation because of lack of water. A cactus soil should contain 25 percent decayed leaf mold and humus, 25 percent loam and 50 percent coarse sand.

Cacti for dish gardens

Cacti not only need organic matter to grow in, but they also need water. Outdoors, you must water them twice a week, but brought indoors, a cactus needs water only every two weeks. Make sure your soil mixture is light and airy. A heavy soil that remains too moist can cause a succulent to rot. Most insects do not constitute a problem for cacti, except mealybugs, which should be treated by touching them with a cotton swab dipped in rubbing alcohol. Do not use Malathion or other strong insecticides. These will damage cacti.

Cacti and succulents can be propagated from cuttings. Slice a stem off with a sharp knife, allow it to dry for several days, then place it in sand to root.

While lacking the lush foliage of other plants, cacti are an interesting variation in an indoor garden and are not to be overlooked when planning your selection of plants.

FLOWERING AND COLORFUL FOLIAGE PLANTS

Chrysanthemums, lilies, azaleas and poinsettias often are thought of as indoor plants as well as outdoor plants. But any potted specimen of these plants did not get that way in a house — rather, in a *greenhouse*! They give a house a welcome splash of holiday color, but these flowering plants do not survive well indoors. When their blossoms fade, move the plant outdoors and sink it into your flower bed for further growth.

True indoor flowering or foliage plants include a fairly wide variety, from crotons with their variegated leaves, to orchids with their breathtaking blooms. African violets, of course, are an old standby that have the unique advantage of being able to bloom under artificial light. Plants with variegated foliage require more light than all-green plants.

276   The following is a selection of some of the more popular indoor plants grown in Florida:

Aluminum Plant

This attractive plant grows from eight to 24 inches high, with silver, waffled leaves. Tolerates medium to high light levels.

Aralia

A large plant, Aralia grows as high as 20 feet outdoors, but normally grows five to eight feet indoors. This plant branches freely and has bright green leaves, some with white borders.

Asparagus sprengeri — Asparagus Fern

Not a true fern, this plant is a member of the lily family. The Plumosus variety has very delicate leaves and reaches a height of six feet. For a hanging basket, use the Springeri variety. It likes rich soil and filtered sun. Low-light conditions will cause the needle-like leaves to drop.

Begonia

Begonias offer dark, flat, green leaves and a variety of shapes and colors in the flowers. They need bright light to maintain their rich leaf color. Some of the thousands of varieties, such as the Rex Begonia, have marbled red and greenish-white leaves. It is truly a rewarding houseplant with its colorful blossoms and lush appearance.

The Asparagus Fern creates a colorful display

Nephrolepsis exaltata bostoniensis — Boston Fern

The Boston fern needs high light levels. It is the most common of the many ferns available. In a hanging basket, it can fill out to an impressive size, with long, drooping leaves. It needs protection against temperatures below fifty degrees. A similar and very popular variety is the Fluffy Ruffle fern. The Boston fern does best in rich, moist soil.

Bromeliads

Grown epiphytic (in air) or terrestrial (in soil), these spiny plants reach two to three feet tall, with beautiful multi-colored, spiked flowers on bracts similar to the poinsettia. The pineapple is a bromeliad. So is Spanish moss. The most common variety grown in Florida is the Billbergia. Another member of this family is the Aechmeas, which grows to three feet with spiny leaves and brightly colored bracts that bloom most of the spring and winter. Most bromeliads respond well to liquid fertilizer and to water held inside the cups of the plant.

Aspidistra elatior — Cast Iron Plant

This hardy plant thrives almost anywhere indoors, including dark corners, and is unaffected by drafts and low temperatures. Often seen in shady gardens outdoors in Florida, it does well inside the house, where its paddle-shaped leaves form a dramatic arrangement that can complement any decor. The leaves often are used in floral arrangements.

Codiaeum Variegratum — Croton

Used indoors and out in central and south Florida, crotons have variegated leaves in red, yellow and brown. Like all plants with multicolored foliage, the croton needs plenty of light to maintain its rich colors. *Caution:* Croton leaves are toxic.

Crotons are well-adapted to the indoor environment but need plenty of sunshine.

Dieffenbachia is an all-time favorite indoors, partly because it thrives with little attention.

Cryptanthus

Cryptanthus is one of the smallest bromeliads. This plant grows from a few inches high to 12 inches with some varieties. It is often used in dish gardens because of its multi-colored, multi-patterned leaves. The plant responds to liquid fertilizer and can be started from small off-shoots of the main plant.

Dieffenbachia picta — Dumb Cane or Dieffenbachia

Another very popular indoor plant, the dieffenbachia has wide green leaves with white-patterned centers. They grow well in rich soil that should be kept on the dry side, with only occasional watering. As this plant gets older, it loses its bottom leaves. To rejuvenate the plant, it should be cut off at the base. New shoots will grow up from the main root. The top portion can be rooted, just as pieces of the bare stem can be dried out, then placed sideways in moist sphagnum moss or similar propagating material for rooting and growing new plants. *Caution:* The name "dumb cane" stems from the fact that all parts of this plant are toxic. If chewed, the tongue will swell up so badly that speech becomes impossible; hence the name "dumb cane."

Dracaena is another favorite which does very well in low light conditions.

Dracaena marginata — **Dracaena**

With a tall main stem and graceful, drooping, dark-green leaves, the dracaena ranges from the small variety (Florida Beauty) about 12 inches high to the larger types (Dracaena Marginata) that can reach a height of 15 feet. Dracaena survives low light conditions but does better with plenty of filtered light. Allow to dry out before watering.

Fittonia verschaffeltii argyroneura — **Fittonia**

Sometimes called the Silver Nerve Plant, this attractive plant has leaves netted with white veins. The Red Nerve Plant has red veins in the leaves. Fittonia require high light levels and must be protected from temperatures below forty degrees.

Cissus rhombifolia — **Grape Ivy**

With a mass of tendrils and attractive shiny green leaves, this plant is excellent for a hanging basket. Grape ivy actually is a member of the grape family. This plant likes filtered light and moist, rich soil. Spider mites can be a problem, but frequent overhead spraying with water usually will control this pest. New plants can be started from stem-tip cuttings.

Hoya carnosa — **Hindu Rope Plant**

The Hindu rope plant sometimes is called the wax plant because of its unusual, twisted stems and leaves that have a waxy surface. This plant needs moist soil for best growth.

280 IVY

There are many different varieties of ivy. The most popular include the following:

Hedera helix — English Ivy

Needing temperatures under 70 degrees, and suffering from red spider mites, English ivy is difficult to grow but well worth the effort because of its rich-looking, variegated leaves. It likes rich soil and low light conditions. Saturate the soil when watering and allow it to dry out before watering again.

Senecio mikaniodes — German Ivy

A slow grower, German ivy prefers cooler temperatures and strong, filtered light. Plant in rich, moist soil but water sparingly. Soggy soil can kill this ivy.

Scindapsus aureus — Golden Pothos

Particularly suited to indoor culture, Pothos ivy can grow halfway around a room. Sometimes called a "variegated philodendron" because of its leaf patterns, this plant should be grown in rich, moist soil in good, filtered light. Allow the soil to get almost dry before watering. New plants can be grown from stem-tip cuttings.

Crassula argentea — Jade Plant

With fleshy leaves and waxy stems, the Jade plant is one of the more common succulents. It does best in full sun when it gets a reddish margin on its leaves. The soil can be allowed to dry out slightly between waterings without endangering this plant. When grown in partial shade or limited indoor light, the leaves are pure green.

The bright green leaves and long tendrils of the Pepperomia make it a popular hanging basket in sunny areas.

PALMS

Several palms make very appealing indoor plants, especially the dwarf varieties that vary from 12 inches to eight feet in height. One of the more attractive varieties is the *Chamaedorea Elegans*, commonly called the *Neanthe Bella*. Others include: the Bamboo Palm *(Chamaedorea erumpens)*, the Arecas *(Chrysalidocarpus lutescens)* and the Dwarf Date Palm *(Phoenix Roebelenii)*, which is used outdoors but will grow inside the house near a bright window. Most palms require a high light level and moderately moist soil. Fertilize every two to three months with a liquid plant food and protect them against temperatures below 40 degrees.

The Ponytail Palm *(Beaucarnea Recurvata)* is not a true palm. Growing long, thread-like leaves from a large, bulbous base, this slow-growing plant lives a long time and makes an unusual floor or table decoration. It can go for months without being watered.

Pepperomias

Pepperomias has heart-shaped or round leaves and varies from a few inches to 18 inches in height. This plant (of the same general variety as the table pepper) prefers high light levels but not full sun.

Peace Lily

Tolerating low light levels, this unusual plant grows dark-green leaves up to 30 inches in length from a stalk, with a striking white shield around the flowers.

The Peace Lily grows well in partial shade.

282 *Tolmiea mensiesii* — Piggyback Plant

A long-stem favorite, this plant is interesting in the way new plantlets "ride piggyback" on mature leaves. These "babies" can be rooted by cutting them off and planting in moist vermiculite. This plant has rich, green leaves with a crinkled, frilly appearance. It prefers rich, moist soil and filtered light.

Maranta leuconeura kerchoveana — Prayer Plant

A splotchy maroon pattern runs evenly along the middle of each velvety leaf. This plant folds its leaves at night — hence the name. Because of the pattern on the leaves, it is sometimes called rabbit tracks. It likes moist soil, but slightly drier from December through February.

Gynura sarmentosa — Purple Passion

A striking plant for a hanging basket, this plant needs moist soil continuously. It is sometimes called the velvet plant because of the texture of its green leaves with soft purple undersides.

Trifasciata laurenti — Sansevieria

Also called the snake plant, or mother-in-law's tongue, this tender perennial has stiff, erect leaves about two feet long, marked with white and green, or yellow and green. Overwatering is harmful, but this plant can take more neglect than any other house plant.

Sansevieria, or Snake Plant, thrives on neglect and is a popular potted plant indoors or out.

Schefflera, or Umbrella Plant, is great for patios and sun rooms.

Brassaia actinophylla — **Schefflera**

Schefflera is sometimes called the umbrella plant. This attractive and very popular specimen grows leaves over 12 inches long, with a total plant height of six or seven feet. The dwarf variety has leaves only four inches long, with a plant height of five to six feet. These plants need moderately high light levels and should be watered only after the soil dries out. They are sensitive to temperatures below 40 degrees. *Caution:* Over-watering will cause the leaves to fall, one of the commonest complaints about this plant. It also is subject to spider mites.

Chlorophytum comosum 'Vittatum' — **Spider Plant**

Ideal for a hanging basket, spider plants (also called airplane plants) send out long, flowering racemes which form new baby plants that can be cut off and rooted. Foliage is slender and graceful in green and green-and-white. The tips sometimes will turn brown, a condition that does not indicate disease. Merely snip off the brown tips with scissors. The spider plant prefers filtered sun, rich organic soil and does better if allowed to dry out between waterings.

Monstera deliciosa — **Split-leaf Philodendron**

The split-leaf philodendron is one of the most popular indoor plants in existence. Extremely easy to grow, it will tolerate low light but needs bright conditions for the leaves to split well and attain their maximum size. It prefers rich, organic, moist soil. Aerial roots will hang from the stems of this plant. Do not cut these off, but direct them down into the pot. New plants can be rooted from stem sections placed in damp sphagnum

Philodendron is one of Florida's most popular plants.

moss. *Caution:* Allow plenty of room for this plant. It may start off relatively small (12 to 18 inches), but in a very short time it can climb to impressive heights.

A smaller table variety, the heartleaf philodendron *(Philodendron oxycardium)*, has the same characteristics and makes an excellent basket planter or floor plant, climbing up a totem pole staked in the soil.

Aphelandra squarrosa 'Dania' — Zebra Plant

With dark-green, white-veined leaves that resemble the hide of a zebra, this is a most attractive plant, especially when it produces its bright-yellow blossoms with showy, golden-yellow bracts. It prefers filtered light and moist, rich soil. Ideally suited to high humidity, the zebra plant flourishes in a terrarium, which is the only way to truly cultivate this plant to its maximum potential. If allowed to dry out, the leaves will fall. Lasting only a few months, the zebra plant nevertheless is worth having for its exceptional beauty. It should be pruned after flowering to prevent the plant from getting leggy.

Final Word

This book has been an attempt to answer many of the Florida gardener's most-asked questions. I hope the information presented here on adjusting to Florida gardening and the particular plants in your landscape will help you in your happy gardening quest.

pH, soil, 12-14
Phaius Orchid, 178
Phalaenopsis Orchid (Moth Orchid), 178
Philodendron, Split-Leaf, 283-284
Phlox, 141
Phoenix canariensis (Canary Island Date
    Palm), 50
Phoenix roebelenii
    Dwarf Date Palm, 281
    Pygmy Date Palm, 49
Photinia glabra (Red-Leaf Photinia), 80
Photosynthesis, 15-16
Phythium, 229
Piggyback Plant *(Tolmiea mensiesii)*, 282
Pindo Palm *(Butia captita)*, 49
Pineapple *(Ananas comosus)*, 104-105
Pinnaspis strachani (Snow Scale), 222
Pinus elliotti (Slash Pine), 38-39
Piricularia grisea (Gray Leaf Spot), 228
Pittosporum tobira (Pittosporum), 78-79
Plants
    diseases of, 225-229. *See also* specific plant
        diseases
    indoor. *See* household plants
    protection, 25-27
    selection, 27
Plugging, lawn, 256
Plumbago capensis (Leadwort
    Plumbago), 73
Podocarpus gracillor (Fern Podocarpus), 80
Podocarpus nagi (Nagi), 79
Podocarpus macrophylla (Yew Podocarpus),
    79
Poinsettia *(Euphorbia pulcherrima)*, 74
    summer, 135
Ponytail Palm *(Beaucarnea recurvata)*, 281
Poppy
    California, 127
    Mexican Tulip-, 161
Portulaca (Moss Rose), 141
Potato, 201
Powdery Mildew, 227
Prayer Plant *(Maranta leuconeura
    kerchoveana)*, 282
Pruning, rose, 168-169
Prunus caroliniana (Cherry Laurel), 67
Prunus peraica (Peach), 103
Pseudococcus longispirilus (Mealy Bug), 220
Psidium cattleianium (Cattley
    Guava), 100-101
Psidium guajava (Guava), 100
Punch-bar fertilization, 31-33
Purple Passion *(Gynura sarmentosa)*, 282
Pygmy Date Palm *(Phoenix roebelenii)*, 49
Pyracantha coccinea (Firethorn), 80
Pyrus lecontei (Pear), 104
Pythium, 227

Q

Queen Palm *(Arecastrum
    komanzoffianum)*, 48
Queensland Nut *(Macadamia
    integrifolia)*, 105
Quercus laurifolia (Laurel Oak), 44
Quercus nigra (Water Oak), 43-44
Quercus virginiana (Live Oak), 43

R

Raised beds, 188
Raleigh St. Austine Grass, 245
Raspberry *(Rubus albascens)*, 105
Red Beet, 191
Red Bud *(Cercis canadensis)*, 36
Red Jamaica Banana, 97
Red-Leaf Photonia *(Photonia glabra)*, 80
Red Maple *(Acer rubrum)*, 38
Red-Spider Mite, 270-271
Rhaphiolepsis indica (Indian
    Hawthorne), 73
Rhapis excelsa (Lady Palm), 51
Rhizoctonia solani (Brown Patch), 225, 228
Rhododendron (Azalea), 64-65
Robinson Tangerine, 114
Roses, 162-169
    climbing, 164
    pruning, 168-169
    spacing, 167-168
    Wood, 239
Round Scale *(Saissetia coffeae)*, 221
Royal Palm *(Roystones spp.)*, 45-47
Royal Poinciana *(Delonix regia)*, 42
Roystones spp. (Royal Palm), 45-47
Rubus albascens (Raspberry), 105
Rubus hybrid (Blackberry), 98
Rye Grass, 250

S

Sabal palmetto (Cabbage Palmetto), 50
St. Augustine Lawns, 245- 247
Saissetia coffeae (Round or Hemispherical
    Scale), 221
Salix babylonica (Weeping Willow), 39
Salvia, 142
Sand, 268
Sandankwa Viburnum *(Viburnum
    suspensum)*, 81
Sansevieria *(Trifasciata laurenti)*, 282
Sapium sebiferum (Chinese Tallow), 41
Satsuma Tangerine, 114
Scales, 115, 221-222
    household, 271
Scheffliera (Brassaia actinophylla), 283
Scinadapsus aureus (Golden Pothos), 280

U

Ulmus parvifolia (Chinese Elm), 41

V

Vaccinium myrtillus (Blueberry), 99
Valencia Orange, 113
Vanda Orchid, 178
Vandaceous Orchid, 178
Vegetables, 181-211. (*See also* specific
   vegetables)
   grow-boxes, 186-188
   herbs, 189-190
   insect pests, 186
   organic growing, 188-189
   planning, 183-184
   planting, 185-186
   raised beds, 188
Verbena, 162
Vermiculite, 268
Veronicellidae (Slug), 222
Viburnum odoratissimum (Sweet
   Viburnum), 81
Viburnum suspensum (Sandankwa
   Viburnum), 81
Vines, 231-241
   grape, 236-238
   ornamental gourds, 238-239
Viruses, 228-229
Vitis rotundifolia (Muscadine Grape), 100

W

Walkways, 6-7
Washington Palm *(Washingtonia
   robusta),* 51
Watering, 19-23
   drip irrigation, 22-23
   fruit tree, 94
   hose, 21
   lawn, 256-257
   sprinklers, 21-22
Watering-rod fertilization, 33
Watermelons, 205
Water Oak *(Quercus nigra),* 43-44
Wax Scale *(Ceroplastes ceriferus Fabricius),*
   221
Weather protection, 25-27
   fruit trees, 94-95
Webworm *(Hyphantria cunea),* 224
   sod, 261-262
Weeds
   broadleaf, 252
   control, 251
   grassy, 251-252
   killers of, 253
Weeping Willow *(Salix babylonica),* 39

White Fly *(Dialeurodes citrifolii),* 115,
   224-225
   household, 270
White Grubworm, 262
White Potato, 201
Winter Running Squash, 203
Wisteria *(Wisteria sinensis),* 238-239
Wood Rose *(Ipomosa tuberosa),* 239
Worms, 224, 261-262

Y

Yams, 201
Yaupon Holly *(Ilex vomitoria),* 71
Yellow Crookneck Squash, 202
Yellowing, 226
Yellow Straightneck Squash, 202
Yew Podocarpus *(Podocarpus
   macrophylla),* 79

Z

Zinnia, 146-147
Zoysia Grass, 248
Zuchini, 202